Transmission

Transmission Membership

28 King St Glasgow G15QP t: +44 141 552 4813 f: +44 141 552 1577 info@transmissiongallery.org / www.transmissiongallery.org

A diverse and increasingly high profile art scene has emerged in Glasgow with Transmission at its centre. Transmission provides a place where artists can meet, talk and exhibit along with their local and international peers and influences.

Transmission was set up in 1983 by art school graduates who were dissatisfied with the lack of exhibition spaces and opportunities for young artists in Glasgow. Through sponsorship and support from the Scottish Arts Council and Glasgow City Council they managed and maintained a space in which to exhibit their work and the work of a rapidly growing collective of local artists.

Subsequent committees invited artists who had influenced them to show in the gallery and become part of this dialogue. The range of contacts grew through projects with similar organisations such as City Racing in London and Artemisia in Chicago and this exchange of ideas has continued with Transmission providing a model for other collectives like Catalyst in Belfast and Generator in Dundee.

The gallery is curated and managed by a voluntary committee of six people. Each member of the committee serves for up to two years and is then replaced. Transmission evolves under the influence of each successive committee member and continues to draw in a young peer group as active participants.

The annual members' shows are an important part of Transmission; they are open submission and allow the whole membership to exhibit work – a good opportunity for less established artists and valuable for our future programming. This is also the only time committee members may show their own work in association with Transmission.

We represent the needs and interests of our membership by maintaining an image bank of slides which are made available to visiting curators and artists. Members also gain the use of gallery facilities such as fax, photocopier, video equipment and slide projector and receive ten to twelve mail-outs per year including a newsletter detailing opportunities within the gallery and beyond and invitations to previews at the gallery. Members may 'piggyback' their own information (flyers for shows etc.) on the mail-out. During exhibitions, full members may be asked to invigilate from 11am to 5pm and will receive £15 to cover their expenses. We consider proposals made by members throughout the year – the downstairs space is an ideal area to develop experimental work, present projection based projects and solo exhibitions.

We encourage people to come along and socialise; attend openings, talks, screenings and music events.

One year's membership costs £5 to students or the unemployed, and £15 to those with a wage. If you cannot afford the fee, you may invigilate for a day at the gallery in lieu. For legal reasons we must ask that members choose either a full or associate membership: full members are requested to attend Transmission's Annual General Meeting and may use all gallery facilities; associate members are not requested to attend the Annual General Meeting. Individuals resident in and around Glasgow are encouraged to become full members and to participate more in the running of the gallery.

- -

I would like to support Transmission by becoming a **full / associate** member (please circle)
I enclose a cheque for **£15** (waged) / **£5** (unwaged) / I wish to **invigilate** in lieu of payment (please circle)

Cheques should be made payable to **Transmission Gallery**

Name: ——————————————————————— Tel: ————————————————————————
Address: —————————————————————— Fax: ———————————————————————
——————————————————————— Email: ———————————————————————
———————————————————————
Signed: —————————————————————— Date: ———————————————————————

Please copy and use or distribute this form as needed

THIS book is drawn from the Transmission archive which has been put together by a number of people involved with the gallery since 1983. The archive includes thousands of slides, photos of openings and events, posters, reviews and a mass of correspondence.

A book which celebrated ten years of Transmission had been planned in 1993. Essays were commissioned from Christine Borland, Katrina Brown, Billy Clark, Malcolm Dickson, Douglas Gordon, Thomas Lawson, Ross Sinclair, Simon Starling and Nicola White—all were closely involved with Transmission at different points during its history. The book was never printed but the material forms an important part of the archive.

The current committee decided to produce a chronological account and a visual record of the gallery's history to date, using the unpublished essays to provide commentary, along with texts written to accompany exhibitions.

There is no individual authority on the history of Transmission, but a huge number of personal accounts from various perspectives. As the average age of the current committee is 25, we have relied upon existing documentation and have been advised by our predecessors and other gallery members throughout the production of this book.

We selected material in order to tell a story of Transmission's development and to illustrate the commitment to providing opportunities for less established artists.

This book is an introduction to the continuing work of Transmission. The programme list at the back aims to include every show, talk and event held at or organised by Transmission until August 2001. The whole archive is available for view in the gallery.

Clare Stephenson and Anna McLauchlan
On behalf of Transmission

TRANSMISSION

THE COMMITTEE FOR THE VISUAL ARTS

PRESS RELEASE   PRESS RELEASE   PRESS RELEASE   PRESS RELEASE

TRANSMISSION is Glasgow's first artist-run gallery organised by the Committee for the Visual Arts (C.V.A.), a non profit making association. A varied group of young artists dedicated to the exhibition and promotion of contemporary art and the integration of art into community life.

TRANSMISSION is a street level premises, adjacent to the Tron Theatre Club, providing 800 square feet of exhibition space, organised and renovated by the voluntary labour of the membership. Membership is currently forty artists working mostly in Glasgow but also in Edinburgh and Dundee. Artists may apply by submission of slides in December and June each year.

TRANSMISSION is a venue for new art by young artists. All exhibitions will be organised by the C.V.A., mostly group shows around a particular theme. Work will be selected on the basis of quality, energy and intent. The first show will be "URBAN LIFE", a large and varied group show involving most of the membership. Exhibitions around the themes of Construction Paintings, New Imagery and a social and political show are planned to follow.

TRANSMISSION aims to create a vital art community and a working relationship with the wider community. Newsletters, lectures, slide shows and discussions will be staged in the future, hopefully broadening the audience for the visual arts in the city.

The C.V.A. hopes for reciprocal relationships with other galleries, with the intention of introducing young artists to more established galleries in Great Britain.

The C.V.A. commits itself to the exchange of visual ideas whilst precipitating an artist community committed to art as a vital part of community life.

"URBAN LIFE" OPENS ON DECEMBER 2ND FROM 6PM TO 8PM AND WILL RUN TO THE EIGTH OF JANUARY."

NOTE: Further enquiries about TRANSMISSION should be made to C.V.A. at W.A.S.P.S.
22 King Street, Glasgow. 041-552-2330.

13-15 Chisholm Street, Trongate Glasgow G15 HA

05 Below: 'Gallery gets a splash of help', from a story in the *Evening Times*, 12 August 1983, p. 4 (The gallery was given sponsorship in kind from the paint company Dulux). Committee members left–right: Alistair Magee, Alistair Strachan and Michelle Baucke.

Below left: 'Transmission V. Critics', Frank McNab, *Streets Ahead*, Issue 2, 12–27 May 1983, p. 26.

TRANSMISSION
V. CRITICS...

A group of young artists in Glasgow are planning to open an art gallery in Chisholm St. Called Transmission, this new gallery in the Trongate area will provide motivation for artists who find themselves at present working in a vacuum — a state which faces too many talented painters leaving art school.

The aims of the Transmission gallery will be to provide much needed exhibition space to these isolated artists, and encourage a broader interest in the younger artists working in central Scotland. Artists from Edinburgh are also involved.

Funds are coming from a variety of sources, including private business sponsorship via Tom Laurie, ex-chairman of W.A.S.P.S. Eyes are also being turned to the Scottish Arts Council and Glasgow District Council. The artists themselves are working hard raising renovation funds through a series of functions and dances.

Reactions to this new project are, on the whole, positive, but dissenting noises are being made, even at this early stage. Among these is the argument of financial viability versus cultural value. Kenneth McKenzie, an art-restorer based in the Albany Chambers, is pessimistic about the whole idea. 'These kind of things', sighs Mr McKenzie, 'spring up every couple of years — but they never last.' Mr McKenzie sees art-galleries in purely financial terms. 'And this sort of venture', he goes on, 'can't hope to compete for the custom of rich people who buy paintings as a form of investment.'

The artists involved in 'Transmission', however, believe the patronage of 'rich people', who they say, 'come into Glasgow from the outlying spam-belts and see pound-notes hanging on gallery walls', is fundamentally opposed to their basic aims. Alistair McGee, one of the artists involved, visualizes 'the concept of a gallery for the benefit of, and run by, artists.' Commercial success, over and above the funds necessary for the day to day running, is considered secondary to the boost which the gallery will give to the present state of contemporary exhibition space in Glasgow.

Tom Laurie, 'Lorenzo de Medici' of the Glasgow arts scene, is not at all surprised by the emergence of Transmission: 'It was almost inevitable that something should come from the energy of young artists working in Glasgow', he says. He has a point; artists, no matter how aesthetic, want somewhere to exhibit their work when they're still alive,' and considering that most of Glasgow's present galleries deal specifically in 'dead', investment art, it *is* inevitable that Glasgow artists want somewhere new. The tooth-fairies of 'Transmission' will answer their wishes.

The stock reply to anything like the 'Transmission' from the 'dead-art' galleries is an accusation of naivety and lack of sophistication. To this, founders of the new gallery say that although the main raison d'être of 'Transmission' is cultural, they are not losing sight of the more mundane business side of the project, and they are listening to advice from everyone who is prepared to give it. John Rogan, a founder member, is speaking tongue-in-cheek when he says he is, 'deeply shocked and hurt that someone could be so destructive in their response to our idea'.

Finally, a reaction from Mr Ewan Mundy, who runs a 'D.A.' gallery in West George St:

'To trade in the past, you need a past to look forward to.'

Positive or negative? The people from 'Transmission' don't care — they're too busy thinking about today.

FRANK McNAB

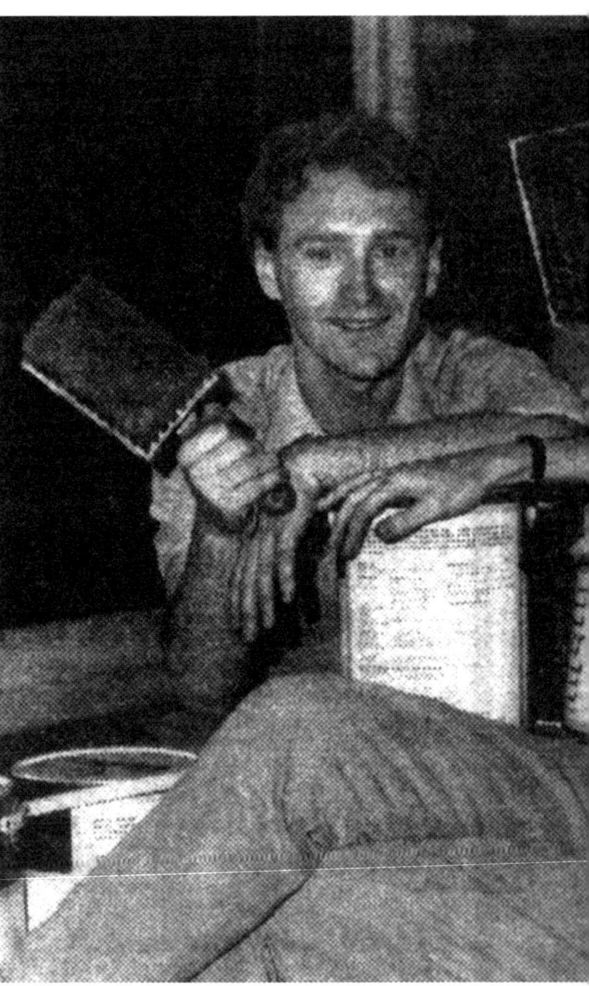

12 Right: Poster for 'Urban Life' and the Benefit Dance at the Mayfair, December 1983.

Below right: 'Urban Life'—left–right: Peter Howson: *Douglas playing the sax*; Lesley Raeside: *Knife*; Alistair Magee: *Mario*; Michelle Baucke: *The Heat*; Andy Walker: *Girl with a towel*.

Bottom right: Alistair Magee (left) and David Linley outside the newly-opened gallery in Chisholm Street.

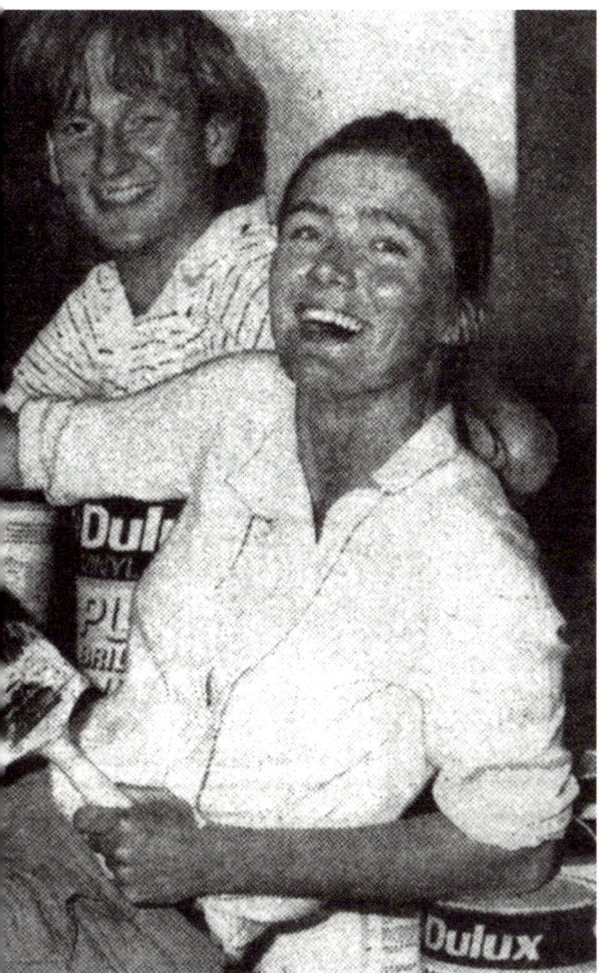

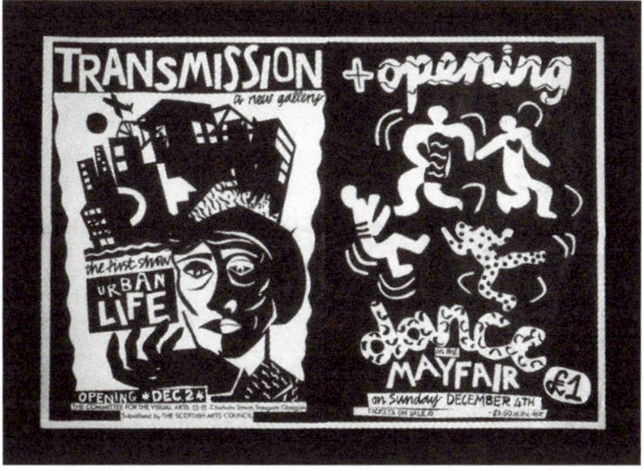

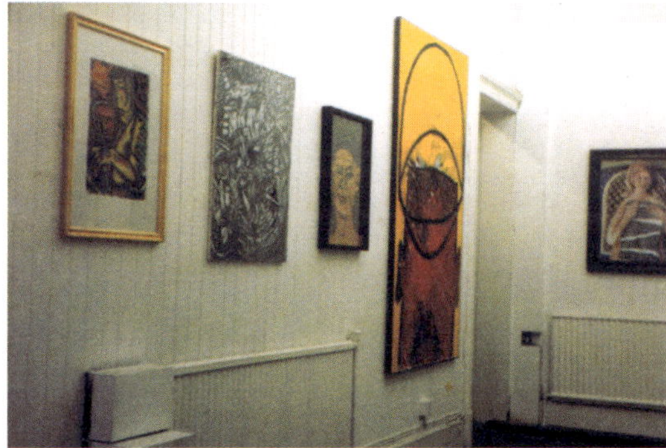

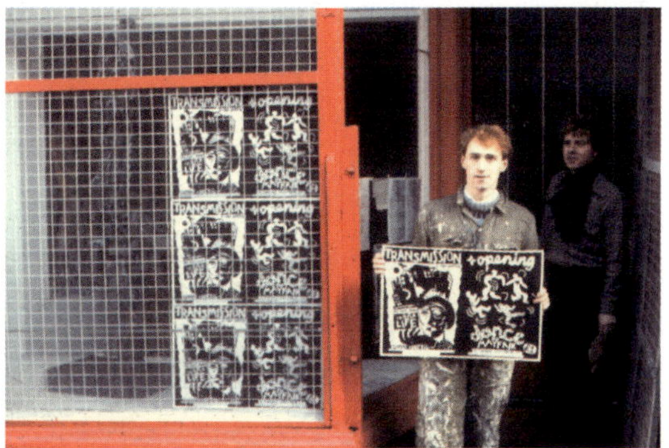

01 Below: 'Construction Painting'—Installation view.

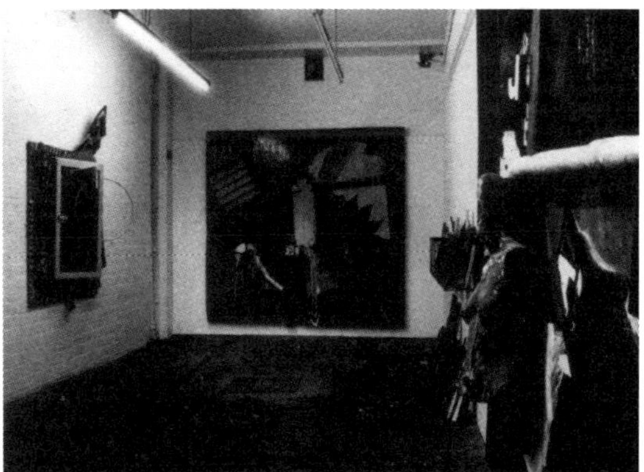

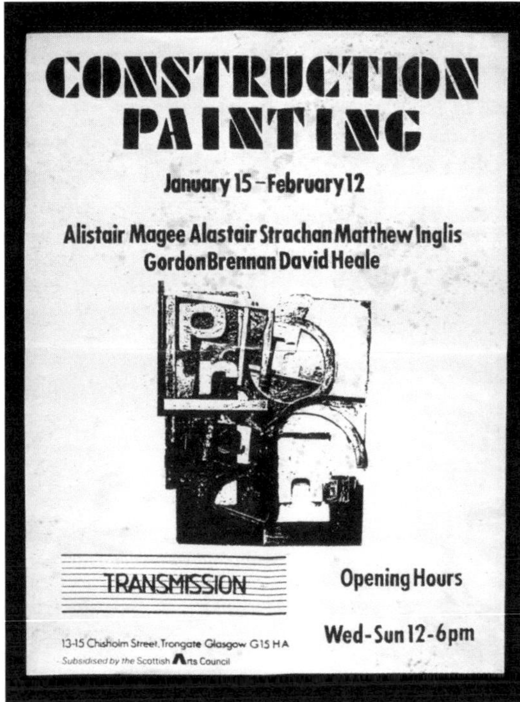

03 Below: 'Winning Hearts and Minds', March 1984, was a group show of drawing and painting with Lesley Raeside, John Rogan, Peter Howson, Helen Gibson, Andrew Squire, Alison Stirling, Gordon Muir, Arlene Stewart, Stephen Barclay, Ken Currie and Adrian Wiszniewski.

Four of these artists (Ken Currie, Peter Howson, Stephen Barclay and Adrian Wiszniewski) were to appear in the 'New Image Glasgow' exhibition at the Third Eye Centre, Glasgow. 'New Image Glasgow' was curated by Alexander Moffat and also featured the work of Steven Campbell and Mario Rossi.

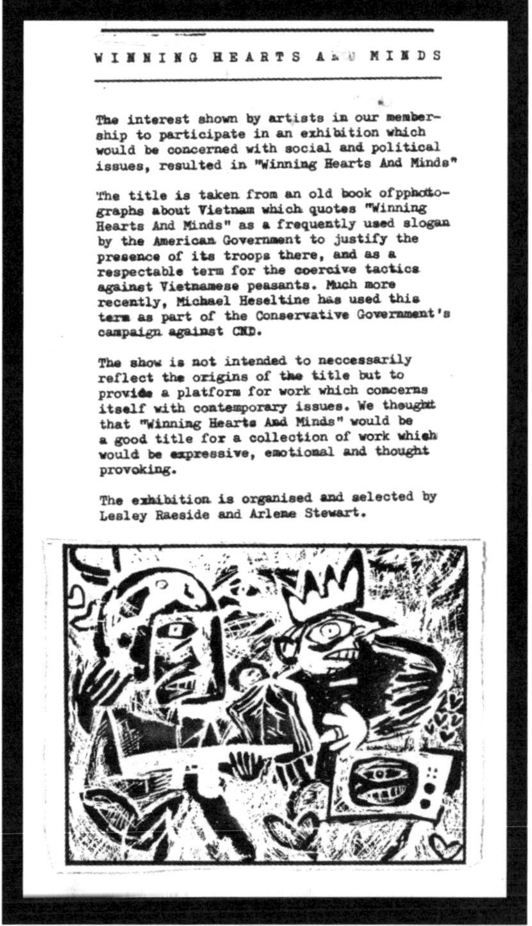

WINNING HEARTS AND MINDS

The interest shown by artists in our membership to participate in an exhibition which would be concerned with social and political issues, resulted in "Winning Hearts And Minds"

The title is taken from an old book of photographs about Vietnam which quotes "Winning Hearts And Minds" as a frequently used slogan by the American Government to justify the presence of its troops there, and as a respectable term for the coercive tactics against Vietnamese peasants. Much more recently, Michael Heseltine has used this term as part of the Conservative Government's campaign against CND.

The show is not intended to neccessarily reflect the origins of the title but to provide a platform for work which concerns itself with contemporary issues. We thought that "Winning Hearts And Minds" would be a good title for a collection of work which would be expressive, emotional and thought provoking.

The exhibition is organised and selected by Lesley Raeside and Arlene Stewart.

05 Iconoclasm: "When I joined the gallery in 85, morale was low. Sewage leaks in the basement had closed the place for nine months, and the serving committee were nearing the end of their tenureship. It is a common occurrence, however, that contraction ensues after initial interest within such projects. In this instance it was also from the wider and immediate art world and media. Perhaps expectations were too high, inevitably resulting in a feeling of disillusionment. Breadth and ambition at the beginning can help avoid such a situation, but the individuals felt seduced and abandoned—mollycoddled at first by the cautious parents of the Glasgow art scene, they were quickly dropped and ignored when 'New Image Glasgow' occurred at the Third Eye Centre in Glasgow, which rocketed several painters to international acclaim on the back of the then popular European neo-expressionism (but here with its own vernacular). New Image was the dawning of a new era, introducing a form of media 'consensual validation' that, if they claimed a 'new renaissance' was upon us and no viewpoints were allowed to debate otherwise, then it must be true." Malcolm Dickson (excerpt from 'Hit The North', an essay written for Transmission, 1996)

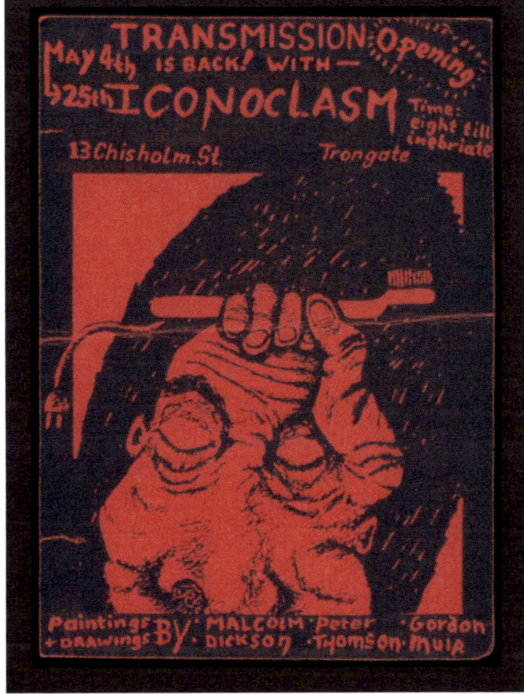

Below: Draft of text to accompany 'Iconoclasm' exhibition.

Guy Debord,– whose thought has certainly been one catalysm among many in this exhibition – wrote that it is through dissatisfaction that a truly radical opposition to capitalist relations grows, and, I speak for the three of us in saying that it forms our point of departure in our art and beyond.

We reject the political, theological, literary, philosophical and academic assumptions which hinge our society to the withered refrigerator of civilisation, and <u>because</u> we believe in creativity as a potent force that everyone should paticipate in, we share a healthy distrust of the culture industry (officialdom), based, as it is on some of the more dubious excuses for Economic Organisation.

The task of the critical post-modernist artist is not one of cluttering up the world with coded ambiguities, but by being part of that vortex of contemporary thought which aims to draw a dividing line between those fighting against an old world, and those trying to maintain it. All that is left of the past or the future is the demand for the present. In our era of streets and dreams, freedom and of thought and behaviour has yet to be tested.

Be cruel with your past and all who keep you there.

Malcolm Dickson. May 1985.

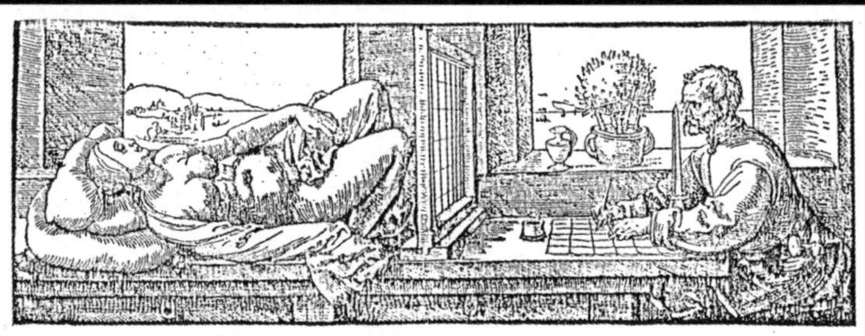

THE MAP IS NOT
THE TERRITORY

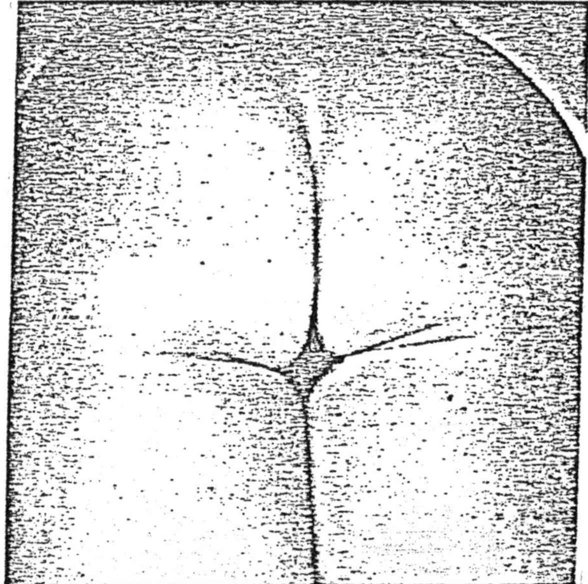

Ralph Rumney

TRANSMISSION
THE COMMITTEE FOR THE VISUAL ARTS
13-15 Chisholm Street, Trongate Glasgow G15 HA
24 Sept-19 Oct 1985
Private View 21 Sept
7pm
Subsidised by the Scottish Arts Council

09 Ralph Rumney—The Map is Not The Territory: "What can one say about someone whose web of the past is spun in many golden and withered threads and whose feet have passed through streets that I have only dreamed. In the 50s, Ralph was one of the few young hopefuls in English painting who one day refused to eat of that bread. Such a rejection of the pseudo-approval of the artworld was fermented by the belief that art had lost its function and that painting was a dishonest way of making a living. As a member of that band of intellectual delinquents—the Situationists—such an analysis and such a break was of the most sincere intentions. That this happened in the late 50s had less to do with prophecy or chance than with plain-to-see facts; art—arguably a previously sacred terrain—was infected by the spread of modern Capital, the artist became a star to compete with the sports hero, TV personality and the pop star. The art object and the artist creator became commodities, and as a result a new dimension was added to the realm of modernist consumption: a trend that has been renewing itself about every five years since. All that is history now. Amongst many swirling encounters, personal grief and theoretical activities, Ralph has since worked for French radio, taught, lectured and continued to write. During the past ten years, Ralph has lived in Paris, Sicily and Venice. In 1981, Ralph 'resolved ontological conflicts and resumed the production of artefacts.'

> Language fails entirely to make one crucial distinction. It assumes that words and the things they describe are identical and so, fails to distinguish between 'maps' in our minds and the territory such maps refer to. (C H Turner, on 'The Semantics of Alfred Korzybski')

If we apply this to a Polaroid photograph of a woman's breasts or body and by stating that 'The Map is Not The Territory', or, in other words, the image is not the reality, a critique of pornography is made. It is here that we apply another Situationist concept—that of 'detournement': strategies of subversion or intervention which turn the ruling ideology's own weapons against itself by creating new meanings within the context of capitalist relations." Malcolm Dickson (excerpts from 'The Image Is Not The Reality', September 1985, written to accompany the exhibition)

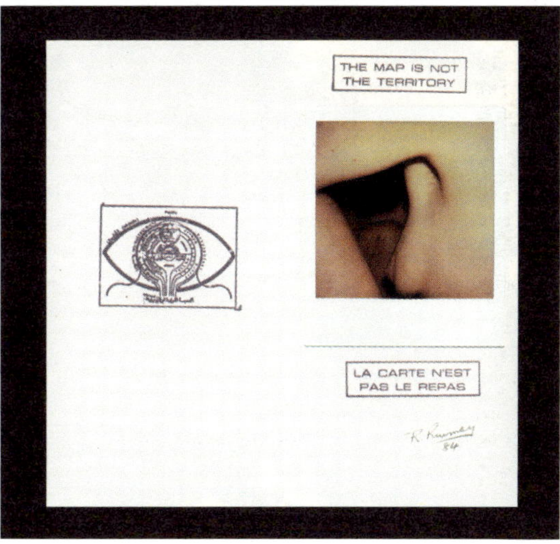

"Douglas Gordon: One of the first shows I saw at the gallery (when it was still located in Chisholm Street) was by Ralph Rumney. This must have been 1986.

Hans-Ulrich Obrist: The 'One and Only' Ralph Rumney. The only ever British man of Situationism. He was expelled by Guy Debord because one of his pieces did not arrive on time for some Situationist publication.

DG: Yes, I think he might have been 'expelled' from Transmission as well. He was big into drinking and arguing and yes, set the tone for years to come. But it was quite important to see this kind of work and attitude, and behaviour, and misbehaviour in Glasgow. It was a lot to do with a certain de-mythologising of art, artists and their supposed aura. On a very basic level it encouraged younger artists to sit around with people like Rumney or Stuart Brisley (who came to Glasgow a little later). Inevitably, for me at least, the art wasn't the important thing. The art was only an excuse to be able to cut through all the dross that was around in the art magazines and actually see real people from other places who were making things and thinking thoughts and talking about ideas. I mean, it's better to sit and hear it from the horse's mouth, rather than just browse through *Artscribe* or whatever." (from 'Ping Pong—A Conversation between Douglas Gordon and Hans-Ulrich Obrist', for Transmission, 1995)

1986

01 War Of Images: 'War Of Images' brought together a diverse range of politically engaged artists from throughout the UK. It was held at Transmission and Glasgow School of Art.

"This group have just the radical and critically aware approach to art that Scotland has lacked until now. They have an openness to an interesting variety of ideas from Situationism, through the music of 1976/77 and its take power-into-your-own-hands ethos, to Foucault.

02 Below: 'Events Space 1' was a festival of film, video, installation and performance; the largest in Scotland for ten years. Video facilities were provided free of charge by local rental firms and the newly established Electronic Imaging Department at Duncan of Jordanstone College of Art in Dundee.

Their commitment to an art of ideas that challenge the Britain we live in today, is also a challenge to the aestheticism of most art chaos and critics. Theirs is not an art of escape." Peter Kravitz (the *Edinburgh Review* no. 72, p. 2). This "endearing commentary" as Malcolm Dickson describes it, and a shared interest in Scottish intellectuals such as Alexander Trocchi and R D Laing, led to an association between the Edinburgh Review and Transmission. This resulted in the gallery hosting a number of events such as the 'Transmission Goes Verbal' series.

05 The Shining City on the Hill: "During the 1986 Mayfest 'celebrations' we hosted 'The Shining City on the Hill' by Coventry based painter John Yeadon, whose homo-erotic imagery created nervous twitches amongst the Mayfest* committee, who quietly suggested that we should not open to 'the public'."

* Mayfest was an international arts festival held annually in Glasgow.

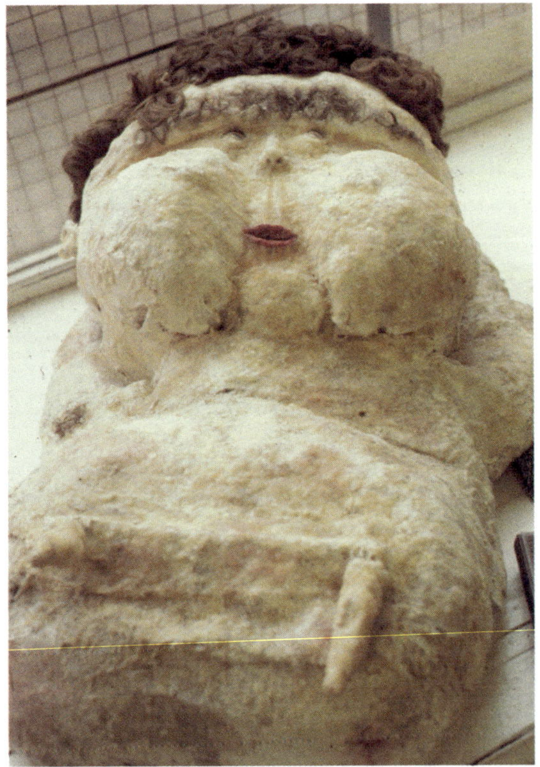

From the street-level Transmission to the renounedly majestic G.S.A. Mackintosh Museum, were the respectful venues for the January show 'WAR OF IMAGES'. At the outset a polemical venture, bringing together artists from Liverpool, London, Glasgow and one each from Edinburgh and Dundee, the show was, in retrospect, a mere caricature of its strategic aims. The aim perhaps was to provide a (very) brief platform proclaiming the consciousness of class issues to the social production of art, to question whether there still is avenues of contestation. There was no answer provided, and judging by the accompanying short article in the fanzine type catalogue, this was intentionally so. There are no easy sign-posts in developing an oppositional voice. This could be interpreted as a cloaked excuse: the inconsistency of the work and the lack of theoretical discourse is simply the result of bad organisation and the fact that all the work here was selected in response to a notice of the exhibition in a small-circulated seditious magazine called Variant - spasmodic hodge-podge of post-political, ZG-ish, anarchist critique and antiaesthetic theory which gained more enemies in its reputation than it did partisans in the cause of doing something really positive about the appalling state of culture in Scotland.

Despite certain inconsistencies, the show was exciting in its diversity, from large paintings to savage graphics, from scratch video to crude and delicate sculpture. Since this exhibition could have been a necessary challenge to the **uncritical** blast to fame of the 'New Image Glasgow' painters, perhaps more emphasis should have been placed on work in time-based media, though given the fact that ideas come and go in Glasgow and absolutely no magazine or publication exists to discuss them or document artists' activities, it didn't really matter. Not that the particular painting included in this show lacked power: Peter Thomson's 'Cityscape' is almost phobic in its portrayal of boredom - an expressionless man stares out from the canvas, objects and experience have gone haywire, the enviroment is transformed into a cold mechanical Trumpton, only in this real life tale Noddy is a sexual pervert and Big Ears is a junkie. The Self objectified and made into a commodity is also the theme of Ian Hughes' 'Night Duty' and 'Anatomy Lesson', the oppressor here being psych-medical control. In Mark Cardwell's crude combination of oil and acrylic, 'Burning Bus', a police surveillance helicopter scans the aftermath of what I presume was a riot.

Much of the painting follows on, in fact, from the gregariousness of the 'Iconoclasm' show in May of '85, an exhibition which brought together three Glasgow School of Art emigres, Peter Thomson, Malcom Dickson and Gordon Muir, who are all represented in 'War of Images'. Gordon Muir's electrifying untitled big pastel painting which graced Transmission's best wall space displays a strong stylistic development which is a triumph to the senses. His massive triptych '...Fruit of the Electric Tree' from the Smith Biennial easily overshadowed all the other exhibits, no comparison with prizewinner Lis Hansen and only just stealing the show from first prizewinner Ian McCulloch in its vibrancy. The accompanying text to 'War of Images' was written, as with the 'Iconoclasm' show, by Malcolm Dickson - only now he has swapped Debordist for Foucaldian plagiarism. Well, it's post-modernism after all. Helen Flockhart - who was with the aforementioned Iconoclasts involved in the selection of this show - was here represented by a revolting fat sculpture figure, reminding me of Polanski's 'Repulsion', the melting wax of the scultpure like translucent white diseased skin easily cutting to the scene of the skinned rabbit in Carol's fridge (here played by Catherine Deneuve). By a strange coincidence, Helen is currently gracing Roman Polanski's mother country (Poland) and is probably half way through her second bottle of cheap Vodka and trying to forge chocolate vouchers - which I am told is extremely difficult to obtain if you are over the age of ten. Communism is capitalism without the good bits, eh?

Pete Seddon's 'Conversation Pieces' comprised four pastel drawings and four texts, both interdependant and essential to the reading of the work, and although a bit thin was loaded with possibilities. The same applies in Tony Rickaby's 'Dialectical Landscape: Watching the Aylesbury Estate', whose use of a large band of bright yellow acrylic proved too much for a young local selfpromotion graffitti artist who inflicted a considerable amount of damage to the work with a black marker. Someone remarked that it improved the work, and it seems to me that this sort of cultural hi-jack is underused method in invading the alienation of privilege of The Artist. Both Seddon and Rickaby are Marxist-Leninists, and are working in the same intellectual area as Paddinton Bear lookalike Terry Atkinson, who, like Komar and Melamid makes a living out of painting political puns and telling us that revolution has been a failure without questioning their own political positions. Terry Atkinson is a Trotskyite, by the way. Mouse Katz coorganiser of the feminist touring art show 'Pandora's Box' drew a lot of compliments with her four piece installation sculpture, which was based on four stages of human civilisation - Celtic, Ancient Egyptian, Greco-Roman and our own computer age - to make the fundamental point that the myths of the time are based on misunderstanding, disrespect and oppression, forces and values that have worked against women since time immemorial. As well as being thematically pertinent, this particular work was quite beautiful. Eric Marwick's satirical sculpture models addressed the cultural colonialism of Scotland by England, his work tinged with the failure of Devolution, his nationalism coming from a socialist perspective, and not from Myopic Nationalism. In a country TODAY, where native culture is still a minority interest, and political and economic inequalities still fall squarely on the North side of the Border, issues pertaining to such need to be reclaimed by socialists, though may the will of buddha keep the Labour Party away. Marwick portrays England as an old Bulldog, and Scotland as an elderly woman with syphallitic warts, an image not compatible with Scottish capitalism's attempts to package its image as everybody's home-from-home.

Marxist-Leninism, feminism, nationalism, all we need now is an anarchist and a black, one-legged lesbian for a veritable ideological mish-mash. The former was provided by Existencil Press, who is primarily a woman called Gee who did all the LP covers and related graphics for punk revolutionaries Crass (who were at one time the most exciting band who lived the political lifestyle that punk was all about - self-management, autonomy, dressing in black and not washing very regularly). The image which sticks in my mind is the one of Thatcher eating a huge turd. So incisive! Mick Duffield is a filmaker who provided the visuals at Crass performances, whose films were seen here on a video format. There were hard-hitting, uncompromising and erratic films, combining, as in 'Autopsy', live appearances by Crass, images from Auschwitz and scenes from a porno film. In 'Choosing Death' an image of a car crashing was intermittedly repeated and intercut with scenes from an advertisement in a butcher's shop. The message was clear: consumerism is banal and barbaric, from eating meat to participating in the market-place. 'Yes Sir, I Will' was a film made to accompany a live performance by Crass of the album of the same - this, in contrast, was irritating, noisy, too long and absolutely hysterical. Produced at the time of the Falklands fracas, it is an extremely angry film which suffers from its anger in saying anything constructive about the event. By the end it had me foaming at the mouth. As this material was made in Super 8 Film, it could only be a taster for the real thing since it was shown in video. The personal appearance by Duffield was not to be, however, as neither was the lecture by John A. Walker, a failure in the latter case which lies with management.

After a gruelling session with the above, Sandra Goldbacher's and Kim Flitcroft's video 'Night of 1,000 Eyes' was a pleasure, combining strong music, intoxicating colour, superimposition and visual collage, characteristics of the currently in vogue scratch video. This work is intended to be a critique of stereotyped images from TV, notably the seductiveness of the female eyes as portrayed through film and advertising. It's a blend of images, repeat shots, the overlapping of abstract shapes, and soundtrack from Donna Summer to Working Week, from hip-hop to high opera tending to overlook the internal critique. In fact, it had me reaching for my cravat and hairspray and off for a pose and to get ripped off down at the Subclub. However, just because it evoked a night-club crawl doesn't ban it from being art and anyway, wo club crwal doesn't ban it from being art and anyway, who says you can't write political criticism and dance at the same time. What did Karl Marx gain from sitting in the British Museum for years on end, bloody irritating arse-sores, that's what.

The difference between Goldbacher/Flitcroft and with Duffield is that where one crosses the boundaries between art and pop, the other is extending theory by other means, both, as image makers, must be concerned with visual pleasure, one for the sake of radical haircuts, the other for alternative politics.

Ralph Rumney's video 'Aids' was apparently so appalling it wasn't even shown. As one who had the misfortune to see this work and meet the man, I can confirm this. It uses overlong footage from the Live Aid concert interspersed with meaningless images - a shoe, a cat and a few shots of tits and navels just to make the connection with his Polaroid photographs which were shown in Transmission Gallery last September. His own navel is undoubtedly going to become his trademark, he's been staring into it since the turn of the sixties. The best thing about the video is the Steve Reich soundtrack, which is even destroyed by the pretentious reading of an old Scots poem above it just to prove that if you have enough verbosity you can do anything and justify it anyway you like with whatever you like. As an ex-Situationist, Ralph feels he can plagiarise anything and boost his own ego with pretentious illusions (my favourite is Ralph believing he was a modern day John MacLean, or after a few pints reminiscing about how he invented Lettrism and detourement). He had some things in his favour; he had known Guy Debord, was the ex-husband of Michelle Bernstein. Ralph was an ex-lot-of-things but not very much in his present political being. Debord had even kicked him out of the Situationists for being a bore. But this is an exhibition review and not a characeeer assasination. This was the case of another rackateer trying to turn Situationism into a career.

Because it was the most useless and disposable, The Intolerants' 'The Wooden Hut' was the most interesting. The Intolerants are a group of 'poets, filmmakers and artists' (parochial stylists and ex-popstars). Their hut was a 'dwelling without a tenant' which was constructed out of abandoned wood collected from skips locally. Built as it was, within the larger splendour of Glasgow School of Art Mackintosh Museum (zzzz), the piece was doubly ironic. Garnethill, where the artschool snobbishly stands, was once one of Glasgow's upper class areas (at the turn of the century), now another ghetto area with (to its credit) thriving indigenous cultures. Gradually, throughout the show, fragments of writing were pinned to the structure (the 'metaphysical demands' mentioned in the catalogue) proclaiming the power of chance of desire above that of order and boredom, reminiscent perhaps of a Blake or a Breton. Since I seen no-one construct the piece, and saw no-one scuffing away after pinning those fragments to it, the hut stood as a fossil to the imagination, someone had once passed through here, and was perhaps hiding

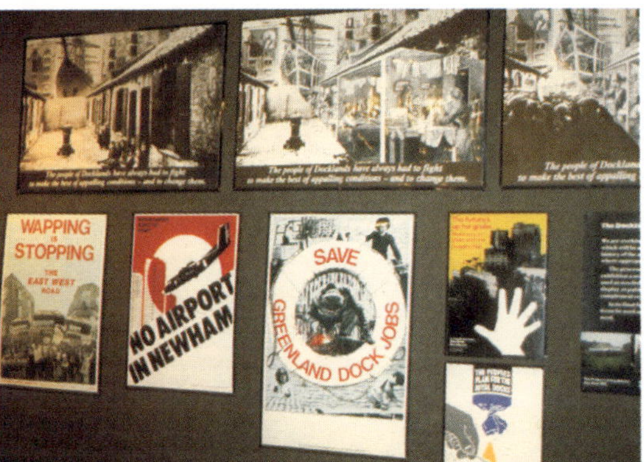

Above: Review published in Transmission Newsletter, March 1986.

Left: Peter Dunn/Lorraine Leeson (The Docklands Community Poster Project), photomural.

Opposite, right: Helen Flockhart, Untitled.

Malcolm Dickson (from 'Hit the North', an essay written for Transmission,1996)

"The exhibition is titled 'Shining City on the Hill'. This refers to the Thatcher/Reagan future capitalist utopia. This arcadia is a myth, as much as it is a

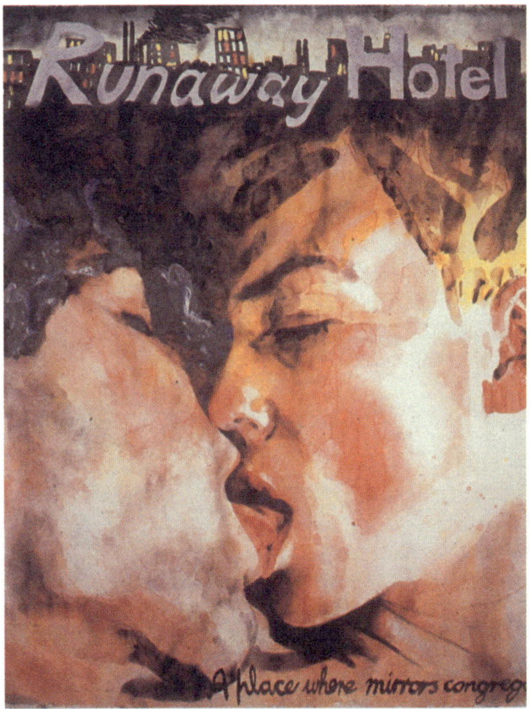

Above: Cover of the catalogue produced to accompany 'The Shining City on the Hill'.

crusade, created by the new style media capitalist, a challenging yet false new world. In my drawings the Metropolis is not seen directly, only glimpsed at, possibly in the window never fully described. Like Kafka's brief description of the Castle, its presence is all pervading…what we do see is the room populated by the vulnerable and confused.

I usually have a particular even popularist starting theme, nuclear weapons, drug abuse, homosexuality, inner city squalor or unemployed youths running away from home only to stay in shabby hotels in the Metropolis. Even though the finished work has a visual clarity, what is actually going on is still usually unresolved and unclear. Painting is still a process of discovery and experiment.

I would like to expose in the cool light of day the hypocrisy of thoughts, feelings and activities that usually exist in the dark corners of anonymous brown paper envelopes. The aim is to hold contradictions and to deal with paradox: paradox as the dialectic of life, the play between truth and falsehood, reality and illusion, the art of fiction, contrivance and artifice." John Yeadon (from artist's statement)

08 Transmission Goes Verbal: "You're in danger of giving literature away to the people who think they own it anyway…. It's like the Stalinist Communist point of view that would say 'Fuck all art because it belongs to the bourgeoisie', now usually the people who say that are themselves bourgeois anyway, and it's a real kind of condescending patronising thing to do because in a sense it's as if they don't want the proletariat to be contaminated by art, as if somehow it didn't belong to them anyway in the first place…. It's important to realise that literature doesn't belong to any one class at all, literature belongs to mankind—it's universal."

Right: James Kelman and Tom Leonard at the gallery.

Below: 'Transmission Goes Verbal' poster.

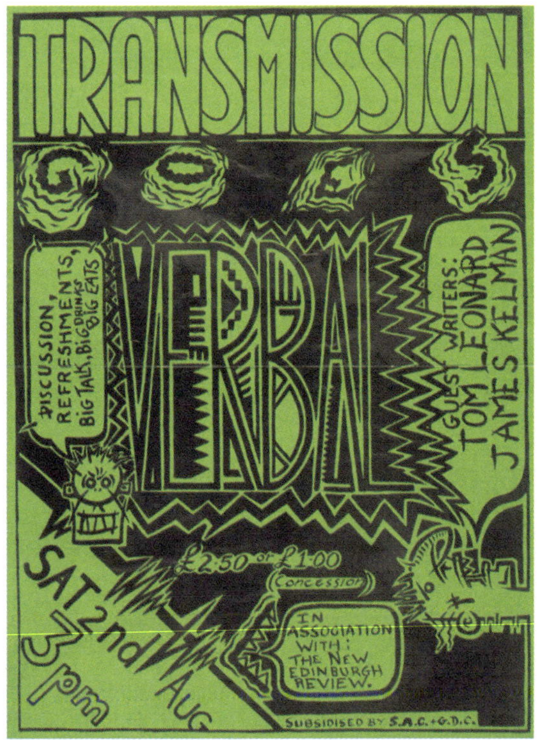

James Kelman (from the press release for 'Transmission Goes Verbal")

08 Stuart Brisley: "In a discussion with Transmission members, Brisley articulated a belief that receptivity to his work was not class-based—only the institutions that he was avoiding were based on such hierarchies—but centred around sensitivity. For him it seemed

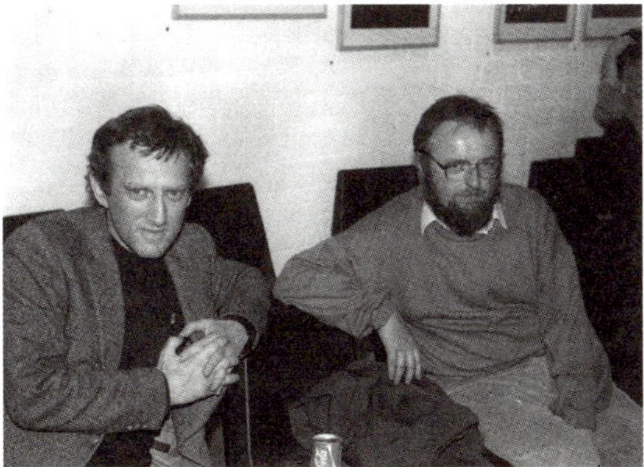

apposite to make his return to performance in a small gallery where the energy existed in people's minds, rather than being manifested in a space. As a mark of recognition, he stated that at Transmission, the artists 'work hard to create something and through that aspirations evolve and things actually happen, you become part of an argument (which is what is happening in Glasgow) which gives life to everything. Take away Transmission and Glasgow loses a lot by it.'" Rebecca Gordon-Nesbitt quoting Stuart Brisley ('When bad men conspire, good men should associate', MA report for the Courtauld Institute, 1995, p. 25)

Below: Stuart Brisley, *Red Army II*, August 1986.

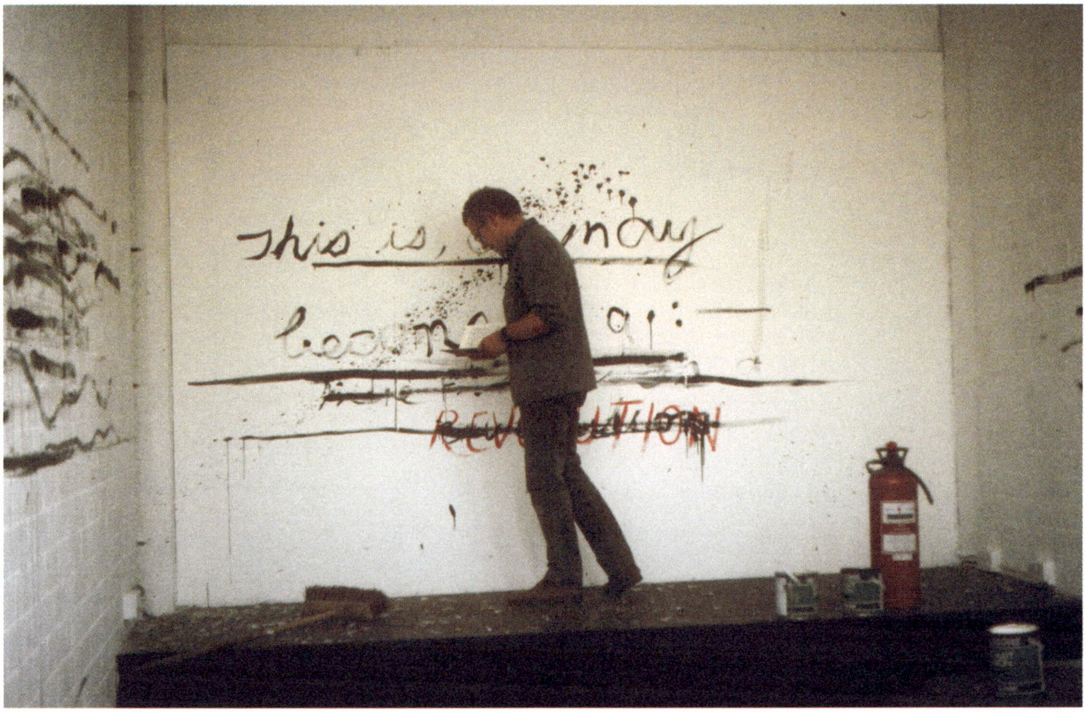

1987

04 Iconoclasm [II]: "Gordon Muir and Malcolm Dickson take a strong line in 'Iconoclasm' at Transmission (till April 25), but having read and heard their polemic, I expected, hoped, it would be even tougher. Based in Drumchapel and Keppochhill, both graduated from Glasgow in 1984 and share similar views but use different methods of expression.

Till 1984 Muir painted in the New Image Glasgow style. 'I soon found it inadequate', he said. An exchange visit to Baltimore produced a swing to graffiti style: loud garish comic strips where pop culture collides head-on with urban tower blocks and hypodermic needles. *Scheme Boys' Revenge*, *Nightmare Gadget*, *Epitaph for 86*, all rage with lurid energy. The Broadwater Farm riots, Barlinnie roof protests, lyrics from The Fall, writings of J G Ballard, all are grist to his mill. 'It's high time fine art shifted gear and put its foot down on the accelerator,' he believes.

Below: Malcolm Dickson with his installation 'Beneath The Cobblestones, The Sewer'; inset: Gordon Muir and 'Iconoclasm' installation.

Dickson gave up painting a year ago to concentrate on video and writing. The installation, *Beneath The Cobblestones The Sewer*, using found objects neatly embedded in plaster squares, returns to an earlier preoccupation. These 'fossils of trash culture' as he calls them: discarded old hammers, chisels, keys, covered in grey graphite dust symbolise for him the demise of Glasgow as an industrial force." Clare Henry (the Glasgow *Herald*, 10 April 1987, p. 4)

05 Desire in Ruins: "DESIRE IN RUINS installation and related events by Ed Baxter, Andy Hopton, Simon Dickason, Karen Eliot, Stefan Szczelkun, Glyn Banks and Hannah Vowles…

This Mayfest, Glasgow's artist-controlled gallery Transmission plays host to a group installation 'Desire in Ruins'. The individuals involved do not form an organised group, though they share mutual interests around pursuing exhibition strategies, text as critical intervention, the non-artwork, performance and installation work, the implications of Punk, the Situationists and Fluxus. These concerns brought them together in the exhibition 'The Ruins of Glamour/The Glamour of Ruins' at Chisenhale Works in London last December." (from press release)

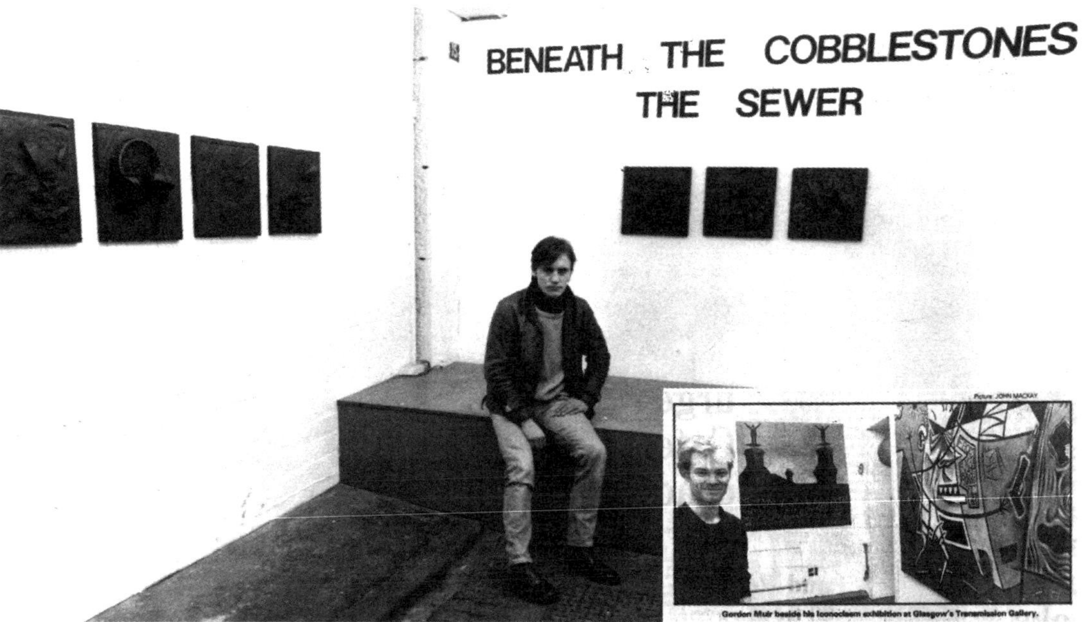

"At our opening the following night we had a shooting range (with Tammy Wynette singing 'Stand By your Man'), the usually cool art students dancing to Glasgow's famous County and Western streetsingers out in the back yard, bottles of Liquid Sky, children's toys and ultra-violet light. For five pounds you could demonstrate your financial support for Glasgow's unofficial alternative gallery by shooting an air-rifle at repeated images of two naked white middle-class children, a boy and a girl holding hands, with inflated white balloons above them, containing white paint which when hit by the pellet splattered their contents all over the children.

Desire in Ruins. No Transmission.

As the *Glasgow Herald* put it, 'What the public will make of it all, heaven knows. Last spring it could have been a sentimental Mothercare ad. Today its message is clear. Their future desires are already in ruins. No safe sex for them. The sins of their fathers are visited even on the unborn'.

In the following days the 'public' started to tear down the posters showing the two children, complaining to the police. The Procurator Fiscal advised Transmission that unless the remaining posters were removed there would be a prosecution under the Obscene Displays Act. Ironically the administrative procedures involved in relaying the reaction of the public to Transmission via the police were so cumbersome that it was only three days before the end of the show that the final ultimatum was received.

Another ruined intention." Glyn Banks/Hannah Vowles (*Art Line*, Summer 1987, vol. 3 no. 8, p. 33)

"DESIRE IN RUINS—'STATEMENT'
1) 'Desire In Ruins', like 'Ruins Of Glamour/Glamour Of Ruins', seeks the negation of all forms of abstraction. It contests the myths of individuality and value built on contemporary art practice. Indeed, it contests art practice itself. The installation stands in opposition to both modernism AND postmodernism…

PLAGIARISM AS NEGATION IN CULTURE

Below: 'Desire in Ruins' installation.

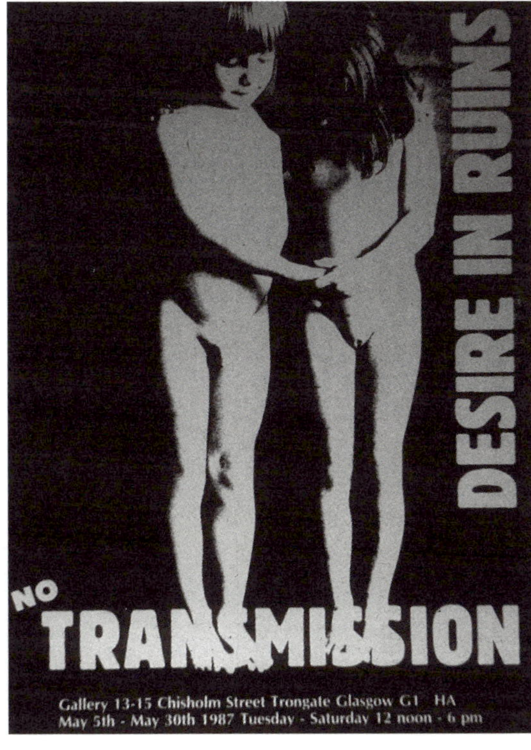

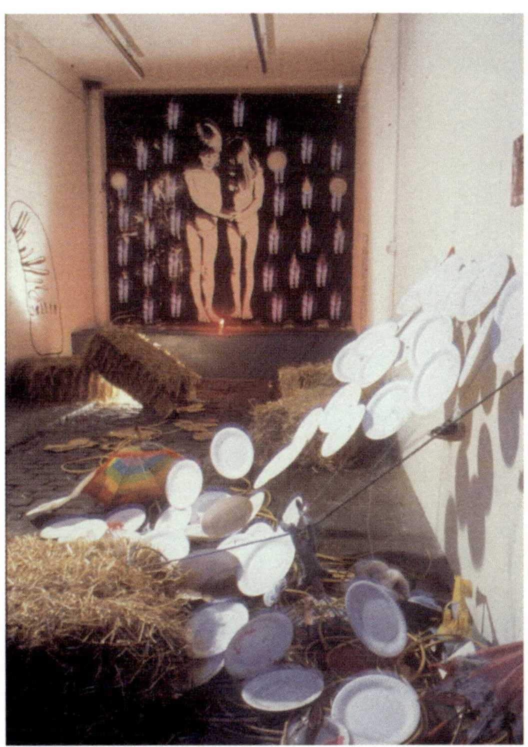

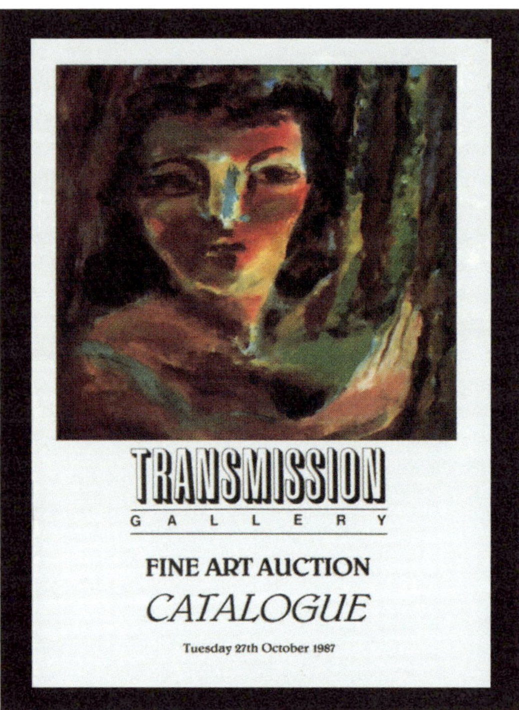

10 **Above:** Catalogue for a fundraising auction for the gallery; this included work by members and supporters of the gallery and raised approximately £5000 for the subsequent exhibition programme.

GIVEN the total colonisation of daily life by Capital, we are forced to speak the received language of the media. It has always been impossible to give coherent expression to thoughts and practices which oppose the dominant ideology. However, we do not seek the creation of new languages. Such an act is doomed to failure and plays into Capital's hands (by reinforcing the myths of 'originality' and 'individual creativity'). Rather, we aim to re-invent the language of those who would control us.

While we refute the concept of 'originality', we do not find it problematic that the idea of plagiarism implies an original. Although we believe all 'human creativity' is accumulative (that is to say, that all 'innovations' are built on the sum total of what has gone before), it does not trouble us that there is, in the past a 'point of origin'. We cannot give an account of this 'point of origin' and will not waste our time making philosophical speculations about such irrelevancies.

Plagiarism is the negative point of a culture that finds its ideological justification in the 'unique'. Indeed, it is only through the creation of 'unique identities' that commodification can take place. Thus the unsuccessful search for a new, and universal, language by 'modernist artists' should be viewed as a high point of the capitalist project. However, this in no way implies that 'postmodernism' is somehow more 'radical' than its precursor. Both movements were simply stages in a single trajectory. Such developments reflect the establishment's ability to recuperate the actions and concepts which in the past threatened its very constitution. 'Postmodern appropriation' is very different to plagiarism. While post-modern theory falsely asserts that there is no longer any basic reality, the plagiarist recognises that power is always a reality in historical society.

Postmodernists fall into two categories. The first of these are cynics who understand the ideological process in which they play a minor role and manipulate it for personal gain. The second category of postmodernists are simply naive. Bombarded by media images, they believe that the ever changing 'normality' presented by the press and TV constitutes a loss of 'reality'. The plagiarist, by contrast, recognises the role the media plays in masking the mechanisms of Power, and actively seeks to disrupt this function.

By reconstituting dominant images, by subjectivising them, we aim to create a 'normality' better suited to our requirements than the media nightmare dictated by Power. However, we have never imagined that this can be achieved solely through 'gallery' exposure. The attitudes used to sell washing powder have a powerful hold over our consciousness precisely because the images associated with them are those most often reproduced in the media. For an image to be effective it needs continuous reproduction in the press and TV. The only viable alternative to our strategy of exposure to images reconstituted by the process of plagiarism, is the physical destruction of transmission stations and print technology." Karen Eliot, from a leaflet to accompany the exhibition. (Karen Eliot is the name invented by Karen Eliot to refer to an 'individual' who can be anyone. In this case, Karen Eliot is writer/publisher of *Smile* magazine. Bookworks and copyart by Karen Eliot can be found in a number of archives including the Tate.)

1988

05 Residue Septik Activity: "The audience line up flat against the wall. Enter London based performer Ivan Unwin under a spotlight video of a giant cow's eye. Throbbing music. Sliding down a rope he covers himself in white powder all the way, landing near a big black slatted box. This he ceremoniously chops with a black pickaxe…" Alice Bain (the Glasgow *Herald*, 10 May 1988, p. 5)

88/06 & 87/12 The Puberty Institution: "Originally working in time-based art, Douglas Gordon and Craig Richardson collaboratively developed their interests in 'Experiments under Nostalgia's umbrella' in The National Review of Live Art 1987 and The Third Eye Centre's 'New Work, No Definition' season under the group name 'tradition:debilitation'.

They now work as 'The Puberty Institution', having performed at the Audio-Visual-Experimental Festival 1987, Arnhem, Holland and at Transmission gallery, 1987.

The Puberty Institution propose to perform a durational installation/event which will take place on JUNE 13TH, 1988. The space is a car park basement, owned by Scotrail, situated in MIDLAND ST., opposite a soup-kitchen, near the River Clyde, in the 'soon-to-be-destroyed' Broomielaw in the heart of the 'merchant city'.

We propose a minimal intervention in a vast and derelict space. We feel that the choice of space is an integral part of our art-process.

07 Below: Transmission's 'Tunnel Party' was held in a disused railway tunnel under Glasgow's Botanic Gardens in July 1988.

Below: Ivan Unwin, 'Residue Septik Activity'.

Bottom: The Puberty Institution, durational performance, June 1988.

Bottom: Tentatively A Convenience performing at the 'Tunnel Party'.

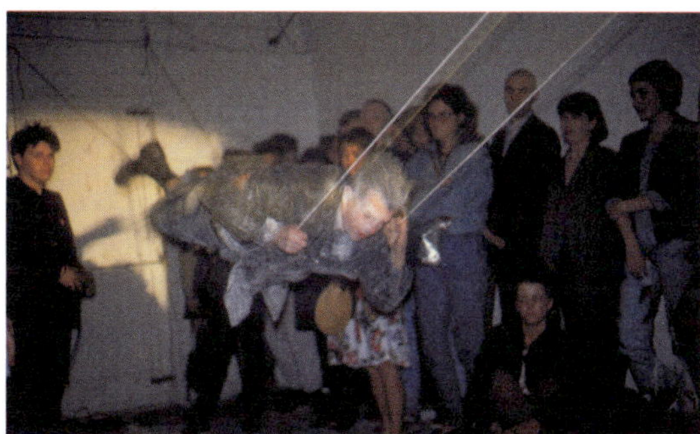

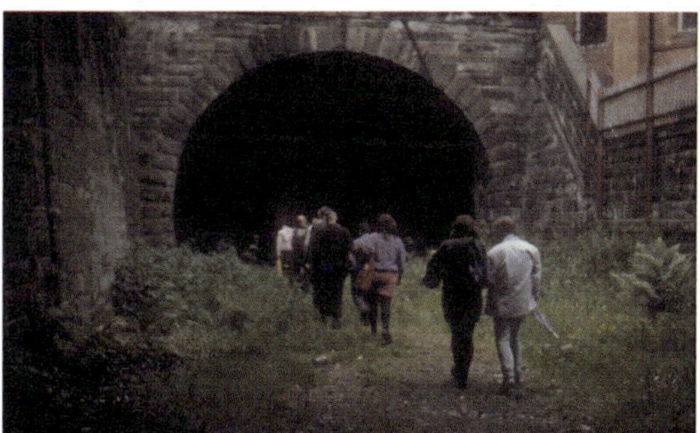

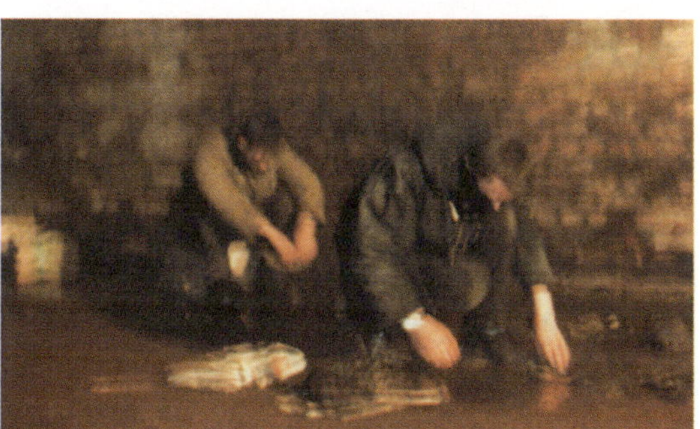

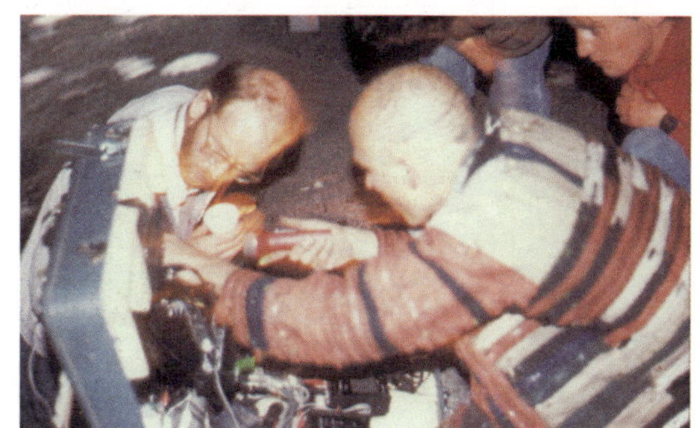

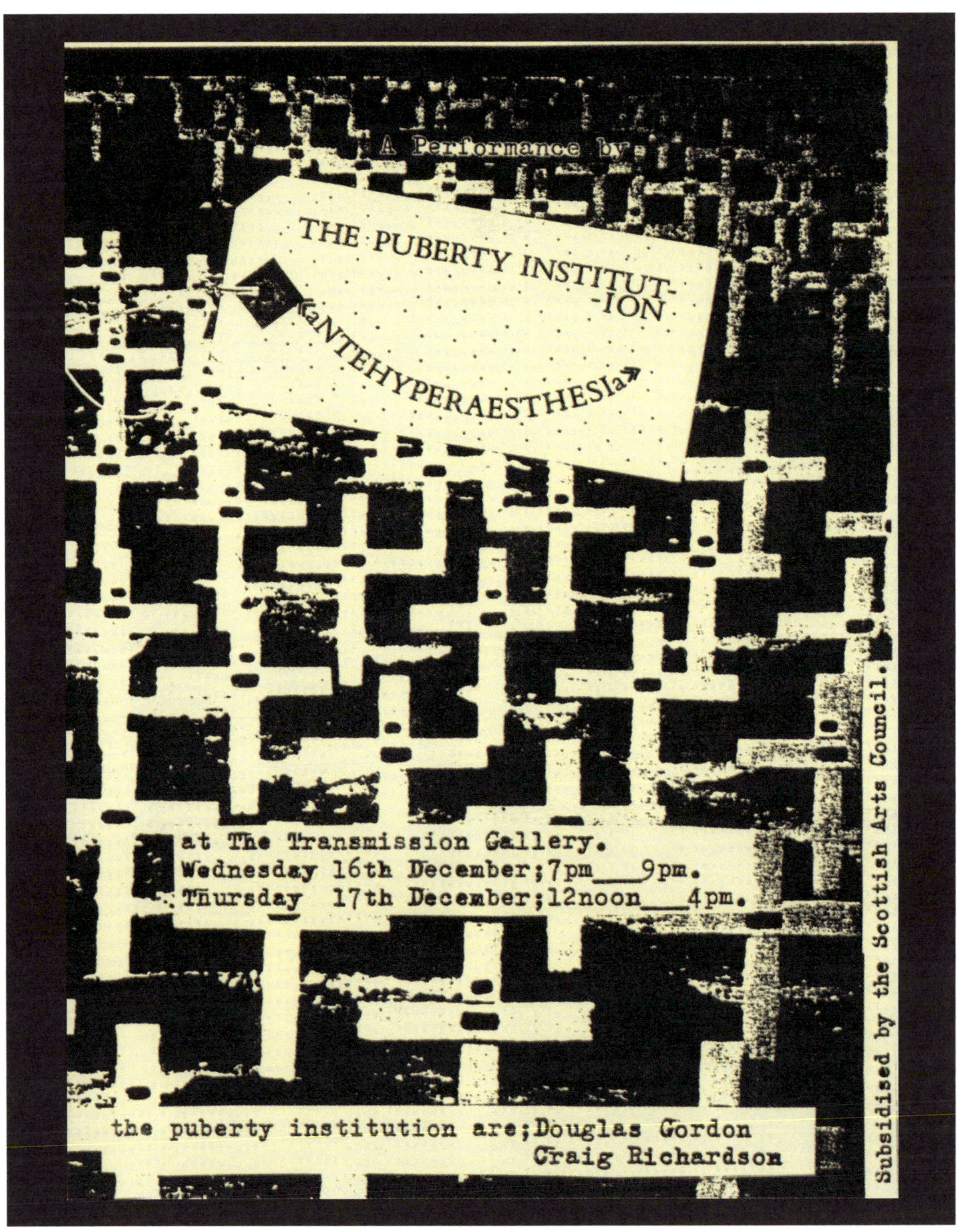
A Performance by
THE PUBERTY INSTITUT-
-ION
aNTEHYPERAESTHESIa
at The Transmission Gallery.
Wednesday 16th December;7pm___9pm.
Thursday 17th December;12noon___4pm.
the puberty institution are;Douglas Gordon
Craig Richardson
Subsidised by the Scottish Arts Council.

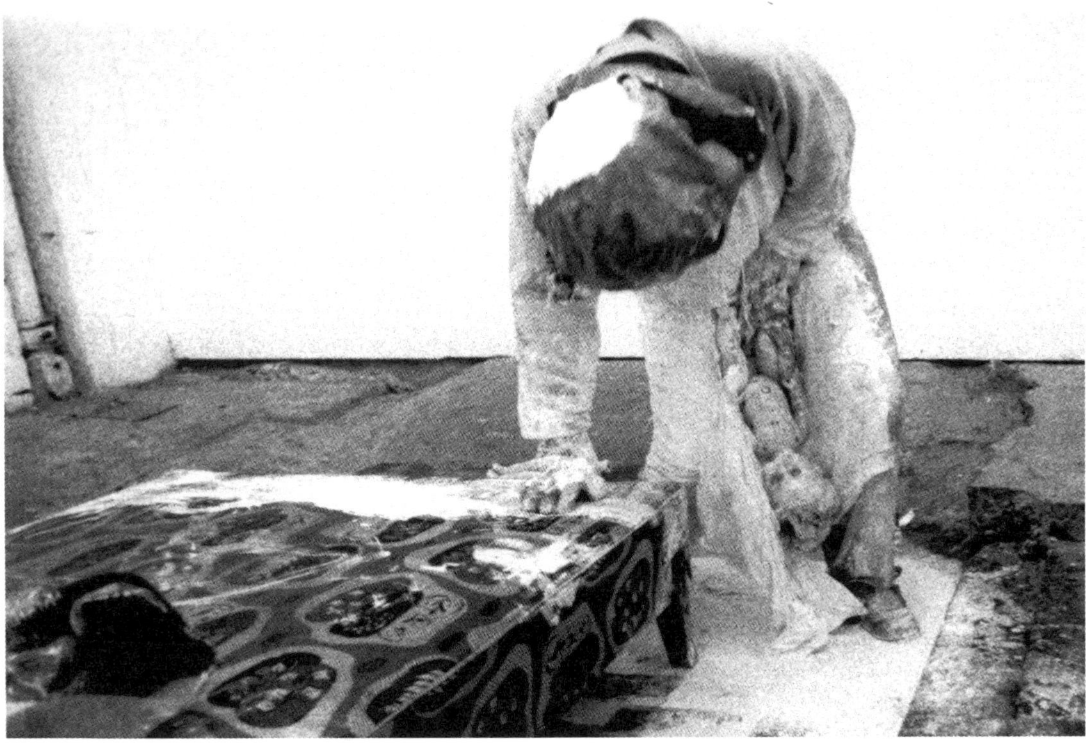

The work strives to create an atmosphere based upon our psychomotor responses to the space and selected objects within that space.

The work will employ all forms of sensory communication.

Our currency is MEMORY.

Our intention is to keep alive the memory of things neglected and disregarded.

We choose to use the 'UNLOVED OBJECTS OF THE WORLD'." (from press release)

08 Shaun Caton — Dark Side Operations: "There are some people in Glasgow who, it appears, have some reservations about all this culture business.

Our tale starts at the Transmission gallery in Chisholm Street, home of a very radical and avant-garde style of performance art. Shaun Caton, a London-based artist, came north last month to perform a 24 hour work called *Dark Side Operations*.

It was strong stuff, as you might expect since the subjects he was exploring included life forms after a nuclear holocaust. For part of his performance Mr Caton was naked apart from a shirt as he enacted the birth of a mutated baby.

As a record of the show, Mr Caton had a colleague take photographs. He took the film along to an instant photoprint shop. When he returned an hour later to collect the prints he was confronted by the manager and two policemen.

The manager had decided that the pictures of a semi-naked man apparently cavorting with dolls should be the subject of a police inquiry. Mr Caton was popped into the back of a police van and taken to the station for questioning.

A very nervous Mr Caton then had the nerve-wracking experience of explaining to Strathclyde's finest the philosophies and reasoning behind his work. He pointed out that he had performed similar scenes recently in Berlin, another European city of culture.

Not impressed but deciding that no crime had been committed, the police released the artist with the traditional advice in such circumstances to 'watch it in future.'" Tom Shields (the Glasgow *Herald*, 23 September 1988, p. 10)

10 **Below, below right and bottom:** Transmission held a jumble sale to raise funds (on the advice of the Scottish Arts Council) during the exhibition 'Work' by Graham Harwood, October 1988; visible in the larger image is a mural in support of the Nicaraguan Solidarity Campaign.

11 Land of Opportunity: 'Land of Opportunity', a five year retrospective held in November 1988, was one of the last shows to be held in the gallery in Chisholm Street.

This featured 'EventsSpace', 'Desire in Ruins', Stuart Brisley, 'Iconoclasm', 'Winning Hearts and Minds', Helen Flockhart, Karen Strang, Alastair Strachan, David Linley, Oladele Bamgboye, Lesley Raeside, Alison Stirling, Peter Thomson and Alistair Magee.

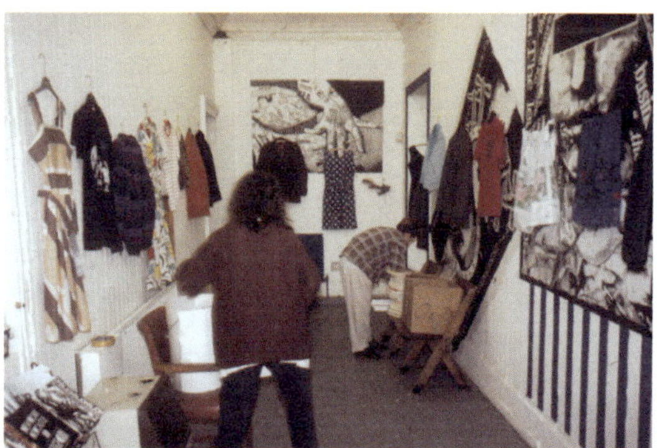

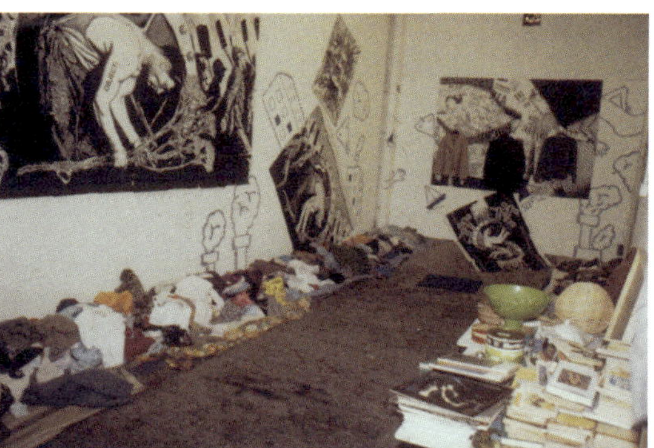

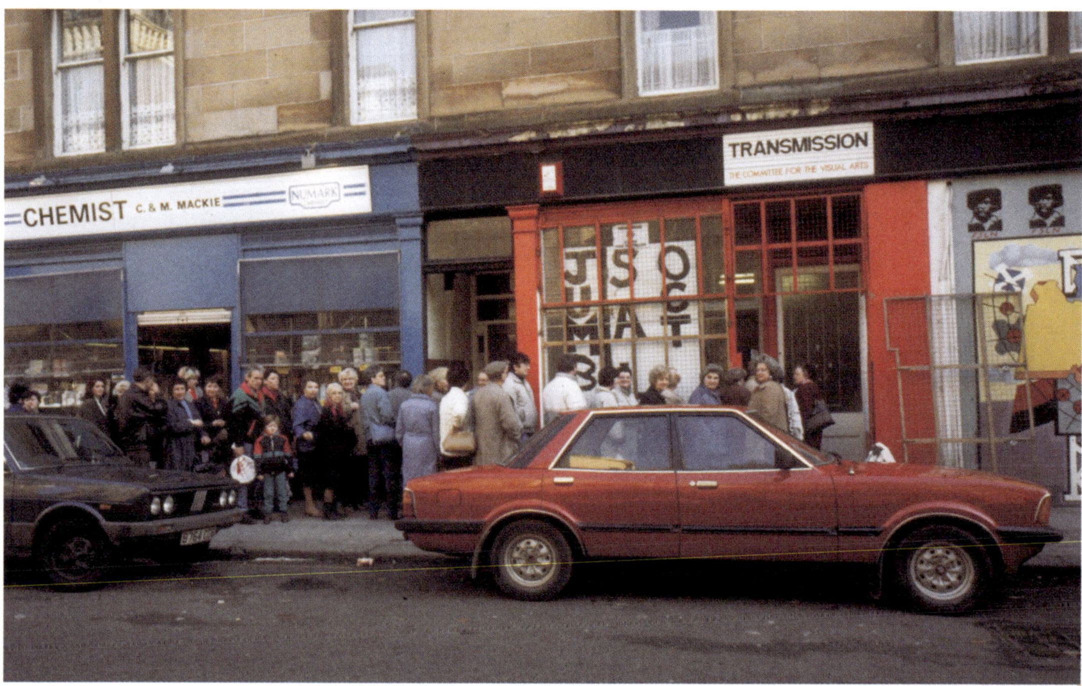

1989

06 Transmission moves to King Street: Billy Clark and Anne Elliot, the committee at the time of the move, approached people to help with the renovation, with a view to enlarging the committee. The volunteers included David Allen, Christine Borland, Jacqueline Donachie, Mike Ellen, Peter Gilmour, Douglas Gordon, Laura Hudson, Euan Sutherland, Ann Vance and Karen Vaughan. Many of these volunteers were graduates from the Environmental Art course at Glasgow School of Art; some had been involved with the gallery while they were students.

"It was Malcolm's [Dickson] interest in the kind of socio-political work that we were interested in in the department that accidentally built a nice bridge between us so that we were the only department in the art school who had the Transmission committee come every year to give a talk to the students." David Harding, Head of Environmental Art (from 1985–2001), in an interview with Rebecca Gordon-Nesbitt, 1995.

Ian Brown (architect), Chris Taylor, Jim Burns and Kenny Little (electrician) also helped with the work.

"After a five month absence from the Glasgow art scene Transmission Gallery is due to re-open in new premises in King Street (burst pipes and a plague of rats had

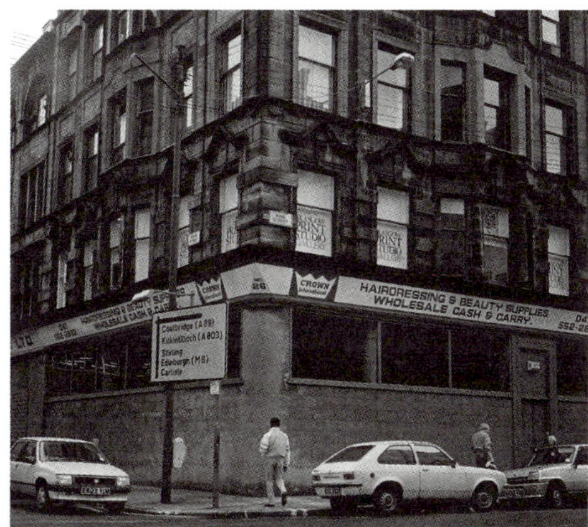

Below and right: The new space at 28 King Street.

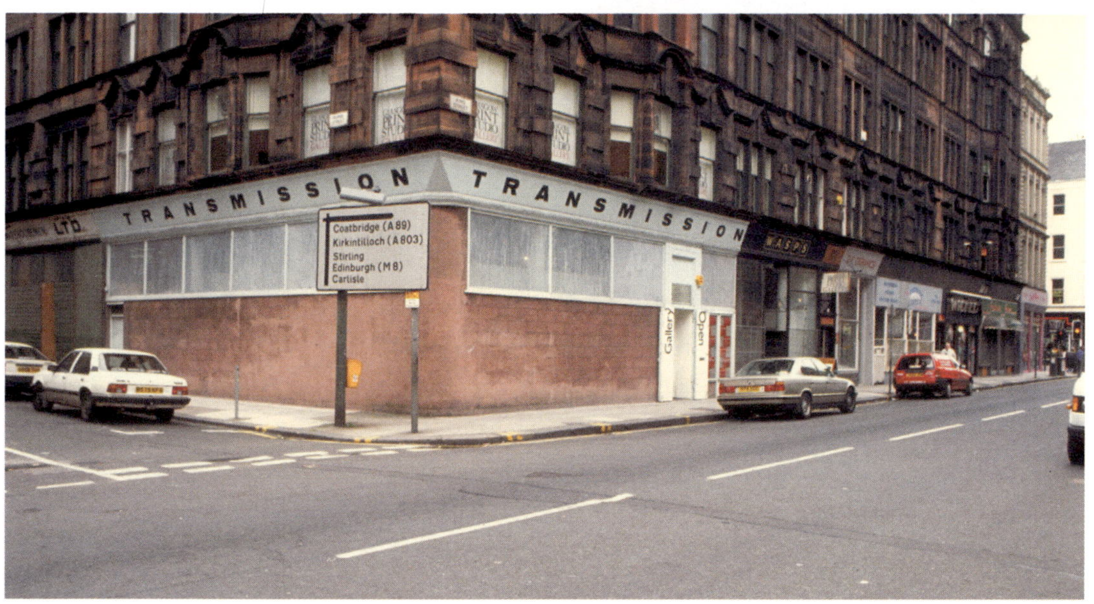

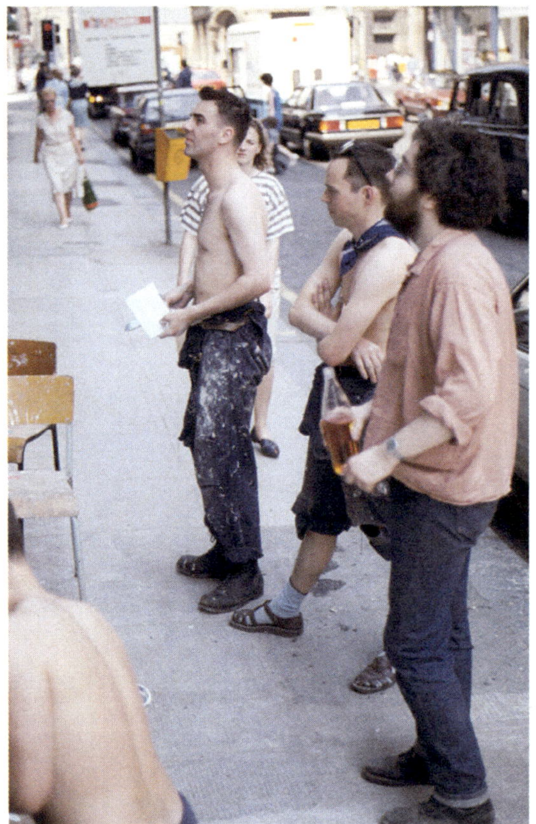

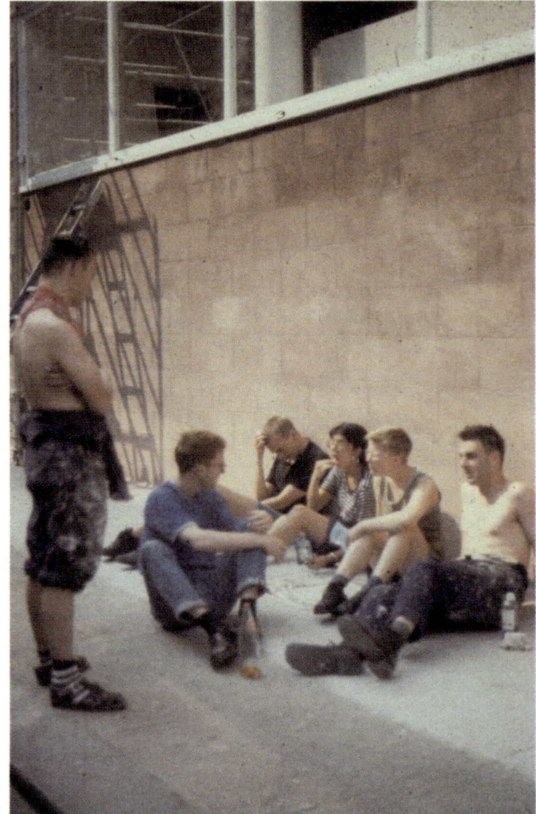

Above: David Allen, Euan Sutherland, Billy Clark.

Above right: Euan Sutherland, Martin Boyce, Peter Gilmour, Helen-Marie Nugent, Karen Vaughan, David Allen.

Right: Ian Brown, Douglas Gordon and Ann Vance.

forced them to abandon their previous location in Chisholm Street!)

Artist-run, the new improved building has one large main gallery with a basement video cinema and a performance installation area.

'It's an ideal space,' enthused Billy Clark, treasurer of the eight-strong committee, 'if anyone had asked me what I'd have wanted in a gallery this would be exactly it.'

With a lack of funding for the move, the committee brought new meaning to the term 'artistic initiative' by

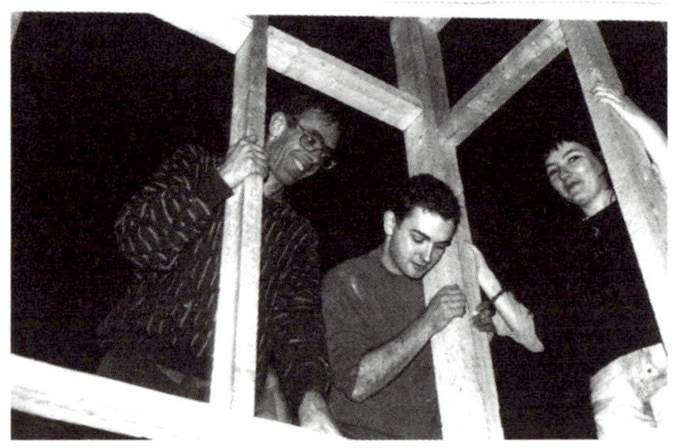

carrying out the renovation work themselves - including the wiring, building walls and creating the public access necessary to pass exacting regulations.

Opposite: Poster by Ross Sinclair.

NOW YOU CAN
REACH THOSE WITH A
DISPOSABLE INCOME
BEFORE
THEY DISPOSE
OF THEIR INCOME

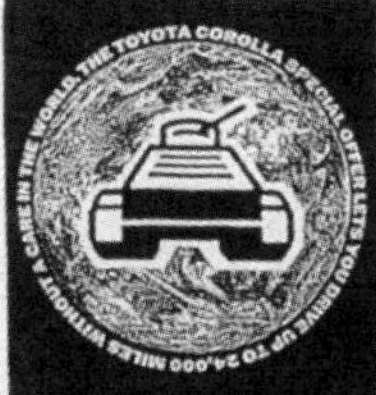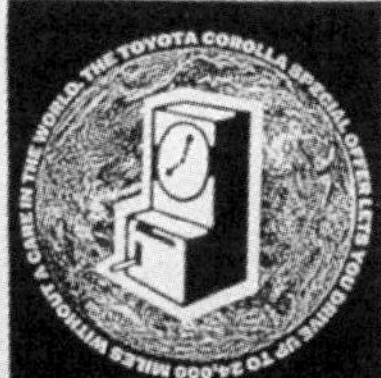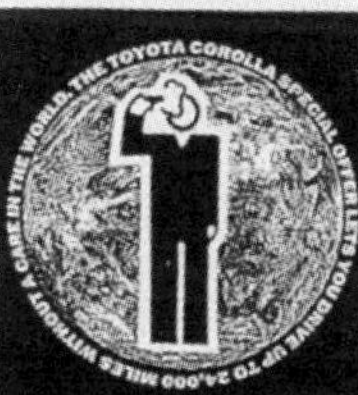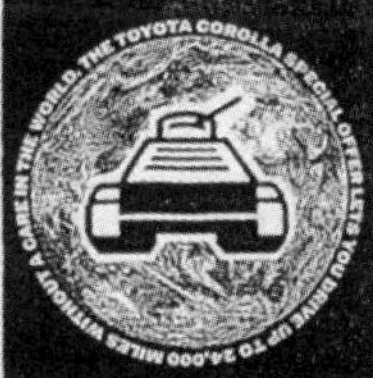

FESTIVAL OF
PLAGIARISM
TRANSMISSION GALLERY   4th-26th August
28 King Street, Trongate, Glasgow G1 5QP   041-552 4813

1989

'We hope to consolidate everything that Transmission has done so far,' commented Clark, 'to do more of what we were doing before—showing work that wouldn't normally be shown in Scotland—but on a larger scale. We will be more of a centre, a place where people will organise from.'

'We can now match the facilities of other galleries,' asserts Clark 'but we also offer a unique, broad-based and unconventional approach.'" Sara Villiers (*The List*, 30 June–13 July 1989, p. 52)

"A bigger, brighter more versatile gallery, but a more conventional space also. Perhaps it is not surprising that the policy of the gallery also shifted soon after the establishment of the new space and with new influences within the committee. Yet when the gallery re-opened in 1989 its anti-mainstream stance was still apparent with events such as the joyful 'Festival of Plagiarism' and performances by the anti-1990 group, 'Workers City'.

Then it was 1990, the year that Glasgow paraded itself as European City of Culture. A year that somehow, beyond the hype and the hoo-ha, did change things in terms of our expectations of ourselves. At this time, Transmission underwent a significant change of direction, and I am sure the timing was not entirely coincidental. A new generation of artists, including Douglas Gordon, Christine Borland and Craig Richardson became involved in the running of the gallery. Previously, the gallery had deliberately positioned itself outside the cultural mainstream. In the early 90s Transmission became, not mainstream, but certainly more allied to the international art scene. Entering the clean-lined space, one could have

been in any city in Europe. Alliances and exchanges were made with like-minded artists and galleries in such places as Belfast, London, Chicago and Cologne. The gallery became increasingly recognised outside of Scotland, and increasingly reviewed in the art press." Nicola White, former Head of Visual Arts Programming at the Centre for Contemporary Art, Glasgow (excerpts from 'Perpetual Motion', an essay written for Transmission, 1995)

08 Fifth International Festival of Plagiarism—Slogans of Reversal/Reversal of Slogans: Mixed media works, lectures and discussions with Mark Bloch, Wendy Lanxtner, The Tape-Beatles, Billy Clark, The Mudguards, AC Acoustics, King Mob, We Are Men, Kola Itch, Jayne Taylor, Stuart Home, Mark Pawson.

August Events:
5th Jamie Reid—Xerox Workshop
6th Jorg Buttigereit—Experimental video work
7th Anarcho/Situationist—Videos
8th The Temple of Psychik Youth—Video Installation
9th Fluxday
10th Decoder—Klaus Maeke—Film
11th Night of the Slack—Florian Cramer—Music and Performance.

'Slogans of Reversal/Reversal of Slogans' in August 1989 followed the Festival of Plagiarism, held in London. The London programme from January 1989 had included contributions from Ed Baxter, Billy Clark, Simon Dickason, Andy Hopton, Malcolm Dickson, Gordon Muir, Karen Eliot, Karen Strang, Graham Harwood, Shaun Caton and Ralph Rumney.

Below: 'Slogans of Reversal/Reversal of Slogans', August 1989.

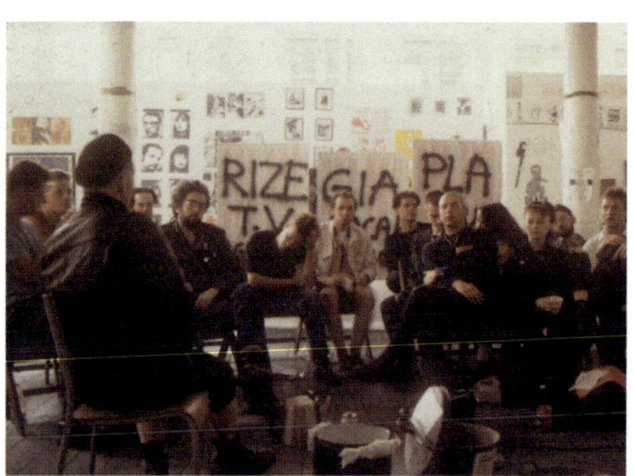

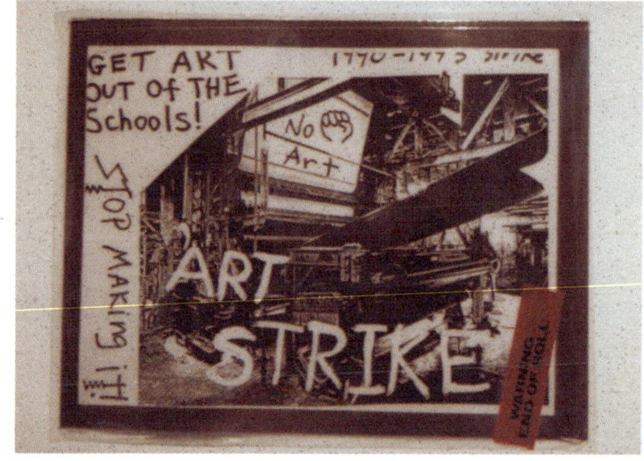

COPY CATS

kidnapping intention cultural

Slogans of Reversal/Reversal of Slogans, Festival of Plagiarism, Transmission Gallery.

Plagiarism is a cultural practice aiming to undermine the hegemony of the concepts of originality and individuality defined as necessary by the social and property relations of capitalism. Creativity, identity, value, truth – how do these categories function in society? By creating the desire of worthy of being bought, words signifying status – the best painter, the most valuable masterpiece – seduce with the power offered to the creator and the attendant superior position bestowed on the artist as 'maker of culture'. The role of most forms of cultural practice is to further alienate those for whom culture is difficult to get to for reasons of political oppression as well as geographical displacement and the elitism of the cultural establishment.

How do you plagiarise? Why plagiarise? Is it art? Art is a concept used to create the illusion of the possibility of attainment of a superior sensibility, but this can be destroyed by appropriating the methods by which these messages reach us – the manipulation of the media, the replication of advertising images and the use of technology. Using xerography, video, anonymity and polemical slogans, new images, worthless in value, high in agit potential, can be created, recreated, replicated, redistributed, recreated . . . Anti-art action therefore becomes free, available to all and most importantly overcomes the imposition of passive consumption typical of most forms of engagement with 'serious' culture.

Slogans of Reversal/Reversal of Slogans is an exhibition which goes beyond the space, has no copyright, involves many nameless individuals and lots of photocopied, reappropriated signs – 'We are the proletariat – the people who like to say no'. 'Real meaning involves another's thought', 'How are the masses made to desire their own repression – Fascination: spectacle seduced by its own promiscuity.' From style culture to nuclear war rhetoric to TV to the glamorization of suffering, involvement with the 'issues of our times' implies critical commitment and accessibility to processes of production – plagiarism implies recreating this. (Lorna J. Waite)

Above: Review from the *List*, 18–24 August 1989, p. 86.

Art Strikes: "In his section of the 'Art Into Society/Society Into Art catalogue' (ICA, London 1974), Gustav Metzger issued a call for a three year strike by artists. Metzger believed that if artists acted in solidarity, they could destroy those institutions (such as Cork Street) which had a negative effect on artistic production. Metzger's strike failed because he was unable to mobilise support from other artists.

During martial law in Poland, artists refused to exhibit their work in state galleries, leaving the ruling elite without an official culture. For months the art galleries were empty. Eventually some mediocre artists were discovered, who were prepared to take advantage of this situation, and their work was shown. The Polish intelligentsia immediately organised an effective boycott of openings, denying the art an audience and the bureaucracy any credibility.

In 1985 the PRAXIS group proposed an art strike for the three years between 1990 and 1993. In 1986 this proposal was extended to a more generalised refusal of creativity. The idea was not to destroy the art world. PRAXIS doubted that enough solidarity existed between artists for such a strategy to work. Instead, PRAXIS were interested in how they, and many other activists, had created identities based on the supposed superiority of their creative and/or political actions to the leisure and work pursuits of the social majority. This belief in individual superiority was seen as impeding a rigorous critique of the reigning society. Put bluntly, those whose identity is based on their opposition to the world as it is,

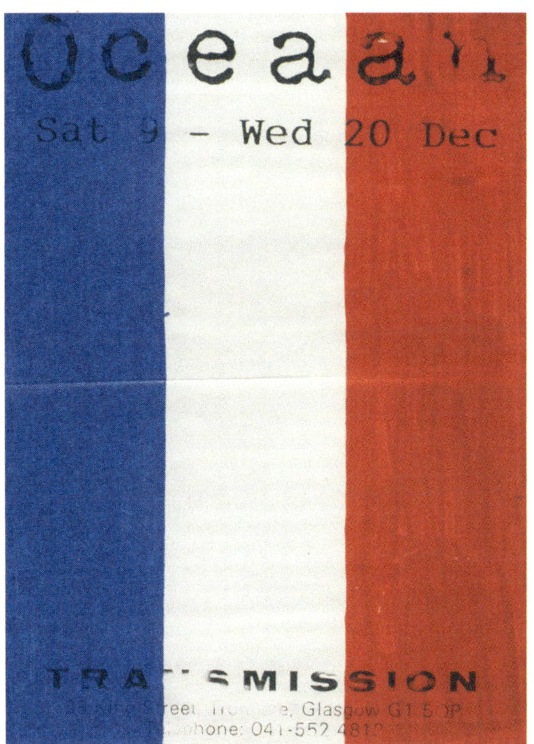

have a vested interest in maintaining the status quo. To change the world it is necessary to abandon those character traits that aid survival in capitalist society." Stewart Home, (from 'Plagiarism: Art as Commodity and Strategies for its Negation', p. 19 [booklet which accompanied the Festival of Plagiarism, London, January 1989])

10/12 Transmission Gallery/Oceaan Gallery Exchange Project, October 1989: Transmission's first international exchange project—with Oceaan (Arnhem, The Netherlands).

A group of artists were selected from the membership of each gallery. The Scottish group—David Allen, Billy Clark, Louise Crawford, Steven Harty and Karen Vaughan—travelled to Arnhem in October with three of the group staying for three weeks and two staying for two weeks, making work and setting up an exhibition in the Oceaan Gallery. The Dutch group—Hester Oerlemans, René Roeten, An van Roosmalen and Wilma Sommers— came to Glasgow in early December.

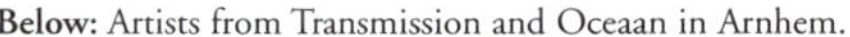

Below: Artists from Transmission and Oceaan in Arnhem.

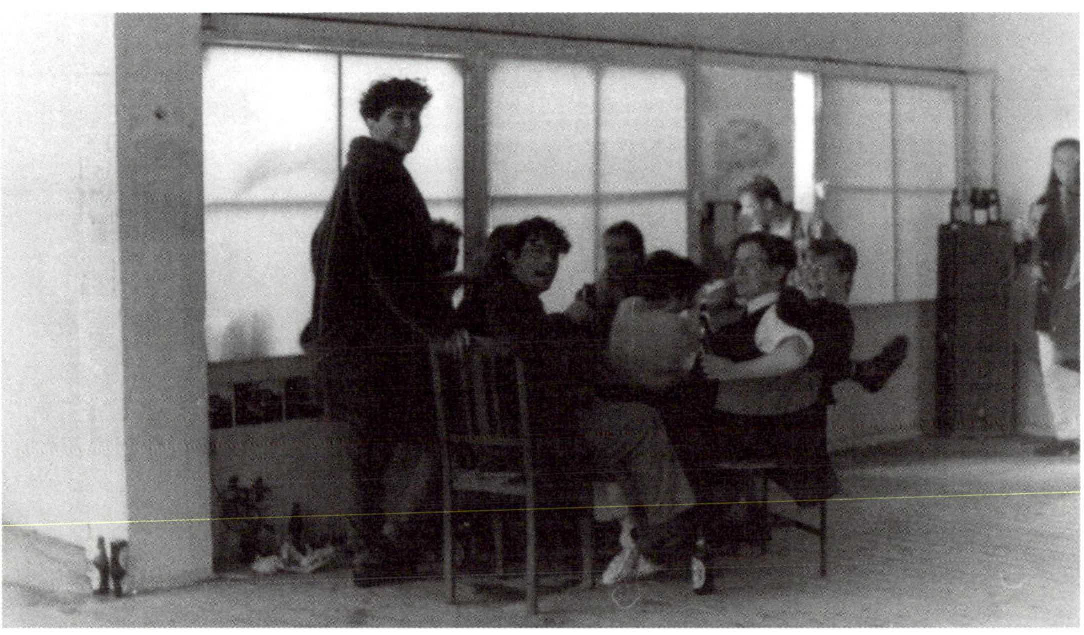

1990

was in the gallery tradition of trying to express those concerns through the exhibition programme. The artists involved addressed the commonalities of human dependence, amongst them the fragility of good health

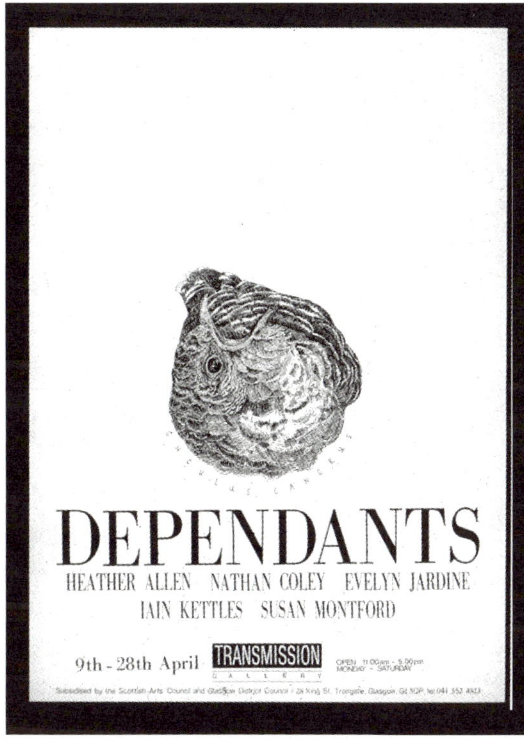

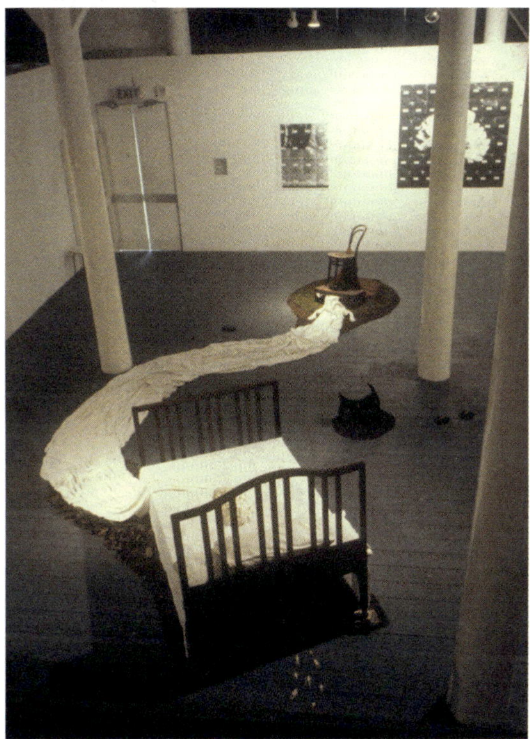

Above: Installation view of 'Dependants'. Foreground: Heather Allen, Untitled; background: work by Nathan Coley.

04 Dependants: "City-wide disaffection with the misguided funding priorities of the 1990 Year of Culture coupled with a genuine anxiety about the future of the gallery's voluntary structure, soon created an uneasy and troubled atmosphere within our new committee. It was difficult to imagine how committee members could cope with the increasing pressure to participate in ineffectual Government retraining schemes while unable to declare the real 'job experience' of working at Transmission. As noted by Simon Ford in an *Art Monthly* article about the phenomenon of the Young British Artist, the Enterprise Allowance Scheme which had been introduced in 1983 and supported around 10,000 artists a year, was becoming more difficult to qualify for, and was on its way to being replaced. The group show 'Dependants' in April 1990

and the ties of home and family. They themselves were united by a financial reliance on the state benefit system. The tiny budget for the show was stretched to give every artist £30 towards production costs. This meagre sum, around the same as a week's dole at the time, could only highlight the inadequacy of income support and the incompatibility of the system with both the 'work' of artists and artist-run organisations such as Transmission.

New Government policies were also reflected in the way funding could be made available to arts organisations. 'Incentive Funding' was a reward for increased revenue earned. Since there was no structure in place to seriously market contemporary art, it was only possible to generate extra revenue through sales of art/craft trinkets and Transmission refused to bid for it. Our other possibility for a funding increase was just as distasteful and unworkable within the self determined structure and aims of the organisation. To engender confidence and create a conveniently consistent point of contact, the Scottish Arts Council wanted Transmission business to be conducted by a paid administrator. In the opinion of the committee there

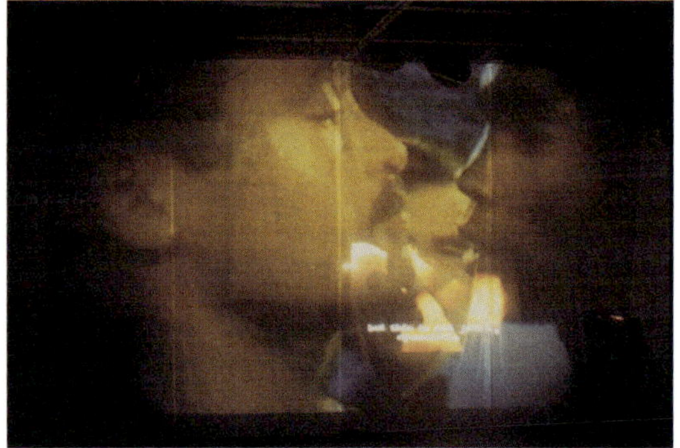

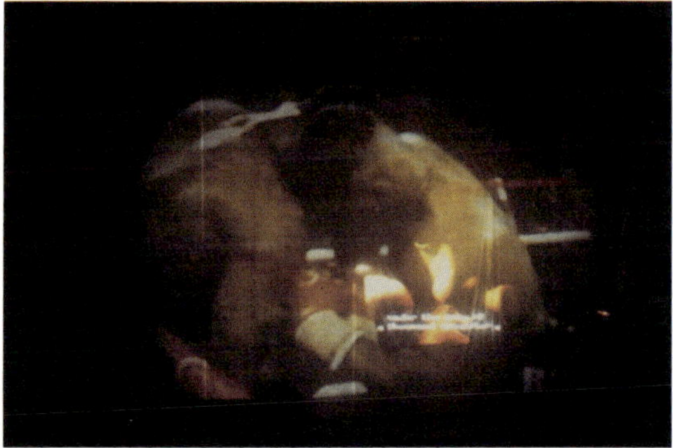

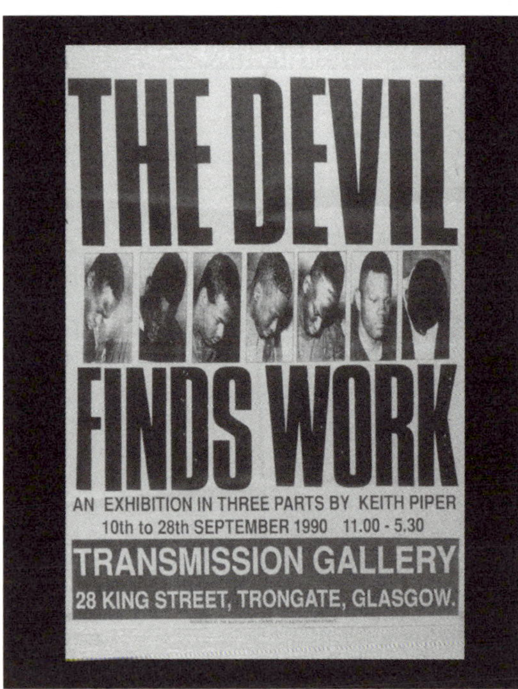

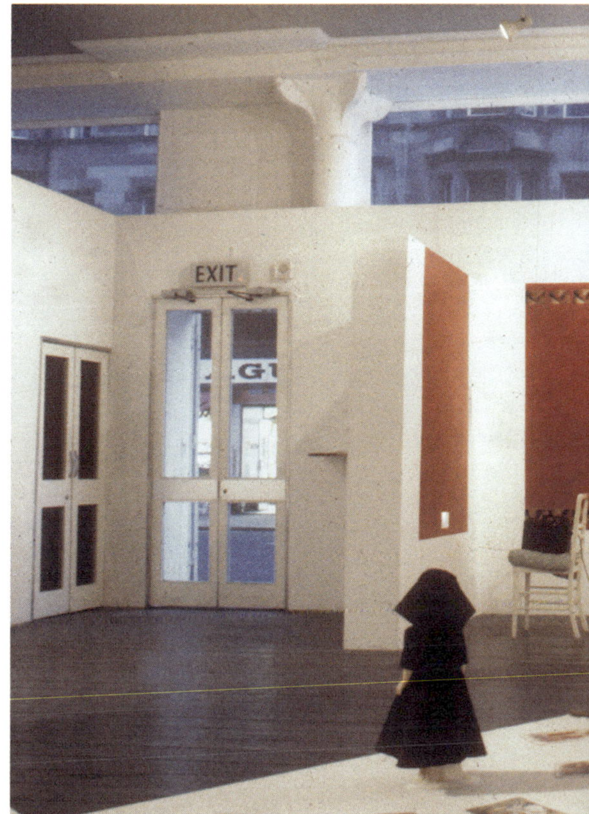

Above and top: Keith Piper, 'The Devil Finds Work'.

was no such rigid division between who dealt with funding, administration and the curation of the programme." Christine Borland (excerpt from 'Dear Green Place, No More', an essay written for Transmission, 1995)

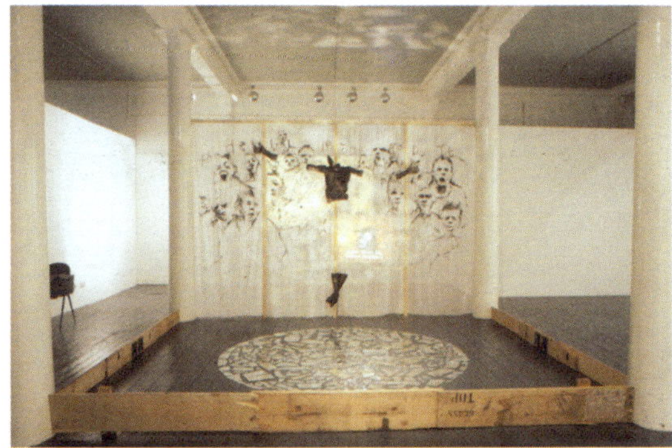

09 'Keith Piper—The Devil Finds Work: "From the 10th to the 28th of September Transmission will exhibit the work of the London-based artist Keith Piper. The exhibition, which has been made specifically for the gallery is in three parts collectively entitled *The Devil Finds Work*. Piper describes the work as taking as a central theme the exploration of contemporary demonologies, their development, their function and our perception of them from within and without. The work combines investigations into the various legacies of imperialism and how these manifest themselves in contemporary society with investigations into various mythologies that have been generated around black male presence in the West. Within this, legacies rooted in the slave trade and the categorisation of the black male in terms of his capacity for brute physical labour are traced forward into a contemporary society which weaves around black male presence a complex cloak of fear and fantasy." (from press release)

12 Wishful Thinking: "'Wishful Thinking' at Transmission Gallery is an interesting show involving four artists who work in mixed media. Jacqueline Donachie previously exhibited in the Saltoun Art Project where she impressed me with her professionalism. Here wall mounted boxes full of cheap multiples: sherbet lollipops, sticky tape, Brillo pads, plastic sunglasses, nylon hair brushes are immaculately positioned on a plain white wall whose slogan, 'An Artistic Treat', is subtle gloss on matt. Karen Vaughan also showed at Saltoun and in Photoworks. This time her fascination with the time-honoured 'fitting' female pastime of embroidery takes the form of film juxtaposed with a photographic zigzag of female hands. Jacqueline Byrne's installation addresses the perennial question of Catholicism and virginity while Rachel Mimiec explores her Polish roots." Clare Henry (the Glasgow *Herald*, 18 January 1991, p. 12)

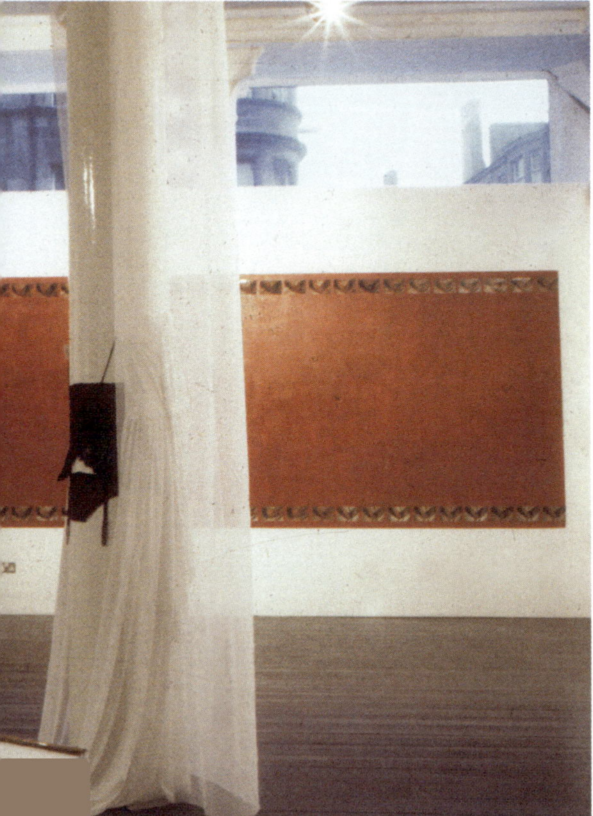

Left: 'Wishful Thinking', December 1990; foreground: work by Jacqueline Byrne; background: Karen Vaughan, *Necessary fulfilment of needs*.

1991

"Transmission has provided a backdrop, a context, a mailing list, or most importantly, an office for several other, though temporary, independent initiatives in Glasgow over the years: 'Information' at Paisley Museum in 1989; the Saltoun Art Project (S.A.P.) in 1990 and 'Windfall '91' in the disused Seamen's Mission, to name but a few." Katrina Brown, former Transmission committee member (from 'Never Being Boring' , an essay written for Transmission, 1995)

From the late 80s groups such as Open World Poetics, Workers City and the Free University used the space regularly as a meeting place.

Free University was an informal network of dissatisfied individuals, interested in aspects of education, art, politics and literature.

"In 1991 a whole series of Free University events relating to the visual arts, power and politics, occurred at Transmission: Jo Spence on Class and Education*, Stefan Szczelkun on art and class, Peter Suchin on abstract painting, Owen Kelly on the opportunities for independent cultural activity and Stewart Home on 'Oppositional Culture and Cultural Opposition'. Many events went undocumented—others, such as Charles Stephens on Beuys and Roland Miller on performance art, were to appear as articles in issues of *Variant* magazine." Malcolm Dickson (from 'Hit the North', an essay written for Transmission, 1996)

*Jo Spence had a solo exhibition 'Missing Persons' at Transmission in September 1991.

05 Workers City: "The month of May carries with it certain overtones of both a cultural and political nature, concerning celebration and a challenge to ideas of official and unofficial culture.

Throughout May 1991 a range of events will be publicly presented by the WORKERS CITY group at Transmission Gallery in GLASGOW.

These events represent a diversity of organisations and individuals who have joined together to go some way towards forming both an analytical and an enjoyable vision of contemporary cultural activity." (from leaflet to accompany events)

"One of the leading lights in Workers City, Brendan McLaughlin outlines the creed of the association which was anti-European City of Culture hype and previews 'Ten Days in May—Review' at the Transmission Gallery ending on Friday May 10.

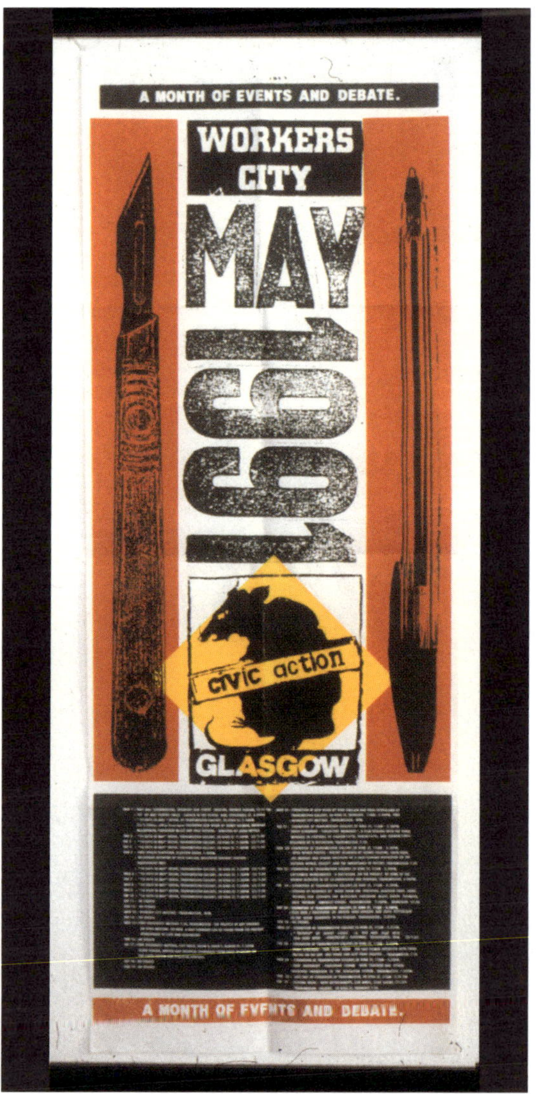

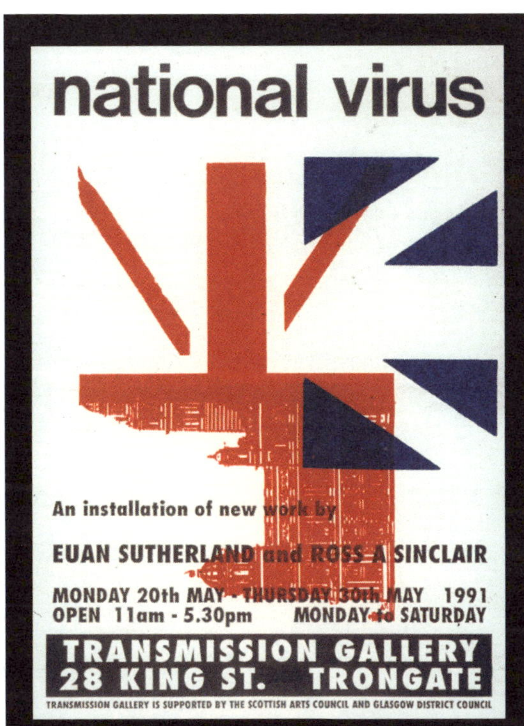

Throughout 1990 and Glasgow's reign as the European City of Culture, certain people refused to get involved opting instead to continue their work as they would do in any given year. However, events conspired to direct their creative skills in attempts to stop Glasgow from being misrepresented and ripped off.

They encouraged people not to be taken in by the vainglorious hype that characterised the year of culture.

They set themselves to publicly question much of the reasoning behind the presentation of Glasgow as a tame, pristine city posturing before would-be inward investors.

They defended Elspeth King and Michael Donnelly against the cynical persecution of Glasgow District Council and Julian Spalding, Director of Museums.

They exposed the outrageous cost to Glaswegians of the Glasgow's Glasgow exhibition and the attempts to sell off valuable public assets to pay for that and other misconceived fiascos.

They stopped [local councillors] Pat Lally, Danny Crawford and [Director of Parks and Recreation] Bernard Connolly from selling off the Glasgow Green to private developers.

Left: 'National Virus', an exhibition by Euan Sutherland and Ross Sinclair, was held concurrently with the 'Workers City' events programme.

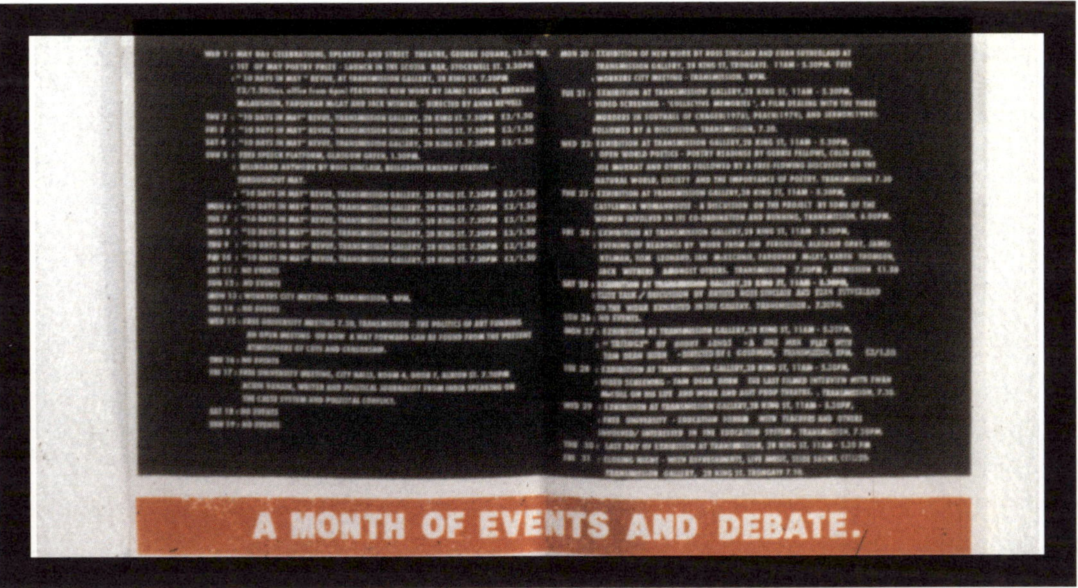

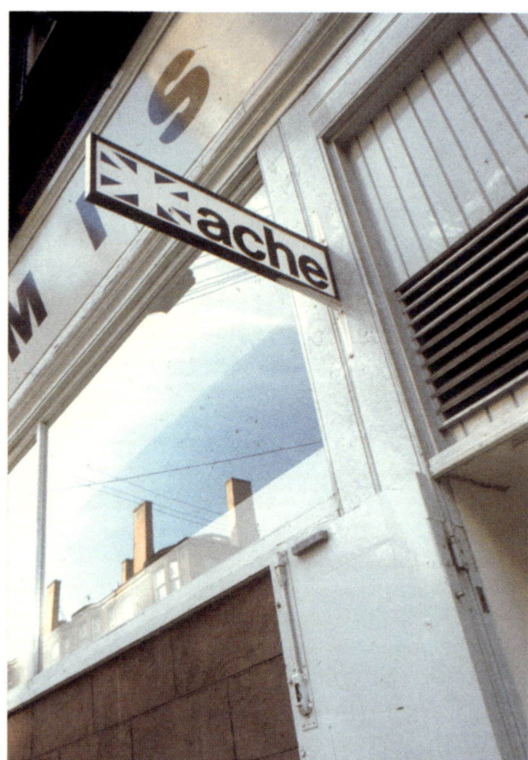

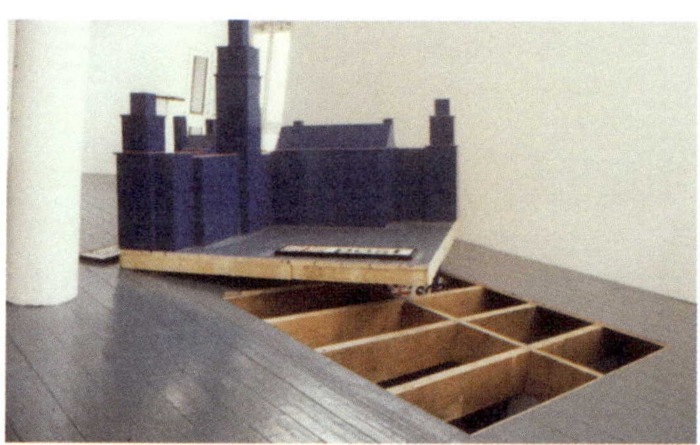

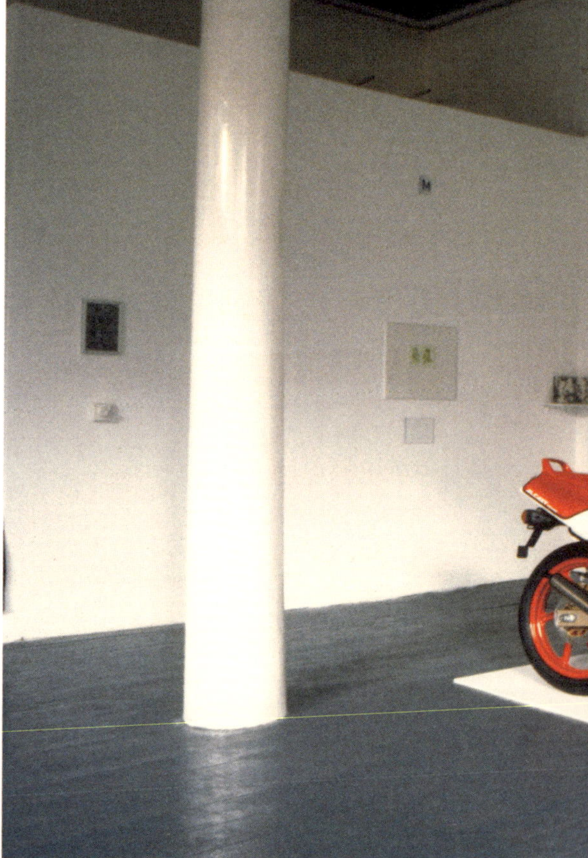

In 1991 they reclaim May Day for the people and then stage a revue and an exhibition which will take place in the Transmission Gallery in King Street.

There will be a visual exhibition interspersed with readings and discussions.

There will be sketches, poems, readings and songs from various members of Paranoid Productions plc., while the exhibition will be set up by members of the gallery. One of those who wrote and organised the revue was author James Kelman. The exhibition is being presented by Euan Sutherland and Ross Sinclair. So do yourself a favour, come along and see the real Glasgow stand up." (from unknown publication, April 1991)

05 National Virus: "This installation of new work by Euan Sutherland and Ross Sinclair continues to investigate and confront some of the themes already raised in the first half of this month's events. The exhibition is site specific. The site of course is an art gallery in Glasgow, 1991. The installation explores the relationship between the 'centre' and its 'margins'. It focuses on the problematic relationship which has always existed between:

National Government/Local Government
National Culture/Local Culture

The artists wish to question the assumption that ideas and culture must be created by, or defined (approved) through, the 'centre', and then disseminated (imposed), through its local representatives (politically and culturally), in the various areas of society, those representatives see fit to target." (from leaflet to accompany events)

07 Speed: "We were organising an exhibition of Cathy Wilkes', but she broke her arm or something a few weeks before the exhibition so she couldn't make the installation. So we went to the membership and we made this exhibition called 'Speed'. Really it was the fastest exhibition that we ever made and it was packed full of 50, 60, 70 objects and pictures. But the overwhelming sense of the gallery was not that it was crowded; it was just full of small statements by people that made one large conversation. It was one of the noisiest exhibitions we ever had, in a way." Douglas Gordon (from 'Ping-Pong—a conversation between Douglas Gordon and Hans-Ulrich Obrist', for Transmission, 1995)

10 Cathy Wilkes—Like Moth: "'Like Moth' takes as its source the work of another artist. Cathy Wilkes' exhibition is 'like' that of the other artist, without being mimetic. The text that publicised the show situated the work of Cathy Wilkes in relation to the work of the

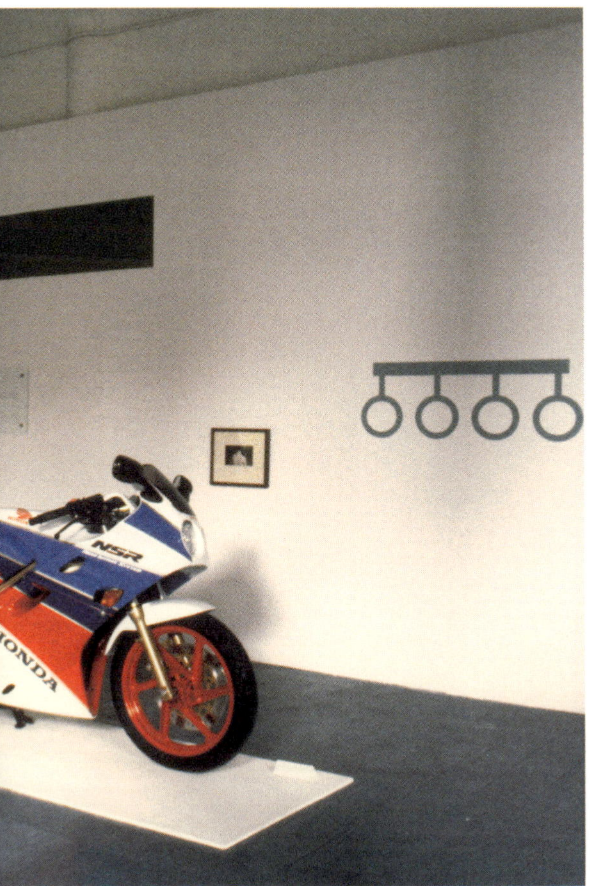

Left: 'Speed', June 1991; foreground: David Allen, Untitled.

Below: Flyer for Cathy Wilkes' 'Like Moth', September 1991.

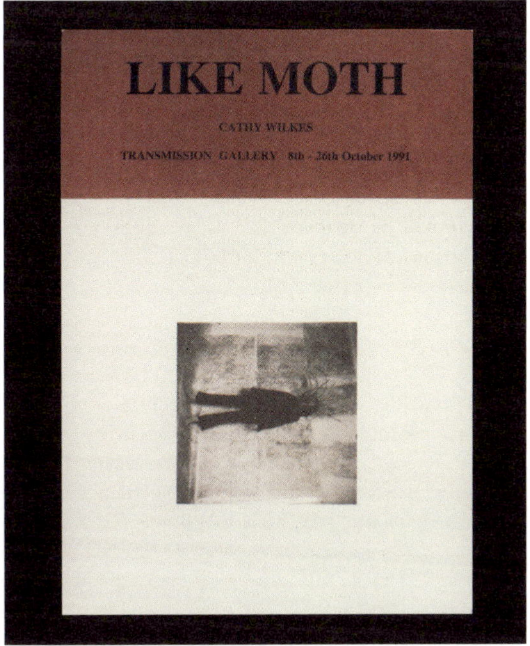

Romanian performance artist Elekes Károly. Following her own cultural exchange to Hungary and Eastern Europe, Wilkes has taken inspiration from the work of this particular artist, and the movement that he was part of, to create works which are a product of her own experience of that culture…

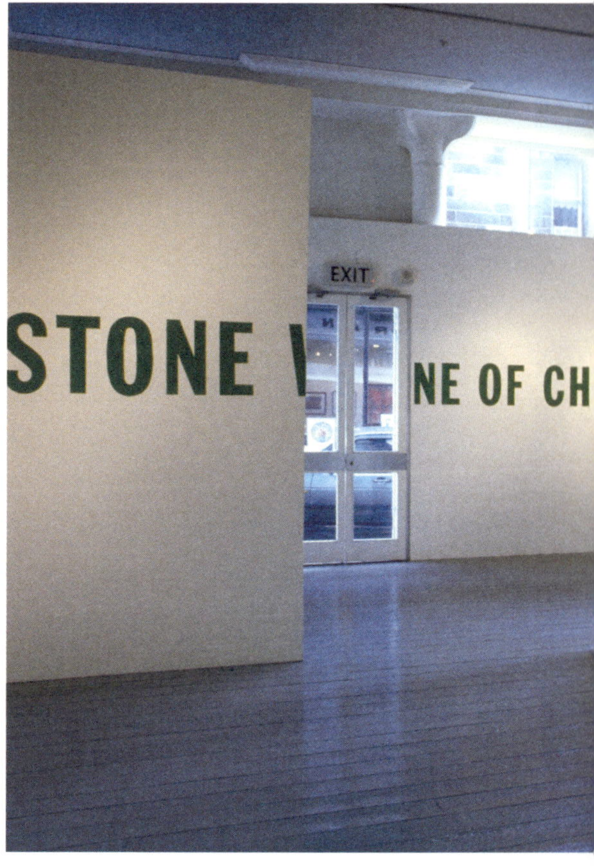

Above: Cathy Wilkes, 'Like Moth', September 1991.

Wilkes' work is unusual in that it sits uncomfortably between Eastern and Western European notions of radical art practice. It seems at once to reflect Eastern European modernist art and at the same time to be reminiscent of the anti-object art of the 70s and early 80s in Western Europe. It is possible that Wilkes' own tentativeness with this show is representative of the difficulty of creating art which negotiates between these two culturally specific art practices and these two politically different cultures. What her work does propose by addressing Eastern European art and presenting it as a relevant issue within our culture is the need for an art practice which challenges the political background in which it is made, be it under an institutionalised hierarchy or within a commodity economy." Ewan Morrison (*Alba*, December 1991–January 1992, pp. 34–35)

11 Lawrence Weiner: "Although Weiner visited Glasgow as early as 1963, this will be his first one-man show in the city. Weiner will install a text in the gallery and will produce an edition of stickers to be distributed and posted up throughout the city." (from press release)

"Language succeeds in the presentation of art, by making it possible to carry across / to convey / to communicate a relationship of objects without having to have with it the entire psyche involved in the production of a realistic object…

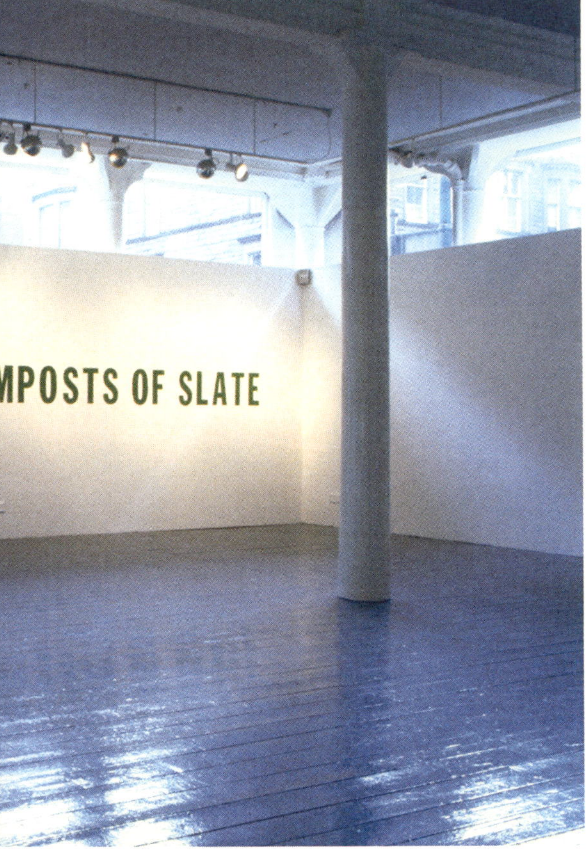

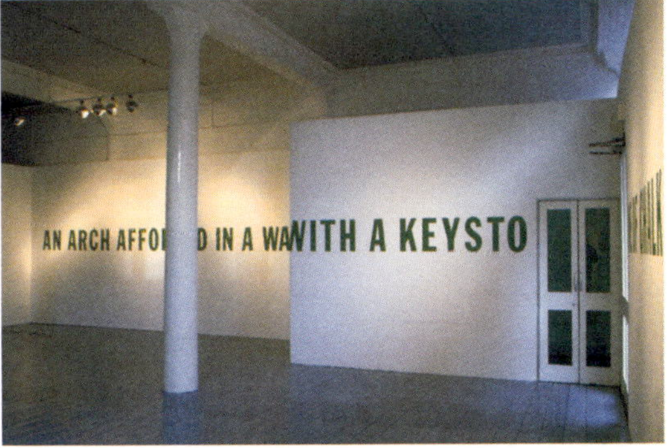

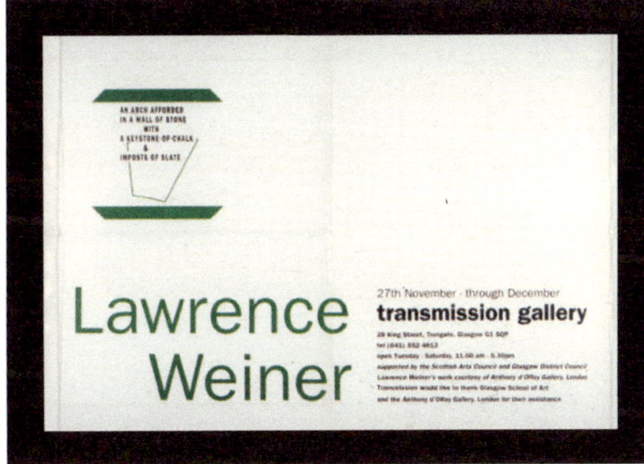

Left and above: Lawrence Weiner, November 1991.

The sticker operates in this context where, economically and culturally, most people are feeling really rather under attack. This economic situation encourages the general attempt to put art back in its place… But when one talks about the billboard and so on—the billboard is a total imposition. That's a taking up of a public place, that's buying space, that is essentially paying the dominant culture to let you put up what you feel is functioning as art at that moment. The poster can, of course, be flashposted, but a poster is advertising something. A sticker, though, functions in a different way. If it is available at Transmission Gallery, if it goes out through *Variant* magazine, then that sticker, if it does stand as art, can be stuck anyplace, by anybody, anytime…. But it's not any kind of counter-culture, nor any aggression, to put it on a sticker. It just takes it out of the context of the average advertisement. The sticker is something that you put on. It's a temporary tattoo on the something that it sticks to." Lawrence Weiner (from an interview with Douglas Gordon, *Variant*, Winter 1991, pp. 36–41)

1992

02 Really Saying Something: In February 1992 six artists from Transmission's membership travelled to Flanders to exhibit in the Cultural Centres of Aalst, Berchem, Bornem, Strombeek-Bever and Tielt.

Below: 'Really Saying Something'—work by Colin Pettigrew.

Bottom: 'Really Saying Something'—foreground: work by Derek Scanlan; background: work by Jonathan Monk.

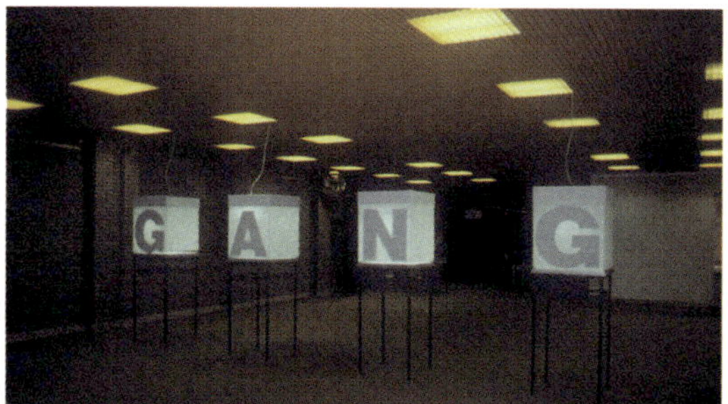

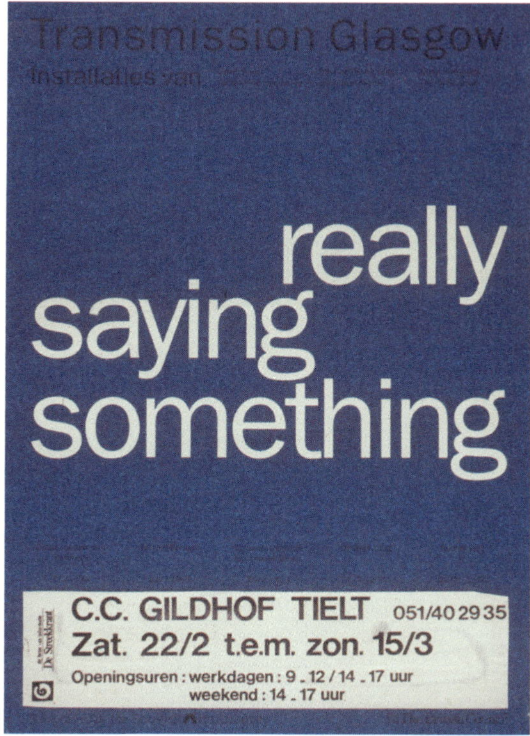

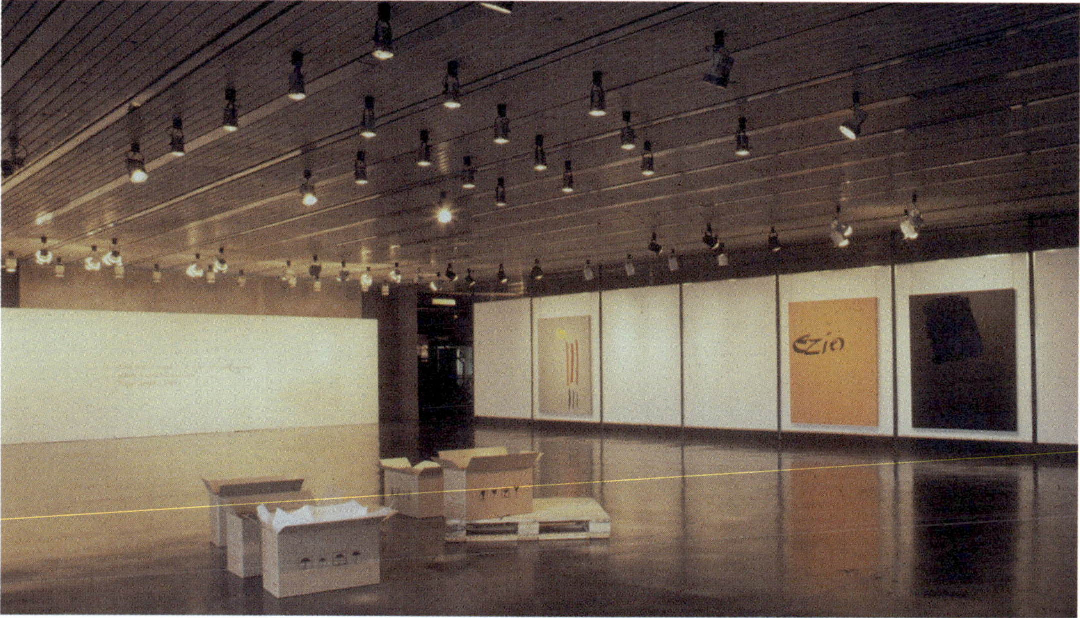

06 **Contact: 552-4813:** "Craving the exhilaration and vitality of 'Speed', last year's show in June (36 artists), we would again like to kick the summer off in a similar spirit.

This is our invitation to you.

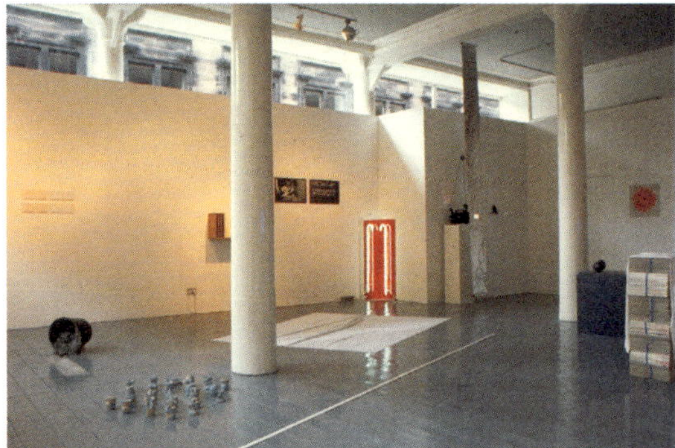

It has also gone out to a good cross-section of artists associated with Transmission. Each of you are being asked to participate in this exhibition, the only restriction being that your work should be small and able to comfortably exhibit alongside the other works in the ground floor gallery." (from letter of invitation, April 1992)

Left: 'Contact 552-4813', June 1992.

09 **Transmission at City Racing/City Racing at Transmission:** "During September, Transmission Gallery and City Racing, London, will mount simultaneous exhibitions.

At City Racing in London, Annette Heyer, Andrew Lockhart, Julie Roberts and Ross Sinclair, four members of Transmission selected by the gallery's committee for this exhibition, show a diverse group of work. Julie Roberts' paintings of medical implements and

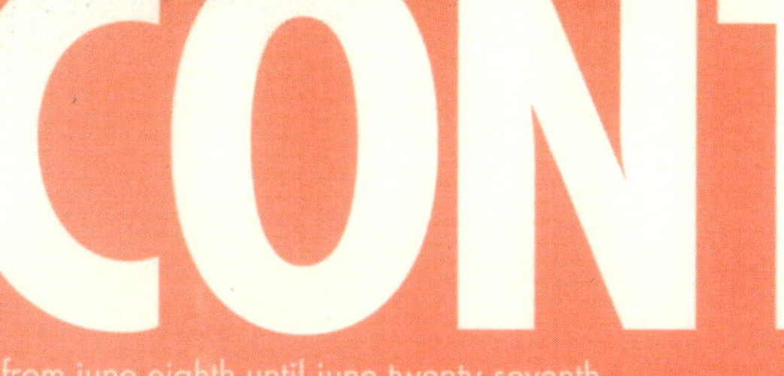

equipment will be shown beside new work, also using paint, by Ross Sinclair while Annette Heyer will show her light-based work and Andrew Lockhart will improvise with one of the gallery's spaces.

In Glasgow, the five originators of City Racing show their own work at Transmission. Equally diverse, this exhibition includes video work by John Burgess, 'liquid landscape lightboxes' by Matthew Hale, Keith Coventry's paintings based on housing estates, an assemblage of comic books and related objects by Paul

Above: Ross Sinclair, *Black Union, Black Flags for USA '92.*

Right: Julie Roberts, *Wheelchair.*

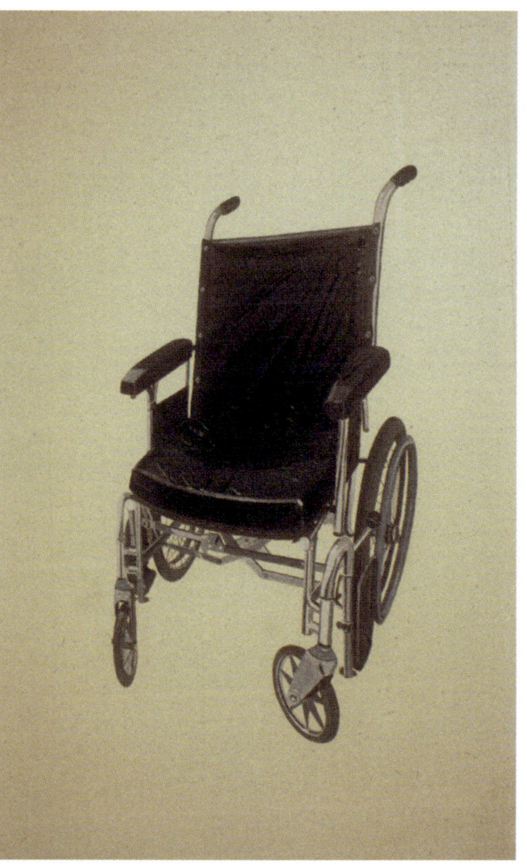

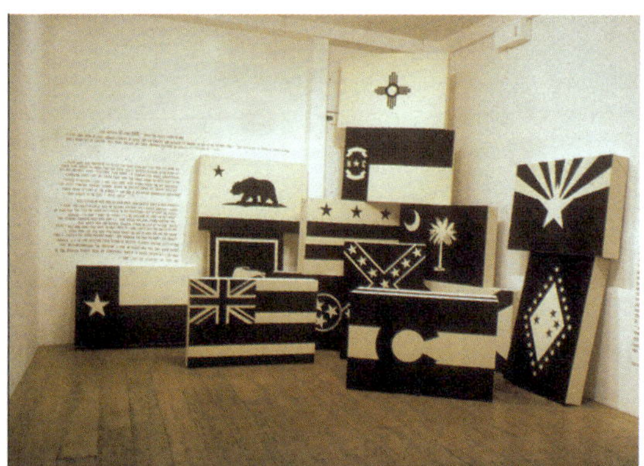

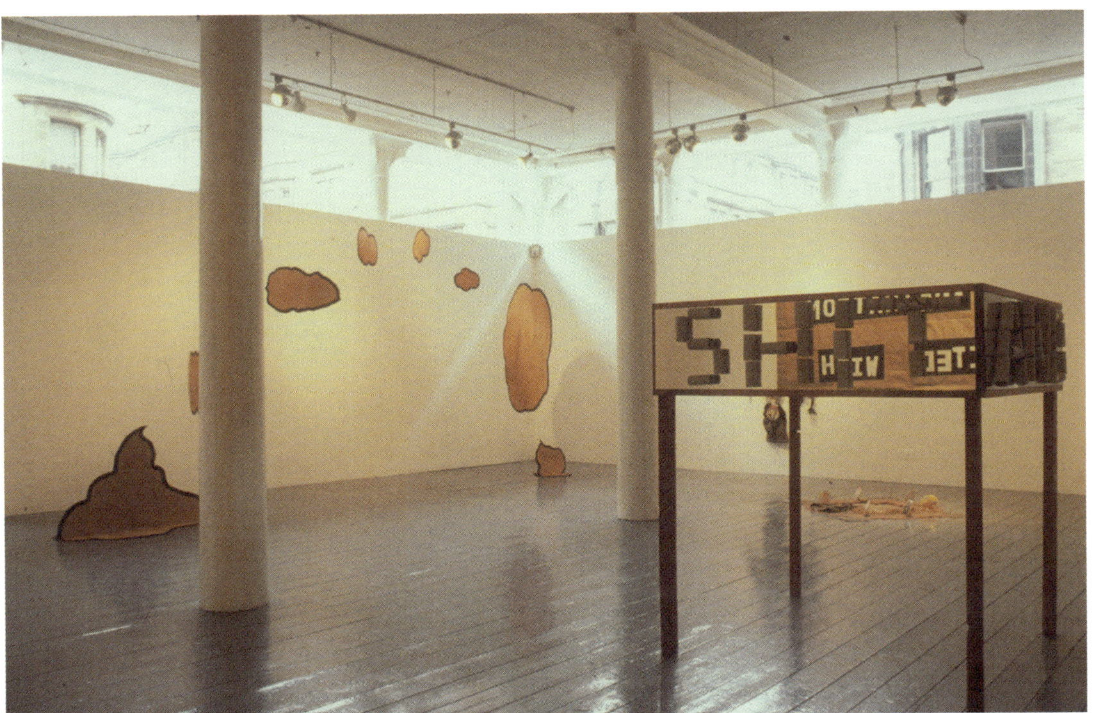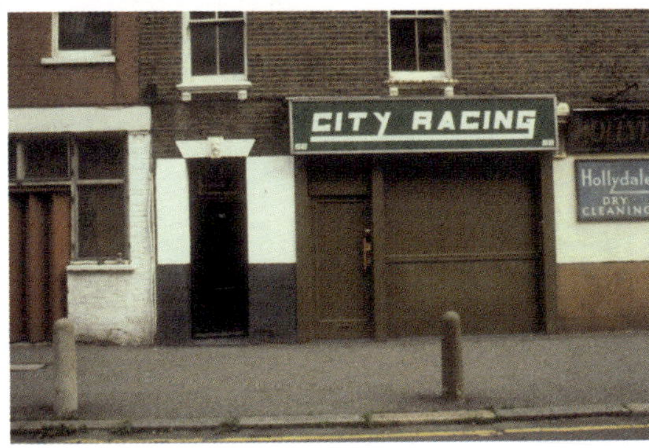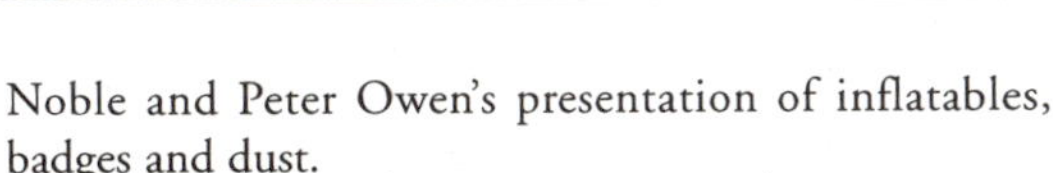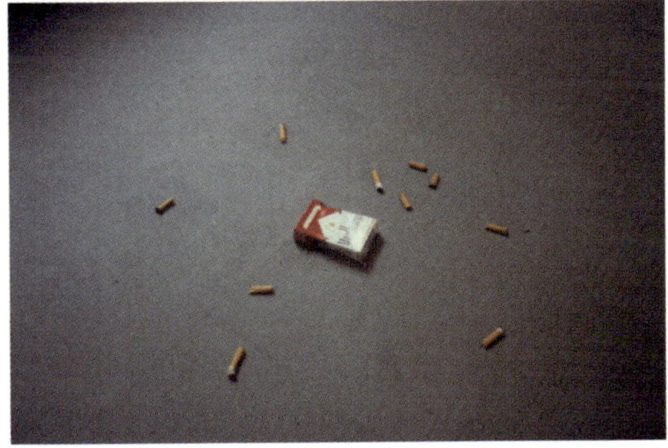

Noble and Peter Owen's presentation of inflatables, badges and dust.

This collaboration is a result of the recognition of the shared aims and ideas by the two artist-run galleries." (from Transmission press release)

Top: 'City Racing at Transmission' — left: Paul Noble, *I Wonder…*; foreground right: Paul Noble, *Common*; (in reflection) Keith Coventry, Untitled; background left–right: Peter Owen, *Dust in the blood*; *Memorial*.

Above left: City Racing Gallery, London.

Above right: Andrew Lockhart, *Dave*.

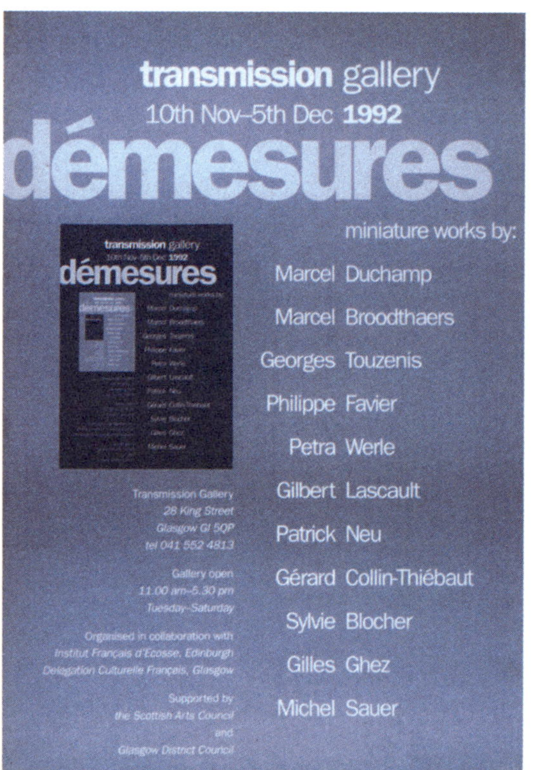

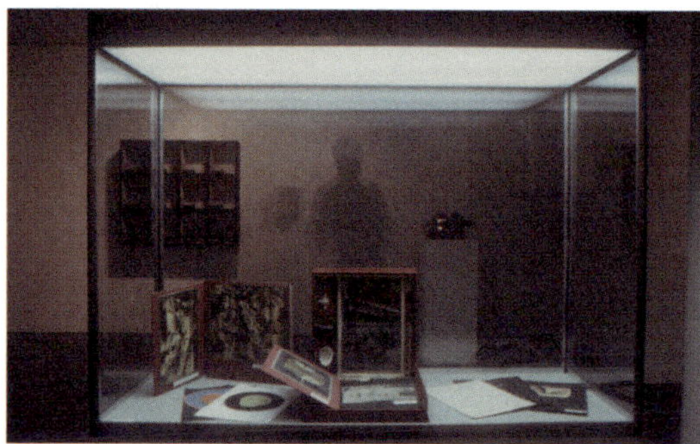

Above: Marcel Duchamp, *Musée en Valise*, 1955/68.

11 Démesures: "'Démesures' is an exhibition of miniature works by 11 artists, all of whom have to some extent devoted their attention to the minuscule, the discreet and the fragile." (from press release)

06 Stan Douglas — Hors-Champs: "'Hors-champs' presents the performance of four Americans who either lived in France during the Free Jazz moment, or who still reside there today: George Lewis (trombone), Douglas Ewart (saxophone), Kent Carter (bass) and Oliver Johnson (drums). The music they play is based on Albert Ayler's 1965 composition, *Spirits Rejoice*, and composed of four basic musical materials: a gospel melody, an attenuated call and response, a heraldic fanfare and *La Marseillaise*. Like many other national anthems such as the

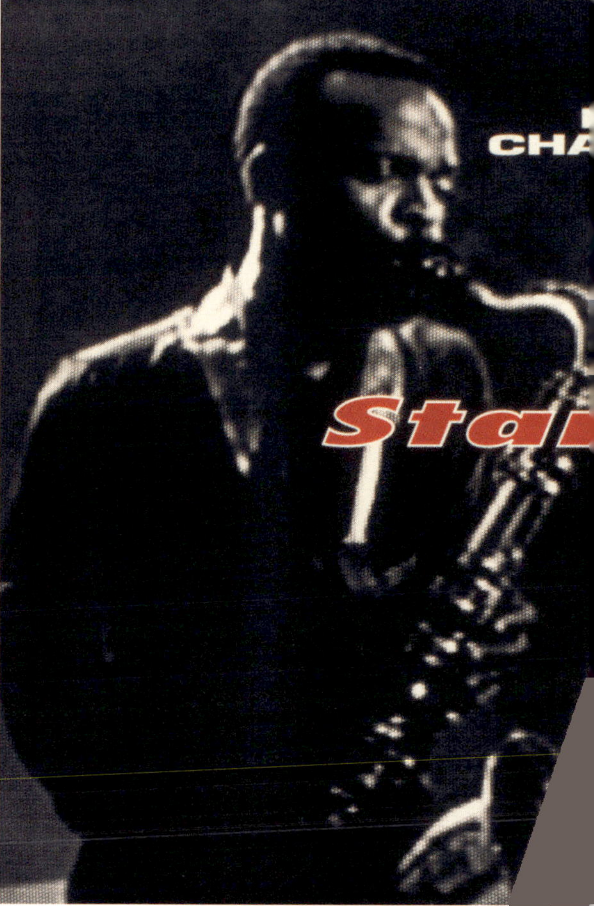

Star Spangled Banner (which also makes a brief appearance), the recollection of its blood-thirsty lyric will remind one of the tacit content of myths of national identity.

Hors-champs was shot en-direct in the style of an ORTF musical television production from the same era as Ayler's composition—notably those of Jean-Christophe Averty. Two video projections are simultaneously presented on recto and verso sides of a suspended wall. While one side of the screen shows a 'programme' montage of the two cameras, the other presents a simultaneous counter-narrative of everything that had been edited out, or relegated to the outside." Stan Douglas (from press release)

'Hors-Champs' was part of 'Fotofeis', a national photography festival.

07 & 09 Transmission in Belfast: In July 1993, a group of artists from Belfast came to Glasgow to exhibit at Transmission. They included Karen Vaughan, Derval Fitzgerald, Sandra Johnston, members of the first committee of Catalyst, now an established artist-run gallery in Belfast. This was Catalyst's first project.

Transmission members Gerard Byrne, Jacqueline Donachie, Anna Milsom, Emma Neilson and Richard

Below: Stan Douglas' 'Hors-Champs' video installation at Transmission, June–July 1993.

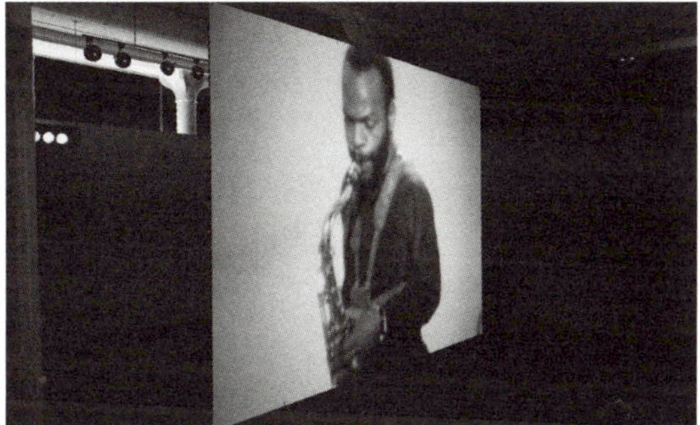

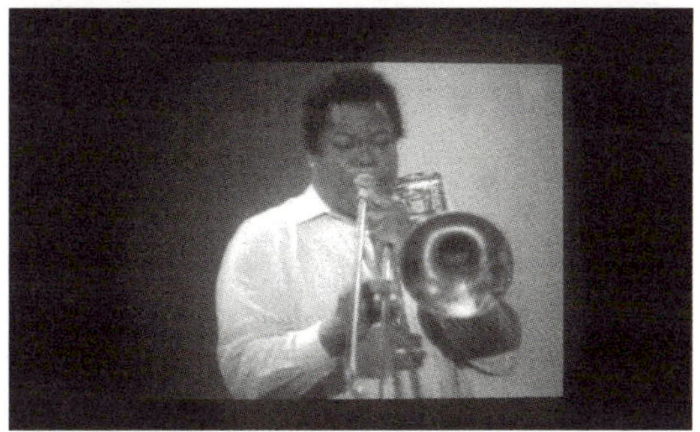

Wright travelled to Belfast in September 1993 to exhibit in a shop unit.

11 & 94/05 Transmission at Artemisia/Artemisia at Transmission: Oona Ball, Nathan Coley, Michael Ellis, Craig Richardson and Heather Allen travel to Chicago to take part in the first half of a gallery exchange project.

They exhibit at Artemisia Gallery, a women's co-operative in Chicago and embark on an intensive lecture tour including the Art Institute of Chicago, University of Illinois, University of Wisconsin, Madison Arts Centre and North Western University.

"'Transmission' was the first instalment in an ambitious, three-part international exchange exhibition between

functioning in the shadows of the art capitals of London and New York, suggests a strong premise that was, unfortunately, not addressed by the work presented.

The familiarity of the photographs and installations in 'Transmission' made it easy for someone unaware of the works' origins to assume it was another group show of emerging Chicago artists. This characteristic lessened the potential impact of the exhibition and questioned

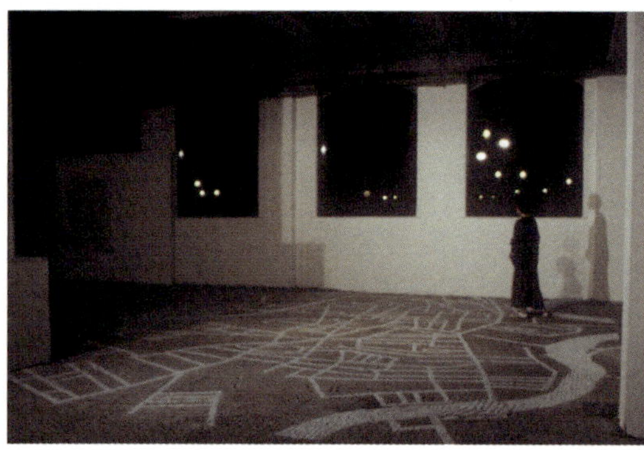

Above: 'Transmission in Belfast'—floor piece by Anna Milsom.

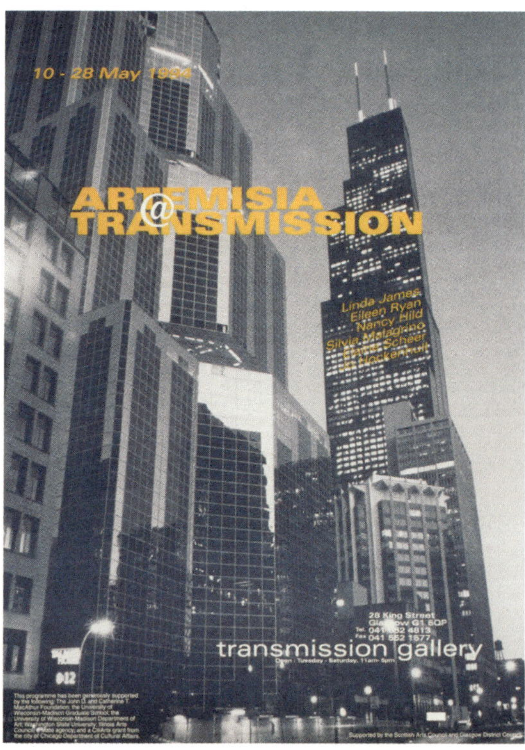

Above: Poster from 'Artemisia at Transmission', second half of the exchange, May 1994.

Transmission Gallery of Glasgow, Scotland, and Artemisia Gallery that for all its good intentions, failed to challenge one's perceptions about art, politics, or culture. The idea for an exchange between two alternative spaces, each with lengthy histories of fostering provocative art outside the perceived mainstream, has the potential to explore unfamiliar territory and fringe topics. In addition, the inherent similarities and differences between the art communities of Glasgow and Chicago, which share a kinship by

the ability of artwork from other Western countries to offer an alternative vision to what frequently appears to be a homogenised contemporary art scene. Of the five artists, the works of four—Oona Ball, Nathan Coley, Michael Ellis, and Craig Richardson—reflected a cool, reductive aesthetic, employing text, photography, and sound in well-worn formats…

Of all the work, only Heather Allen's two crudely fashioned quilts had a toughness to them. They stood

1993

48

apart from the rest of the pieces in the show, not only formally but politically as well, drawing a correlation between the abuse of women and the larger abuse of Scotland as a nation dependent on England for its political identity.

One quilt displays the outline of Scotland with a bull's-eye superimposed over it. An excerpt from the text at the bottom of the quilt reads: 'It's like coming home

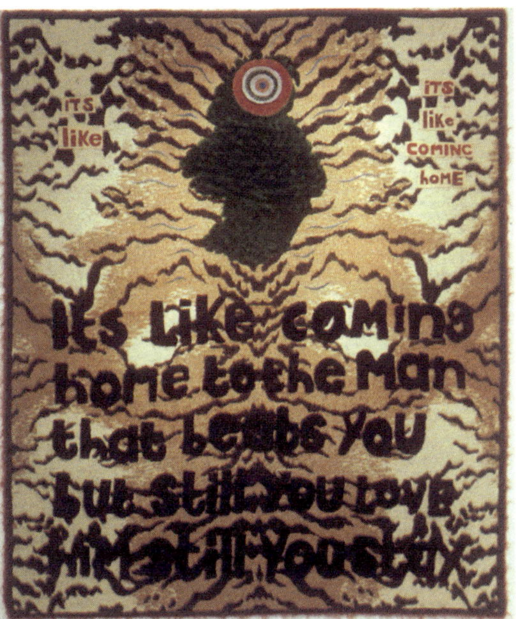

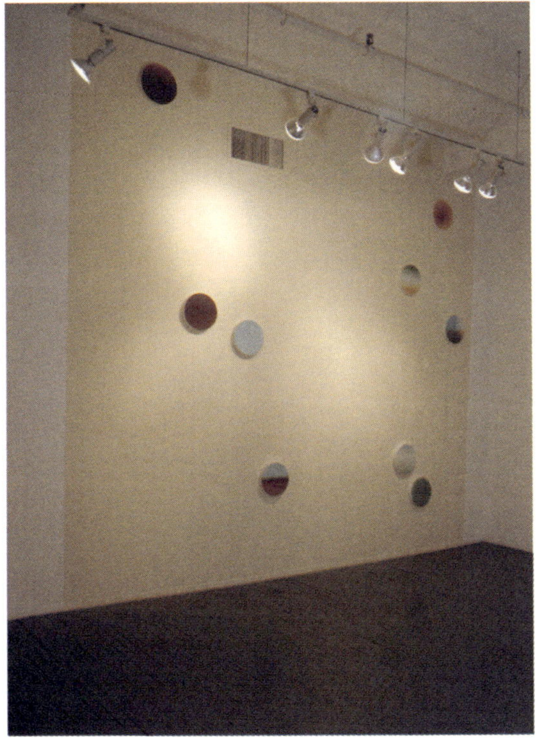

Above: Nathan Coley, *Excerpts from a Florida Holiday.*

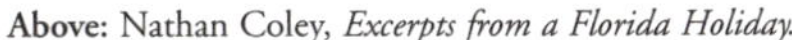

Above right: Heather Allen, *Coming Home.*

to the man that beats you but still you love him still you stay.' …
Allen's pieces felt at home in the Artemisia space. They reflected back to the political climate from which the gallery emerged 20 years ago and tackled uncomfortable issues that now seem increasingly absent from the venue of the alternative space." John Brunetti (*The New Art Examiner*, February 1994, p. 34)

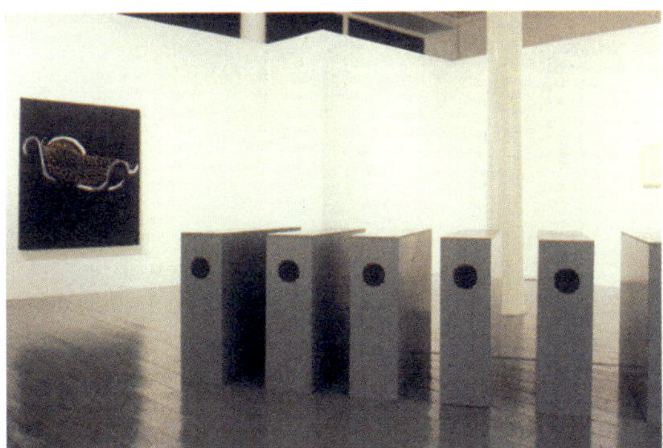

Above: 'Nu-Smell'; foreground: Keith Farquhar, *Six Greyhounds Barking Because They Must Run* (wooden boxes containing recordings of greyhounds barking); left: Diane Main, *Untitled* (computer manipulated Scanachrome 'painting').

12 Transmission Celebrates 10 Years — Nu-Smell: "A great epoch has begun. There exists a NU-SMELL™.

Art, overwhelming us like a flood which rolls on towards its destined end, has furnished us with new tools adapted to this new epoch, animated by this NU-SMELL™.

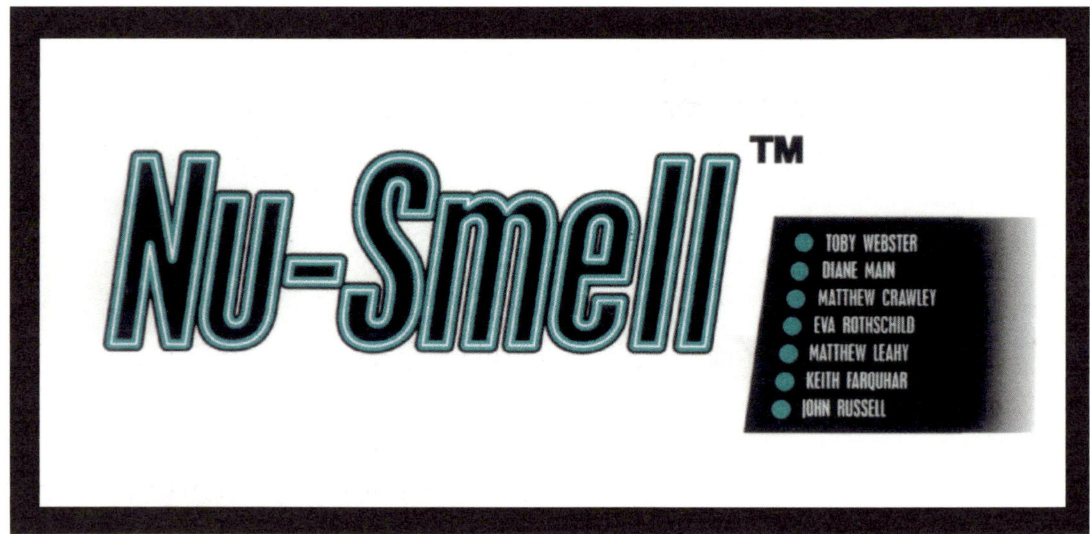

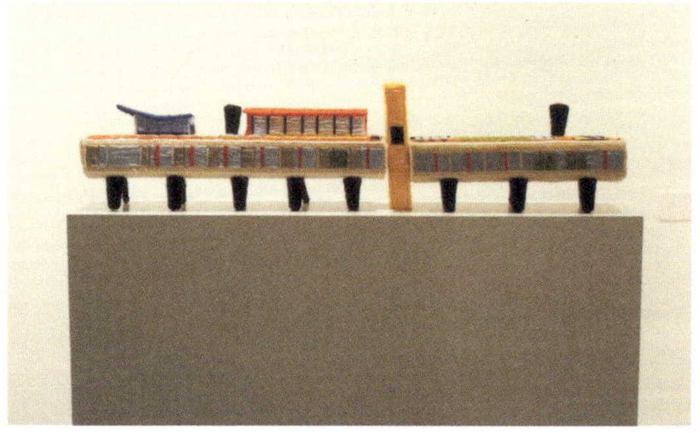

Our own epoch is determining, day by day, its own essence.

Our senses, unhappily, are unable yet to discern it.

Modern life demands, and has been waiting for, this NU-SMELL™.

(after Le Corbusier)" (from press release)

Above left: John Russell, *Unité d'Habitation*, "a reinterpretation of Le Corbusier's 'exemplary' modernist building."

Above: Matthew Leahy, Untitled.

1994

03 Richard Wright: "'By now we are tired of the claims that artists make. Some things are art or all things are art; you choose. I want to do the most straightforward thing. This is neither a lesson nor an argument' — Richard Wright

By applying patches of colour directly to the wall Richard Wright creates flat patterned forms that seem to defy their support (the architecture), creating their own sense of space. His work is perhaps an investigation/critique of the language of painting (its boundaries, its frame) proposed as a matter of experience rather than principle.

Below and right: Richard Wright, March 1994.

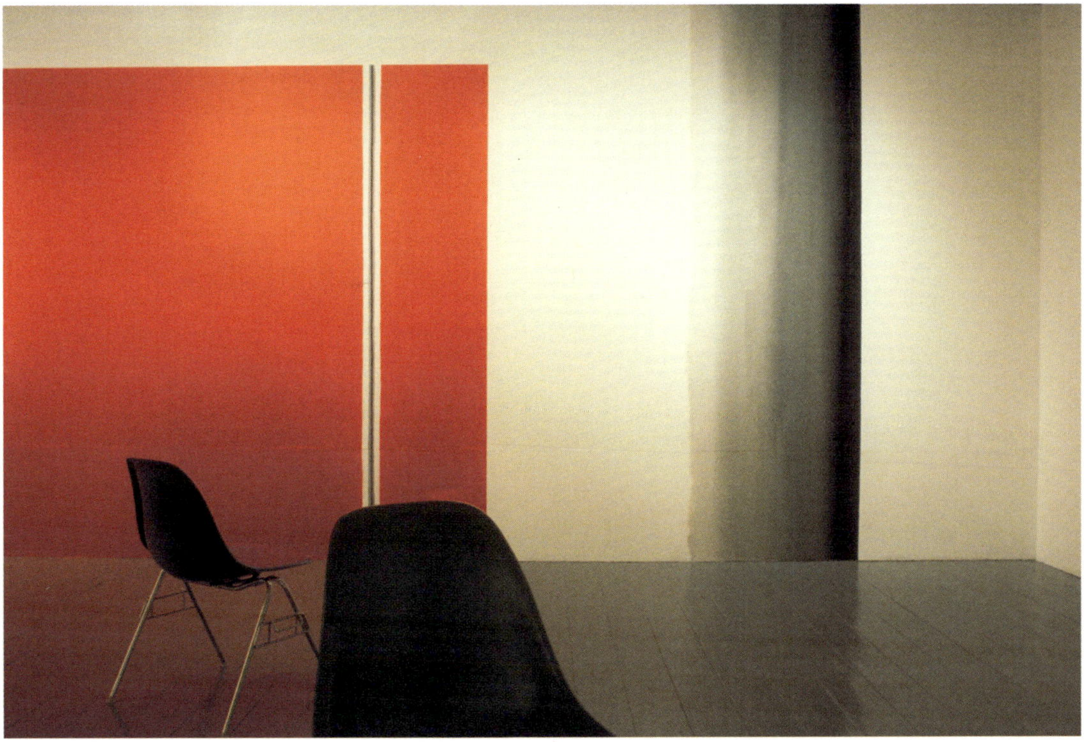

Richard will be working in the gallery during the first week of the show." (from press release)

04 Lothar Baumgarten — Silencium: In April 1994 the German artist Lothar Baumgarten installed 'Silencium' at Transmission. This was part of the 'The Reading Room', a nationwide project involving artists and writers, initiated by BookWorks, London.

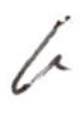

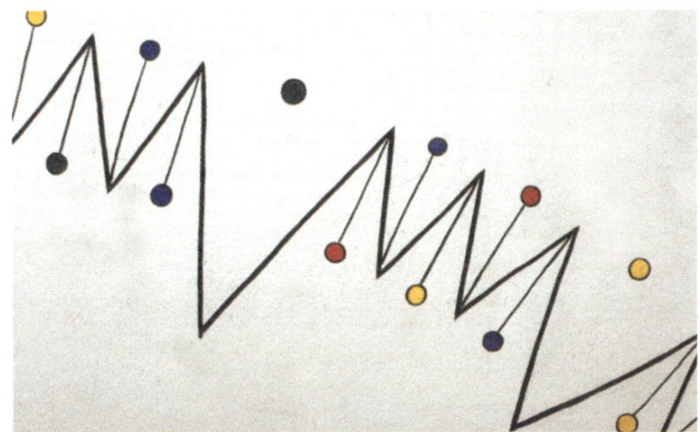

"The structuring guidance and rules of the Reading Room are the metaphysical inventory of 'Silencium'.

Reading tools here mirror ritualised process, the furnished acquisition of knowledge through reading." (from 'The Reading Room' guide)

04 Modern Art: "Over the past decade the circle of artists loosely centred on Transmission have made a name for themselves and for Scotland in a way the Glasgow Boys did in the early 1980s. However, collaboration rather than rivalry is their strength. Modern Art is a very impressive big group show which confirms their strengths. 80 were invited; 79 delivered." Clare Henry (the Glasgow *Herald*, 13 June 1994, p. 6)

"Douglas Gordon: One of the inspirations for the 'Modern Art' show was in anticipation of the fantastic, the glorious new institution in Glasgow which you have just visited today, the Museum of Modern Art.

Hans-Ulrich Obrist: It looks a bit like an Italian Pizzeria with some Memphis design.

Below: Lothar Baumgarten, 'Silencium', April 1994.

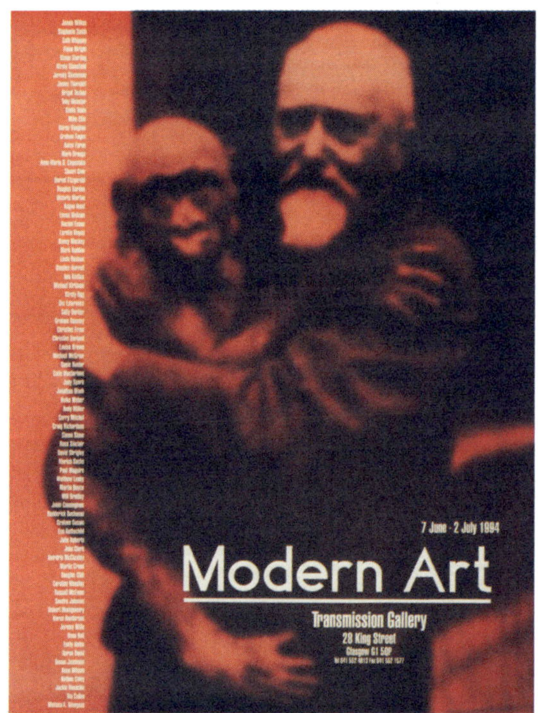

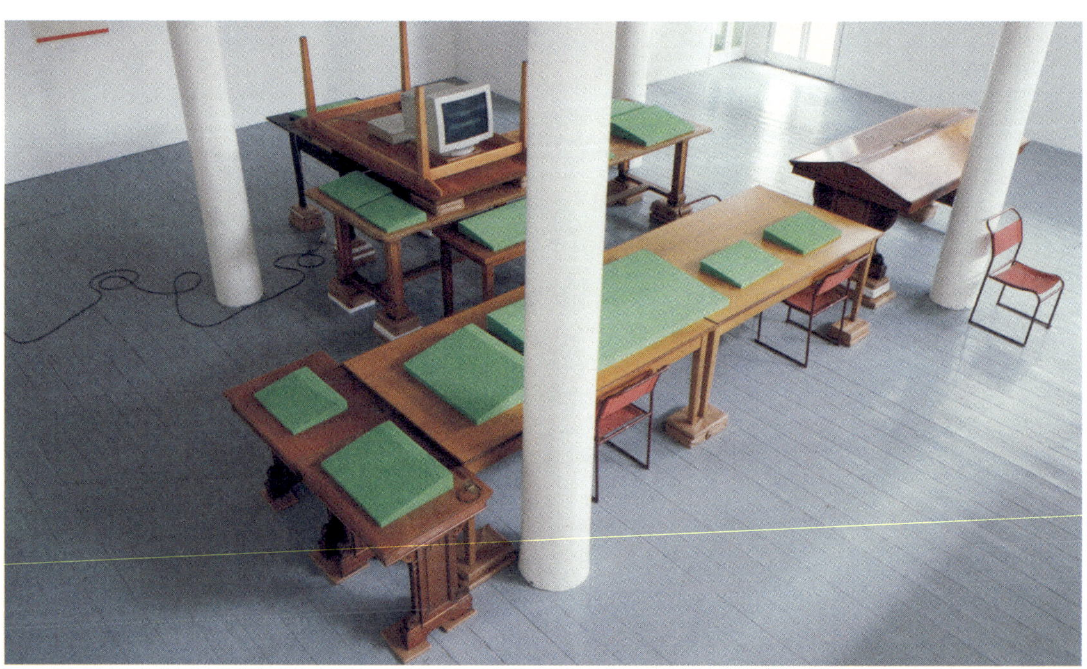

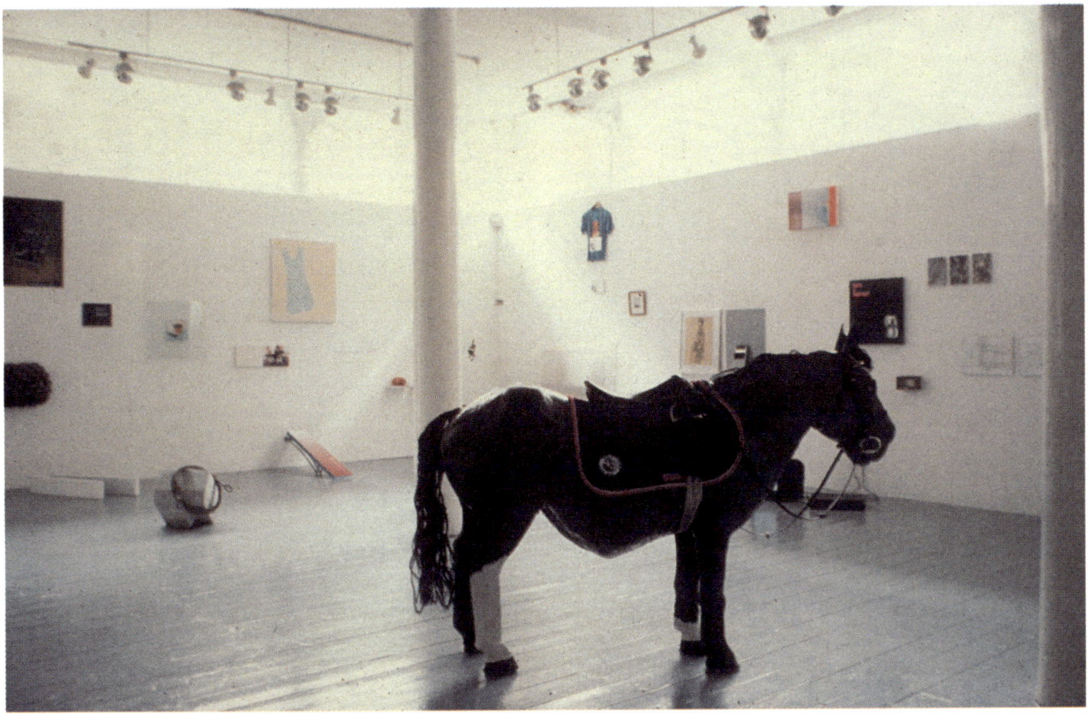

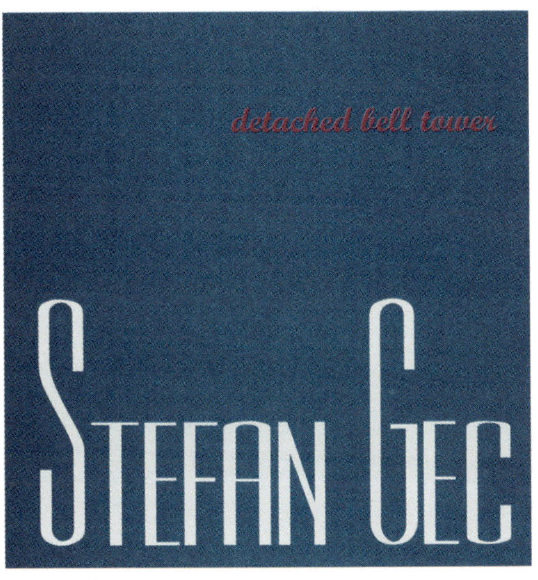

Above: 'Modern Art', April 1994—foreground: work by Louise Brown.

DG: Do you know why it is called the Museum of Modern Art…because when they had a meeting of all the galleries in Glasgow and someone from Transmission (I think it was Simon Starling) asked them a question: 'Why are you going to call this the Museum of Modern Art, because it is not modernism, it is absolutely contemporary art?'

Someone replied, 'Oh, but we couldn't because of the pediment, we couldn't fit Museum of Contemporary Art, the word contemporary is too long, so we needed a shorter word and we thought modern is a good word to use.'" (From 'Ping-Pong—a Conversation between Douglas Gordon and Hans-Ulrich Obrist', for Transmission, 1995)

07 **Stefan Gec—Detached Bell Tower:** "The location of Glasgow on the Clyde, and the industrial activities past and present, particularly the nuclear submarine operations in the area, make it an ideal site for 'Campanil'e'.

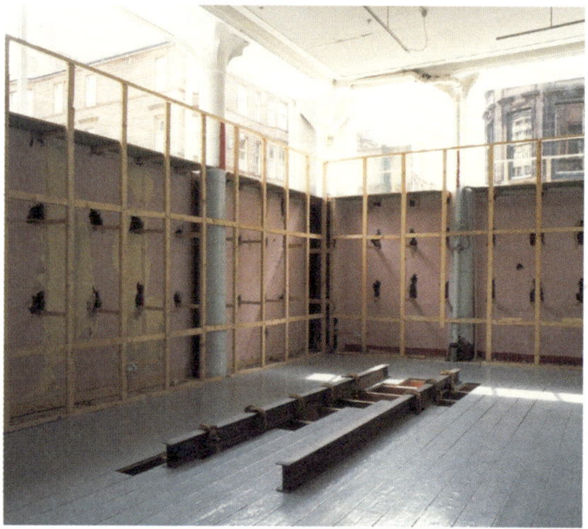

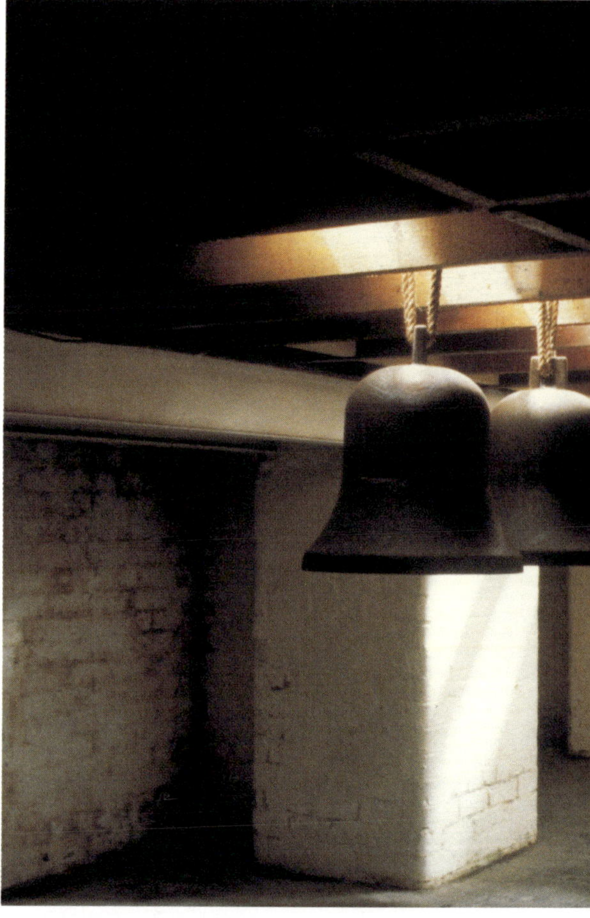

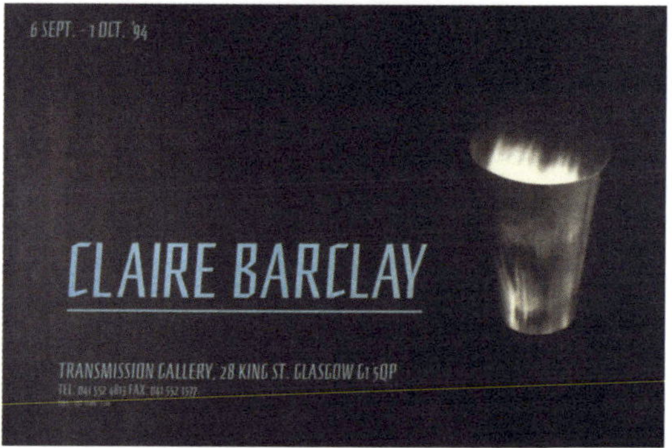

Top and right: Stefan Gec, 'Detached Bell Tower'.

Above: Local newspaper advertisement for the show.

The submarines operating in local waters, and further afield are as a direct result of the perceived Soviet threat, as it existed. The knock on effects of the Soviet disarmament programme has been felt within the community, as jobs come under threat. The process of turning submarines into bells, can be linked to the nature of the nuclear industry, in the transmutation of power. This again draws many interesting connections, politically and geographical." Stefan Gec (from original proposal to Transmission)

09 Claire Barclay: "The body is not far from her work though never figured within it. Use, however, seems close. Each work has the character of purposes not wholly or at all aesthetic, and some appear to be offered to the viewer to find or invent a use for them…

The works uncover an unwillingness to identify with the organic world, the distancing and objectifying of bodily

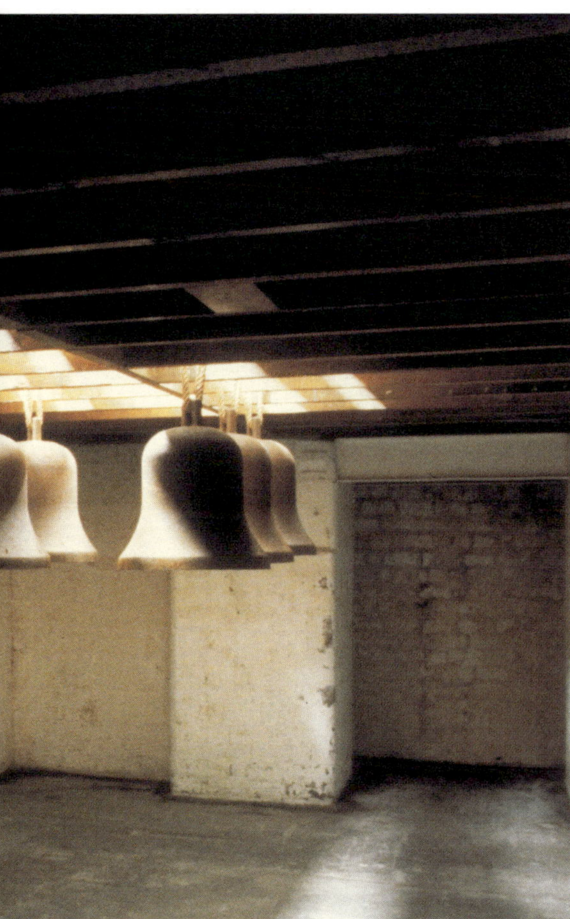

being." Euan McArthur (*Art Monthly*, October 1994, pp. 29–30)

10 & 11 Good Housekeeping—4 event-based projects:

"My name is Hinrich Sachs, I am an artist from Germany and I would like to give you in advance some information about my preoccupations. I've been

Below: 'Good Housekeeping', 'Couch Potatoes'—new video work.

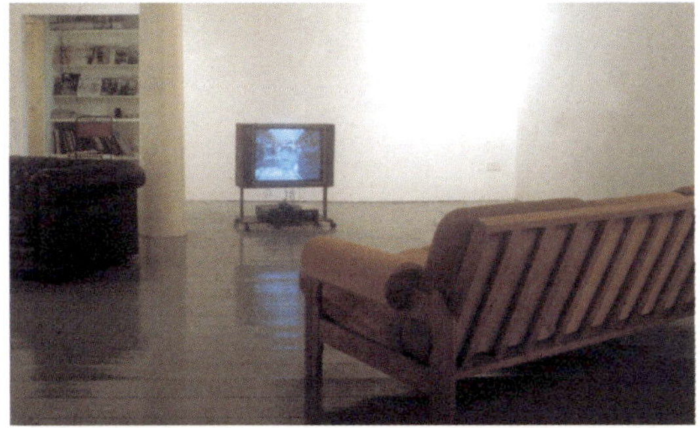

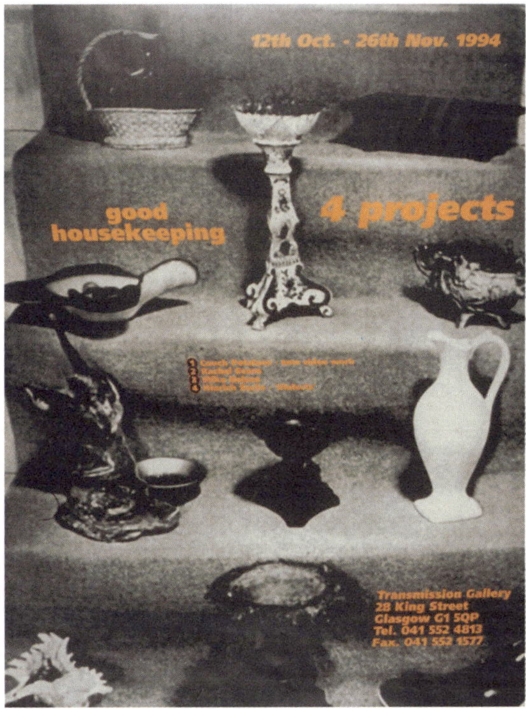

Above: Claire Barclay, Untitled.

Below and bottom: 'That We Know'—invited guests Lisa Goodfriend, Hugh O'Donnell and Karen Lury contribute to a discussion organised by Hinrich Sachs on the significance of the national and international concerns of the 27 nationalised issues of *Elle* Magazine.

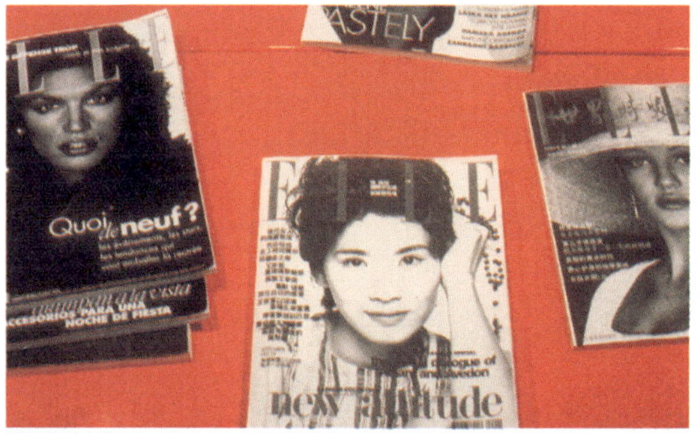

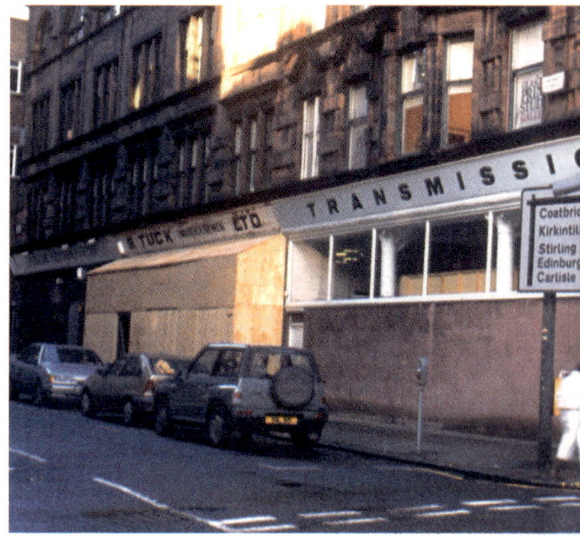

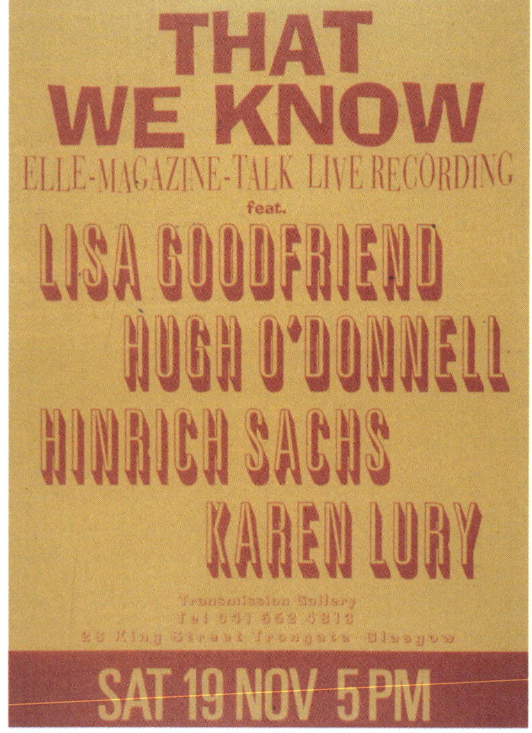

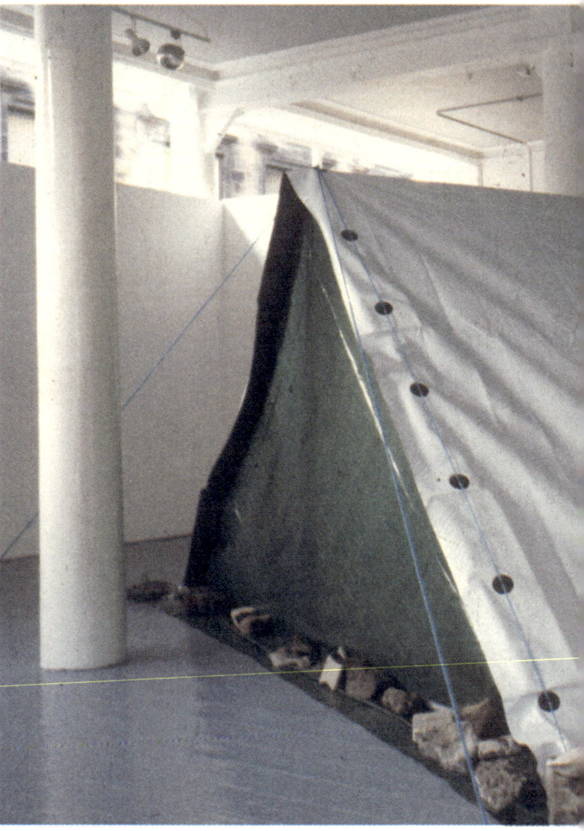

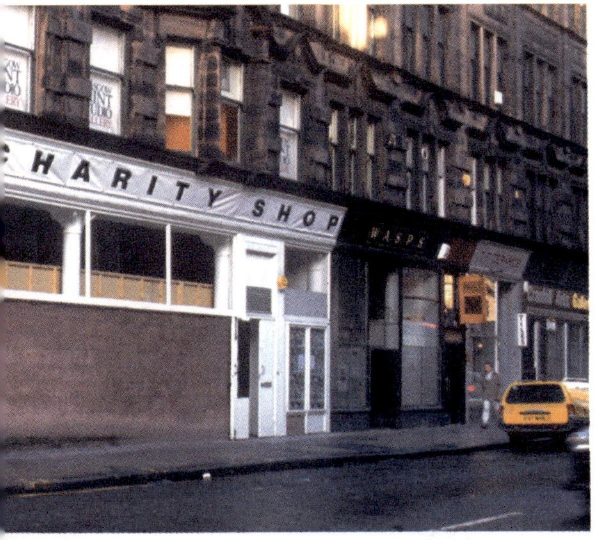

working for some years now with dialogue—situations involving individuals of various native languages and from various diverse professions. The central concern is to look at and investigate interference and exchange in communicative processes, especially the translation and shifting of cultural meanings. This sounds horrifyingly abstract, but in fact it happens naturally and with great ease when talking about simple subjects of our everyday life, e.g. cooking recipes, school books or glossy magazines…imagine those details which belong to our natural cultural heritage existing in an extremely

Left and below left: 'Charity Shop'—Mike Nelson investigates the role of the charitable organisations

Below: 'Rhapsody on a Theme d'Amour'—a romantic evening of dance instruction accompanied by up to the minute news and comment with Rachel Evans.

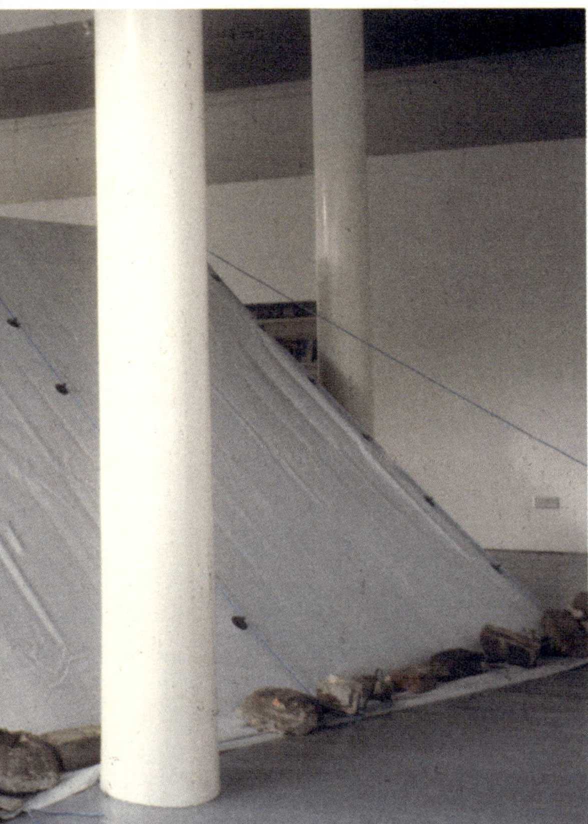

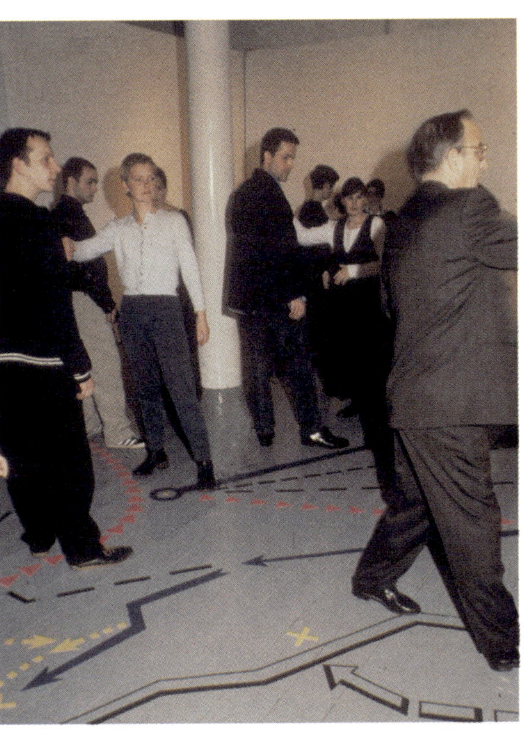

different cultural context, couldn't they become strange things?" Hinrich Sachs (from letter of invitation to the 'That we Know' discussion)

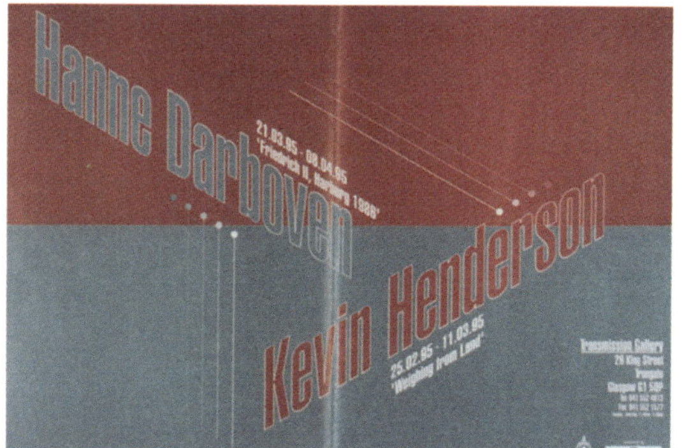

1995

02 & 03 Kevin Henderson/Hanne Darboven: Two projects linked to musical events: Kevin Henderson transposes traditional bagpipe music to the pages of *The Independent* newspaper and works the same music into an evening of improvised Jazz, while Hanne Darboven's labour intensive contemplation of the passage of time is accompanied by a performance of her Opus 26 for string quartet.

04 New Rose Hotel: "From April 22nd–May 20th, Transmission will be re-invented as the 'New Rose Hotel'. Contemporary design and furniture, computer imagery and wall drawings will alter the 'white cube' of

Below left: Kevin Henderson, *Weighing from Land*.

Bottom left: Hanne Darboven, *Friedrich II, Harburg 1986*.

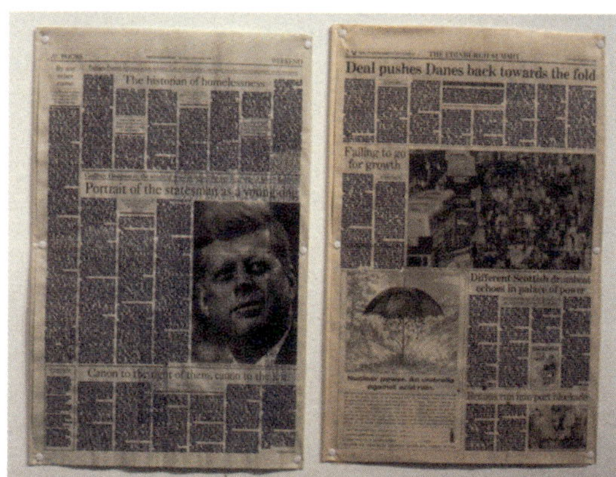

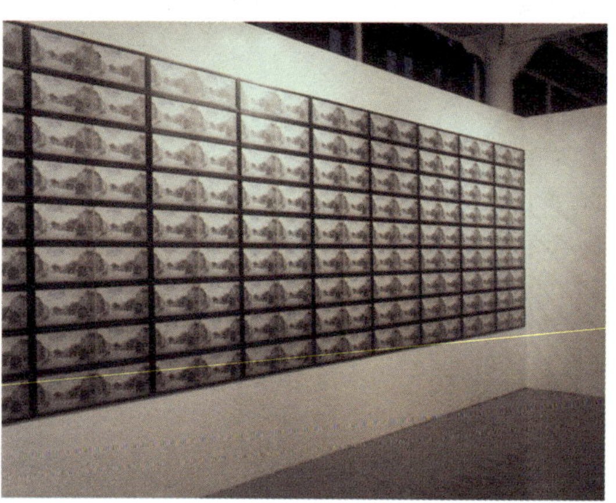

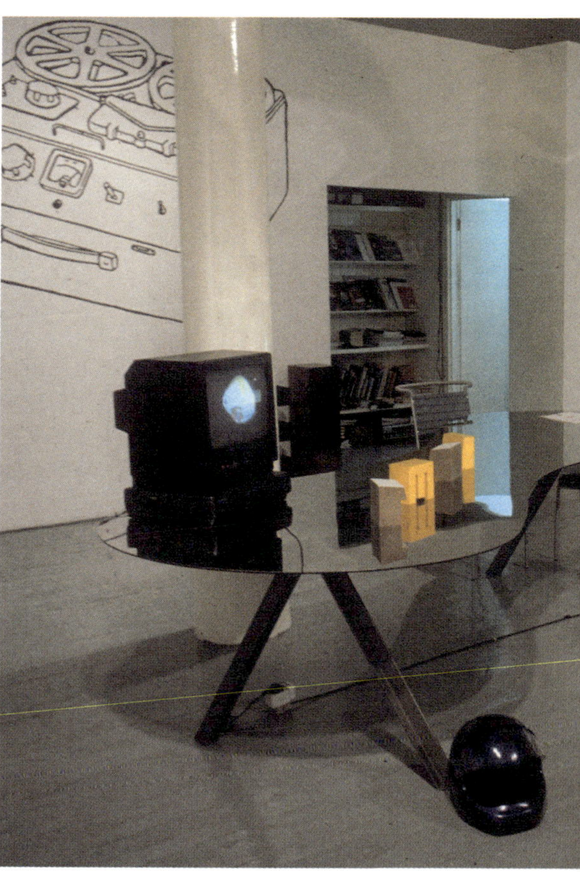

the space; work by artists and designers will be brought together in this new context. It is envisaged as a transformed environment, at the same time optimistic and pessimistic; a place to meet and talk; to exchange ideas about our future.

Work so far confirmed for 'New Rose Hotel' includes paintings by Julian Opie, Victoria Morton; computer-generated videos by Paul Maguire, Su Grierson; designs and models of 21st century dwellings and vehicles (notably 'Project for a Glass House' from Allford Hall Monaghan Morris Architects); furniture by Ron Arad, Susan Hunter; seamless sculpture from Jonathan Ambrose, Toby Webster; Martin Boyce's wall drawings influenced by the futuristic utopian design aesthetics of 1950s and 60s America; an automatic, free espresso machine from Eva Grubinger; contemporary clothing by Glasgow emporium Dr Jives and a selection of magazines from around the world brought together especially for the show by Martin Young. The gallery will be fitted with a state of the art Linn Hi-Fi system from Stereo-Stereo, local DJs Jonnie and Hamish will

Below: 'New Rose Hotel'—left–right: Andrew Megaw (wall drawing); Paul Maguire (video); Ron Arad (table); Nigel Prince, *Perfect Skin No. 1*; *Perfect Skin No. 4* (objects on table); Toby Webster, Untitled (motorcycle helmet); Julian Opie (painting from the series *Imagine that you can order these*); Jonathan Ambrose, *Completion…?* (sculpture); Martin Boyce Untitled (*Exploded Joke*) (wall painting); Alford Hall Monaghan Morris Architects (model).

Below: 'New Rose Hotel'—magazines by Martin Young; furniture by Susan Hunter; video by Su Grierson.

Bottom: 'In Stereo'— Jim Lambie, *Roadie*, July 1995.

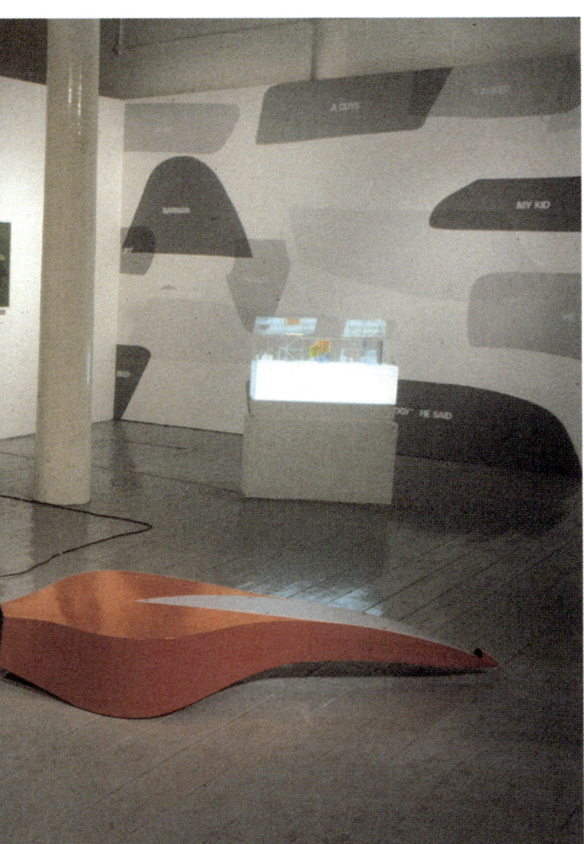

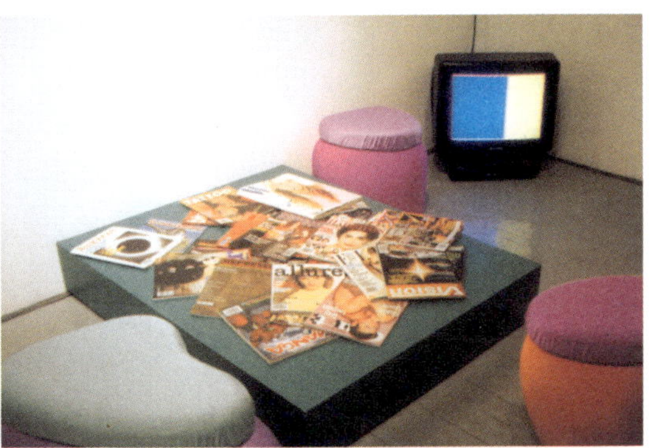

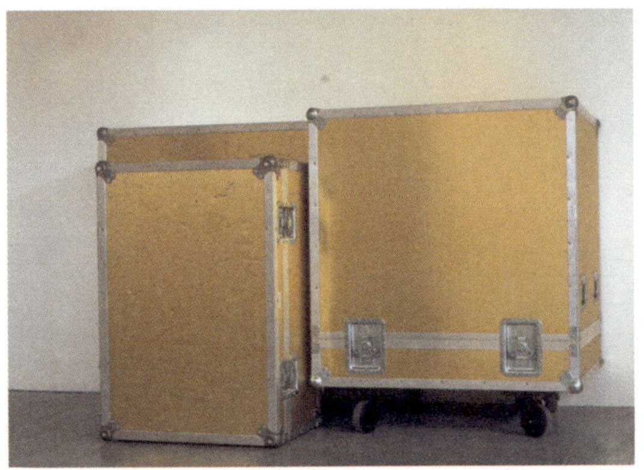

record a CD, a specific soundtrack for this exhibition." (from press release)

08 Guitar Amp Action/In Stereo: Transmission kicks off the summer with a crazy punk rock party featuring local bands Hello Skinny, LungLeg, Superstar and Par Cark.

09 David Shrigley — Map of the Sewer: "For September, Transmission is pleased to present the first solo exhibition of new work by Glasgow-based artist David Shrigley.

Shrigley's unique sculpture, drawings, cartoons and public works are very, very funny. Absurd, satirical, full of random acts of violence and a fascination with the soiled and disfigured, they document a breakdown at the margins of culture as we know it.

Below: 'Guitar Amp Action'—LungLeg.

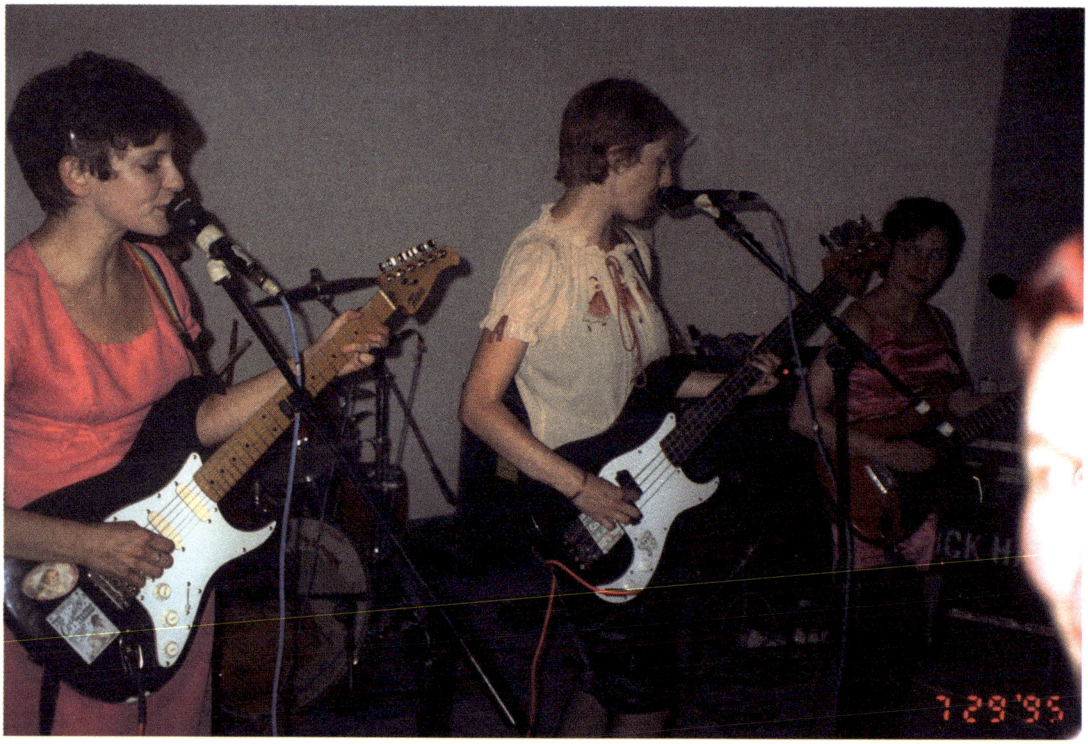

For Transmission he will show several new sculptures, including at least one dog toy and a home-made land mine, along with photographs of two new public works sited in Glasgow and recent books of drawings and cartoons." (from press release)

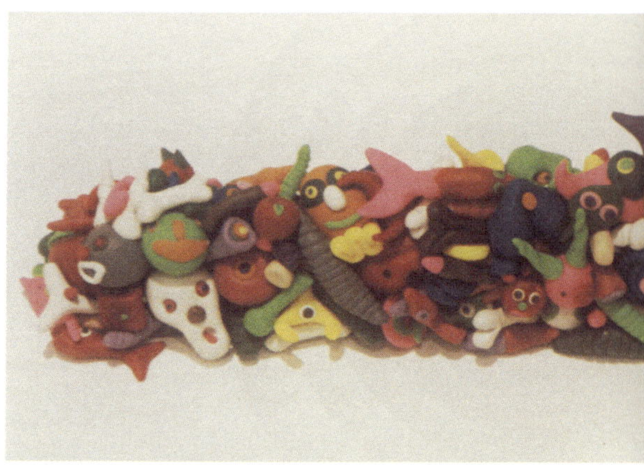

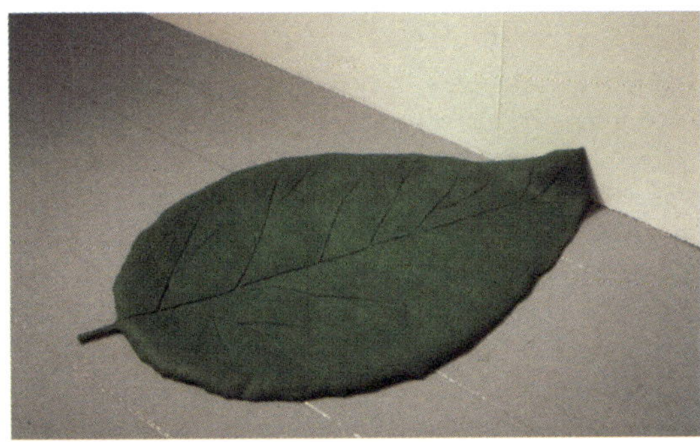

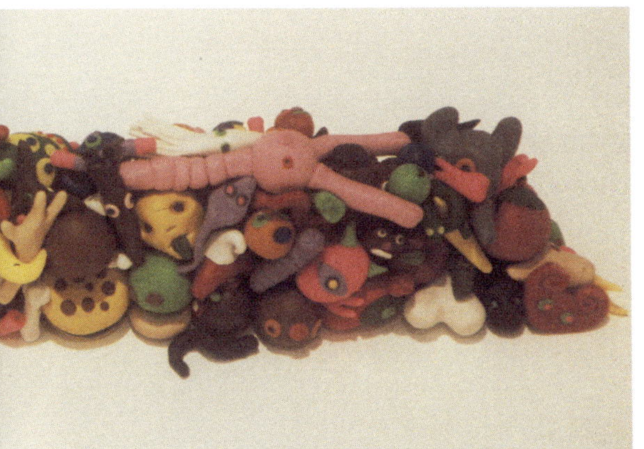

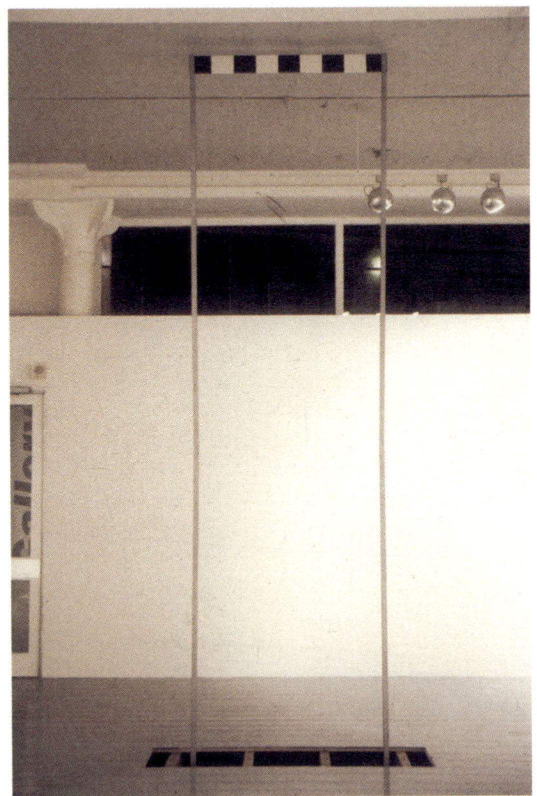

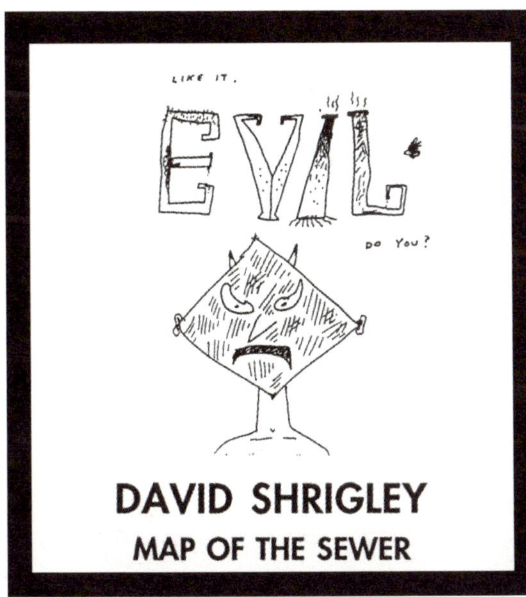

Top: David Shrigley, *The contents of the gap between the refrigerator and the cooker.*

Above: detail from 'Map of the Sewer' press release.

1995

1996

01 **21 Days of Darkness:** "This is strange. I'm standing in Transmission gallery but I'm somewhere else. The walls have been painted black. The curators were teenagers the last time they did that. Of course now they have access to more than posters from Virgin Records—the art on the walls is by artists.

There is a bomb by Gregory Green in the form of a book which lies open on a shelf.

Book Bomb is creepy because it is so quiet and violent, the underside or inner workings of something which on the surface is harmless and normal. There are two photos by Lee Miller—*Dead SS Guard* and *Dachau and The Burgomeister's Daughter, Suicide*. A button has come loose on the upholstery of the couch on which the Burgomeister's daughter lies, and it hangs by a thread. (As they say, God is in the details. It could be that the devil is too). A tiny photographic print shows Pierre Molinier acting out his fantasies in a hotel room in Bordeaux, toying with being both female and male, tucking his penis away between his thighs, using velvet, leather, silk and his own home-made dildo. There is a papier-mâché *Prisoner's Head* by Christine Borland. It is on a pillow on a shelf, crude and weird, with a bizarre child/adult aesthetic, and yet it is functional—escaping prisoners have used heads of this type to fool their guards. Also hanging on the dark walls are photos by Weegee (one of a murdered man lying in a pool of blood) and another by Art Club 2000—a punk/goth, art school death shadow, Untitled (*Cooper Union/Crows*).

Strange sounds come from the basement, where it is dark, cold, and claustrophobic. Videos flicker in the blackness. In Darren Marshall's *Vampire Home Movies*, vampires use blood to make pictures of the last image coming to the minds of people near death. On a double screen video Fanni Niemi-Junkola and an opponent can be seen fighting violently, expertly and relentlessly in the street. Passers-by stand about watching, amused, shocked, or unsure. Søren Martinsen plays a kind of Russian Roulette called *The Man I Love*. With his hand outstretched on a surface before him, he stabs a knife as fast as he can between his fingers. Often the knife cuts into his thumb and fingers. I can hear his groans and see his blood. Vito Acconci tries to pry a woman's eyes open. Next door is a thing called *Baffle* by Douglas Gordon. It is a shape in the darkness from which I can hear noises, a thing wrapped up, gagged, blindfolded.

These are some of the art works in '21 Days of Darkness'. There are other things too: a mummified cat found entombed in a wall, mouth open as if it were

Below: Neil Miller, *Winterland 1*.

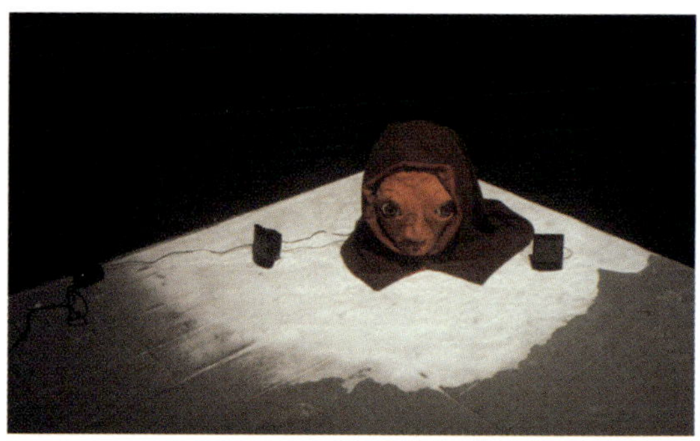

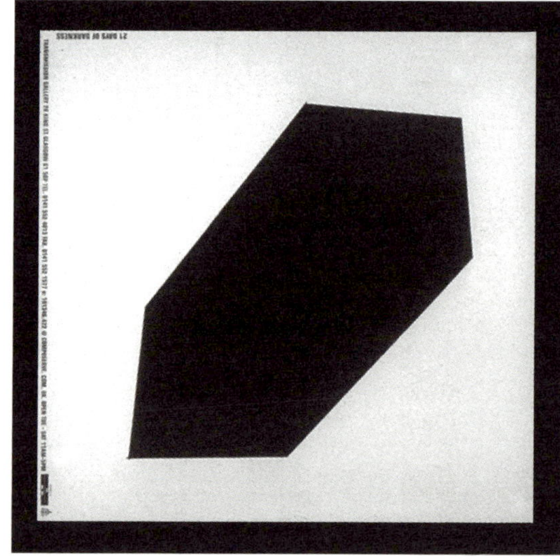

Opposite: '21 Days of Darkness'—left–right: Andrew McWhinney, Untitled; Untitled; Jason Fox, *Blood Fire*; Mabel Palacin, *Suite de las desapariciónes (What has never been cannot end) No.1*; Weegee, *New York (four murdered policemen and murdered man)*; *New York*; Simon Periton, *Thorn Doily*.

screaming, a Japanese mermaid, a box of skeletons, a Jackalope Head and a photograph of the Orion Nebula. To visit this show is to become an adult-child: you can explore places of desire and peril (where classification doesn't count), look for the bogeyman under the bed, wonder what it means to be marked by Douglas Gordon's mirror-image tattoo of the word 'evil', or cut your thumb off for art. It is a dark twin, where things are reflected or played backwards to be understood. Days have been dark for nearly a month now. Sometimes that lets you see more clearly." Judith Findlay (*Flash Art*, Summer 1996, p. 99)

Below: Christine Borland, *Prisoner's Head.*

Below right: '21 days of Darkness'—left: Douglas Gordon, *Tattoo for reflection*, 1995; *Tattoo for doppelganger*, 1995, right: Glenn Brown, *Dali Christ*, 1992; Simon Periton, *Pink Barbed Wire*, 1996; Gregory Green, *Double Bible Bomb*, 1996.

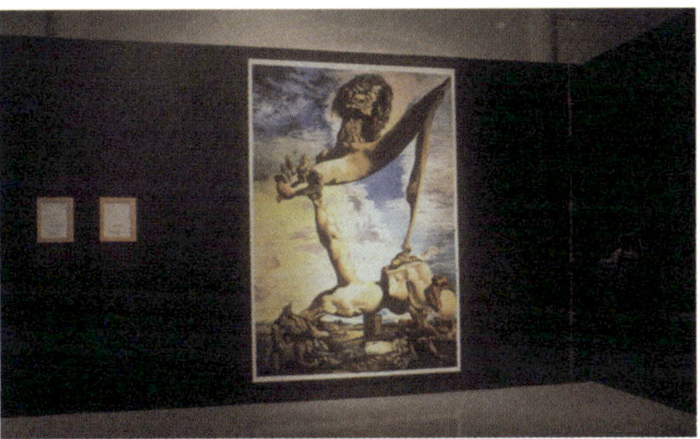

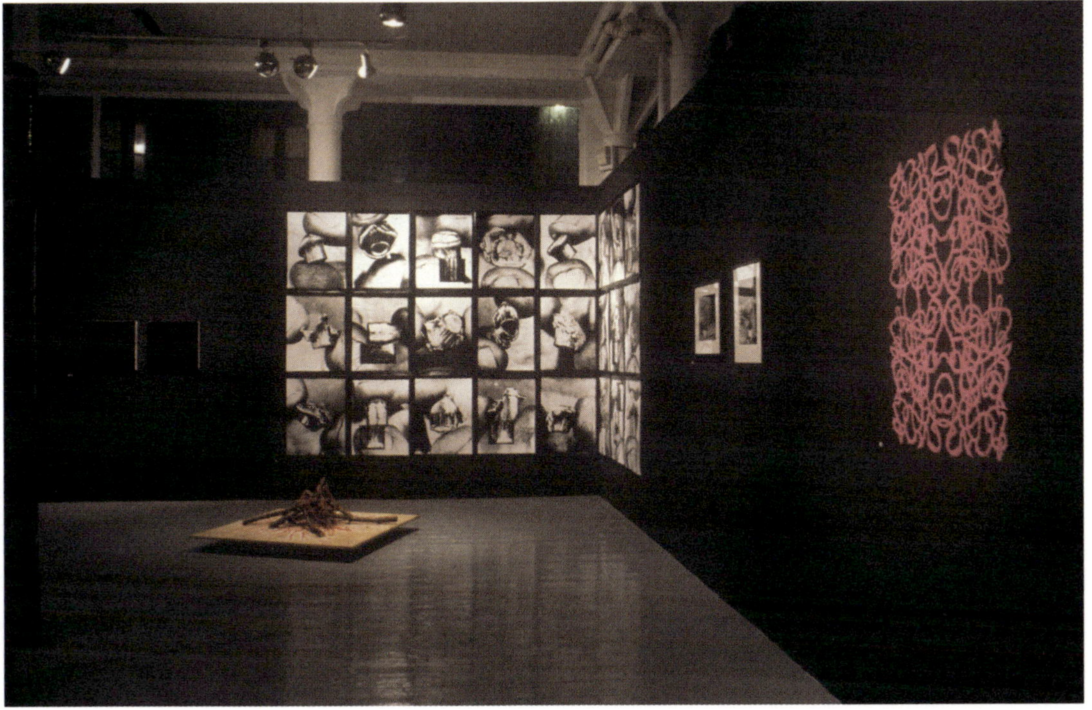

03 Joanne Tatham — The Tower: "A determinedly amateur construction in the basement made from cardboard boxes, newspaper, and paint to form and represent a circular tower rising from the floor to meet the ceiling. The work intentionally recalls a school play stage set, both reassuringly familiar and irritatingly illogical. The Tower relies on confused conventions of representations; a hotch-potch of methods…" (from press release)

Below: Joanne Tatham, 'The Tower'.

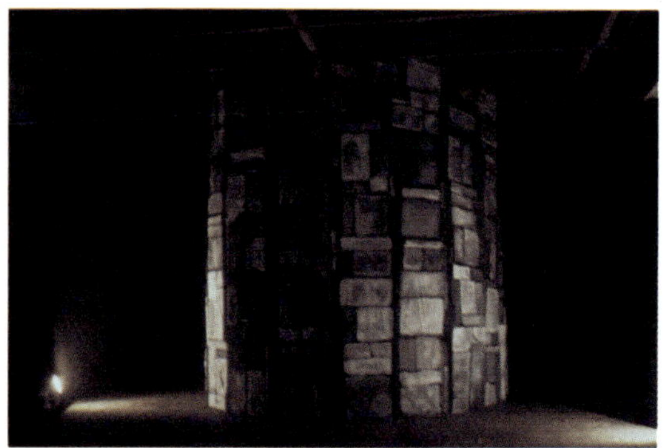

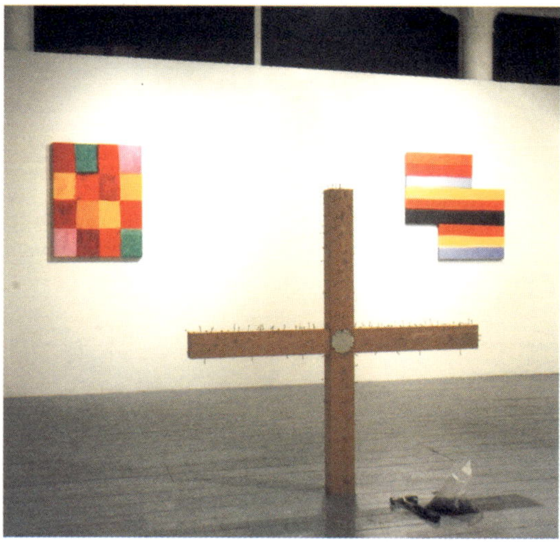

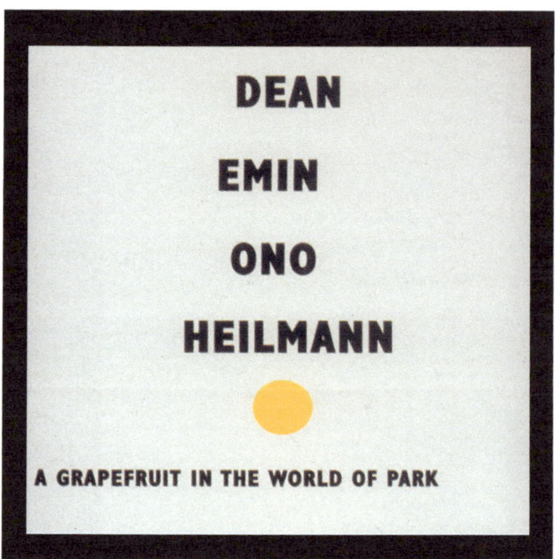

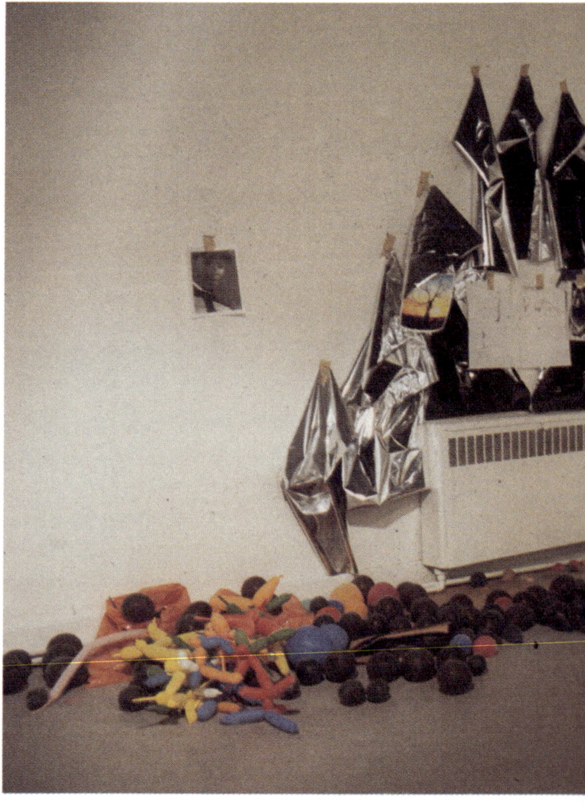

Above: 'A Grapefruit in the World of Park' — foreground: Yoko Ono, *Hammer-A-Nail-In/Celtic Cross (Oak, Mirror Glass, Coffin Nails, Hammer, Container For Nails)*; background left–right — Mary Heilmann, *Chico (Personal version)*, *Barstow*; curated by Cathy Wilkes.

04 Transmission/Brown Spot Exchange: In November 1995 'Brown Spot', a group of artists from Toronto, produced the exhibition 'Forget Brown Spot…Save the World'.

The second half of the exchange project saw Transmission members Martin Boyce, Alan Currall, Tanya Leighton, James Thornhill and Sue Tompkins travel to Toronto to exhibit at 'Free Parking' in April 1996.

Below: James Thornhill and Joachim Koestner, *Sticks and Stones, 1976.*

Bottom: Sue Tompkins, *Breathless Gear.*

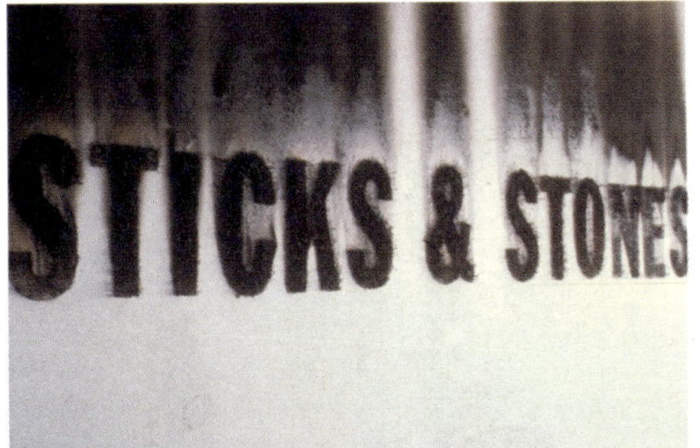

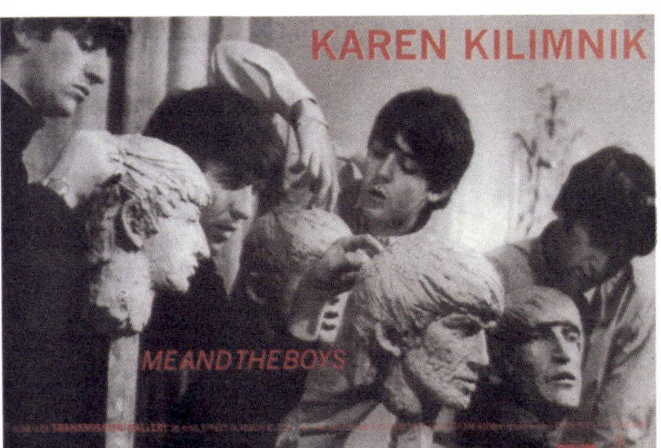

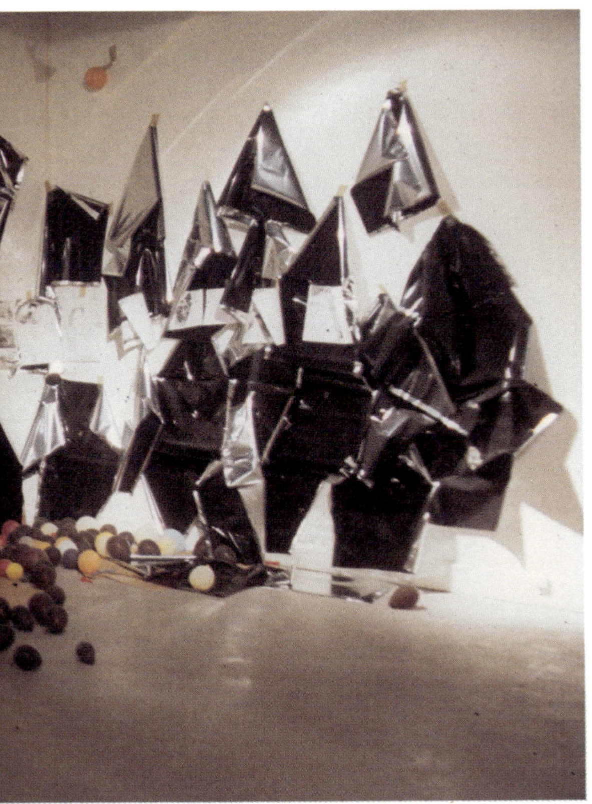

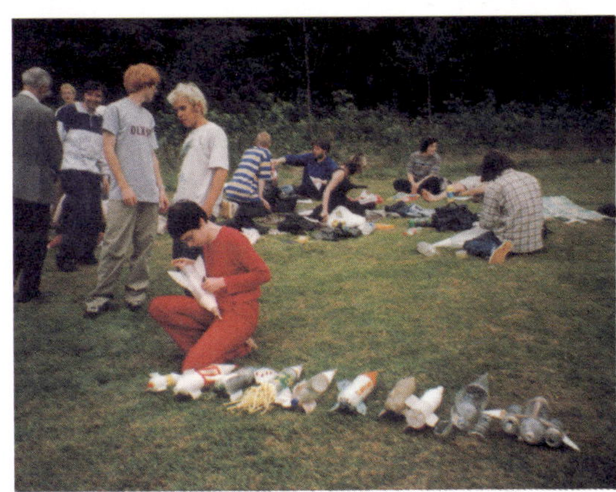

06 Top: Karen Kilimnik, 'Me and the Boys' poster.

Above: 'Rocket Event' with Michael Mulvihill at Pollok Park, Glasgow—foreground: committee member Judith Weik.

07 Jackie Derrida/Rocket Event: "JACKIE DERRIDA aka Graham Bell, Glasgow's (possibly Europe's) only deconstructionist drag queen takes up residence in the basement this month, for a programme of lectures, screenings and performances centred around Ms Derrida's unique lifestyle, beginning with a talk on Saturday July 6th at 8pm.

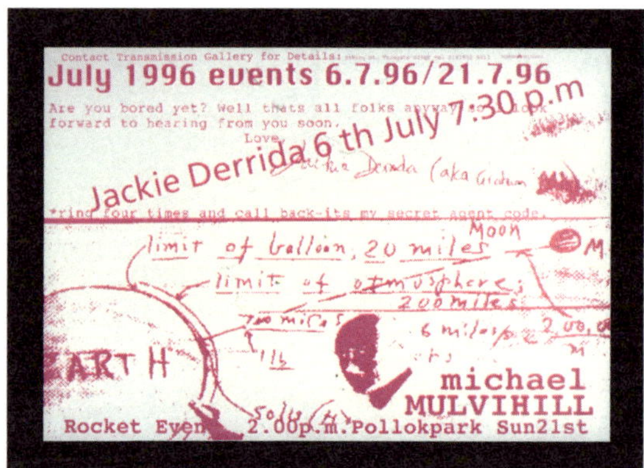

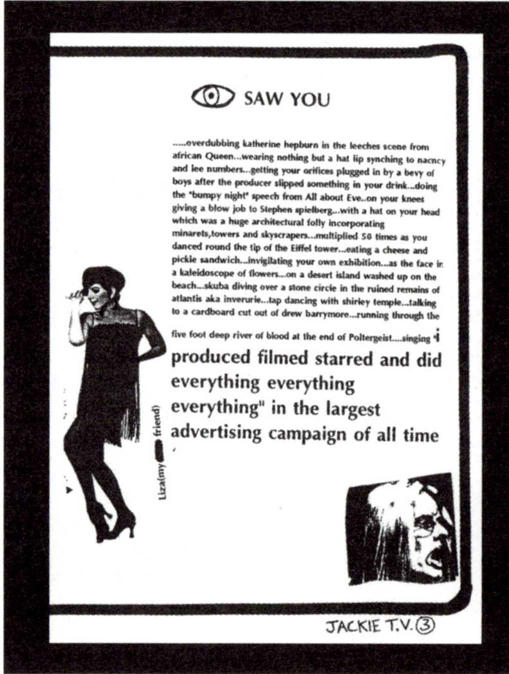

Above: Excerpt from Jackie Derrida's TV guide.

OUTDOORS: ROCKET EVENT Pollok Park 2pm Sunday July 21st

Artist Michael Mulvihill will host an afternoon of home-made 'aquajet' rocketry, including competition for the longest flight with fabulous prizes. Meet outside the Burrell Collection at 2pm. Bring a picnic and a

rocket — easy DIY plans are available free from Transmission." (from press release)

09 **Victoria Morton:** 'Red Eyes' (Victoria Morton interviewed by Cathy Wilkes (extracts from leaflet produced for the exhibition by Transmission and the Pier Arts Centre, Orkney).

"Unintelligible Art is a certain kind of freedom; it is best comprehended in terms of thinking about an Unhappy Consciousness—the tragic conflict inherent in the inner world of your mind and its relation with the world of action. Psychoanalysis is a method of understanding tragic conflict, unhappy consciousness and the self consciousness of art that one can't easily understand. There is a special value placed on unintelligibility and it is difficult to tell what the good and bad parts of unintelligible works are. But, the discrepancy between what bespeaks of psychotic tendency in the artist and what is a stylistic or deliberate development is part of the pleasure of thinking about these paintings — and understanding the unintelligibility as it exists in the work, avoids doing violence to art. (CW)

V:… I'm thinking how do I want this to look—what kind of paint should I choose, what colour should I choose, what thickness should the colour be. What kind of brush should I use.

With this one, *Happiness*, for ages I'd been trying to get a feeling of rapidness…this circular thing was the answer to doing that, they give you the feeling of things moving about and organising themselves… they're almost coming to get you.

C: They're like something…

V:… sometimes it's not important — that they are anything—you see some of these ones (hoops) are really rough. I was painting on these because I wanted them to be whiter so that they give definition to the roughness of the others and so that there's a tonal range going on so that this seems further away than that, so that this grey in the background looks like a separate part of the picture.

C: As well, I'm thinking—you're thinking, what brush should I use, what kind of paint…although in the end

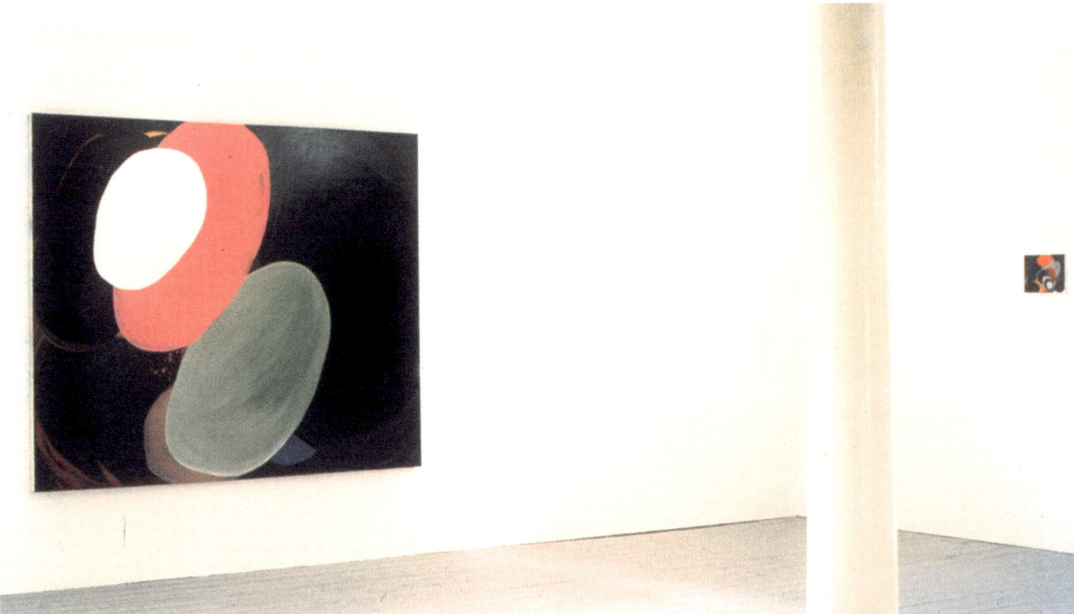

you're painting something that's quite odd and dense and difficult to understand…I mean, it's not a minimalist thing or anything but you're deciding one thing at a time, one thing after another.

V: Yes, well the idea shifts, these aren't pure forms. But I'm clear in my mind I paint something definite—different parts of the painting do happen in different ways. I would paint something very definite like the blue and the black in *Happiness*—quite sort of sluggish—and that would almost be like a labour. I enjoyed putting the paint on but it wasn't something I would do to finish the painting. I've narrowed down the way that I'm painting to such an extent that I'm really only working with four or five different ways of putting paint on. I mean I did something really weird on that painting when I first started it I think I took a marker pen and drew all over it with circles. Then I did something else. Why shouldn't I be able to paint hoops all over?

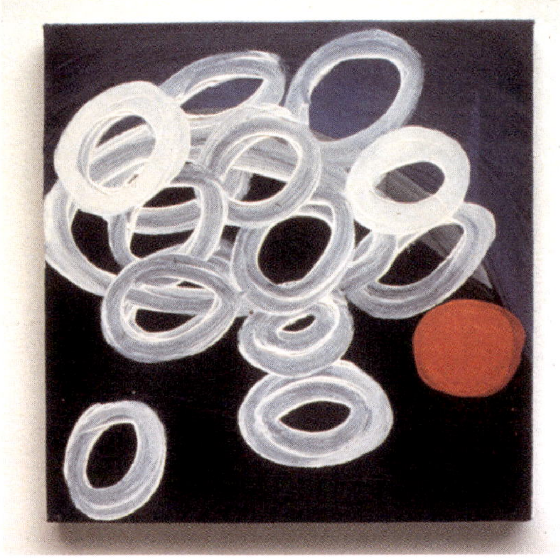

C: So there's an idea of speed, but I don't think it's the speed of the paint going on, it's not out of control speed, it's the speed of being able to move from one painting to another or one picture to another—as I move my head around…

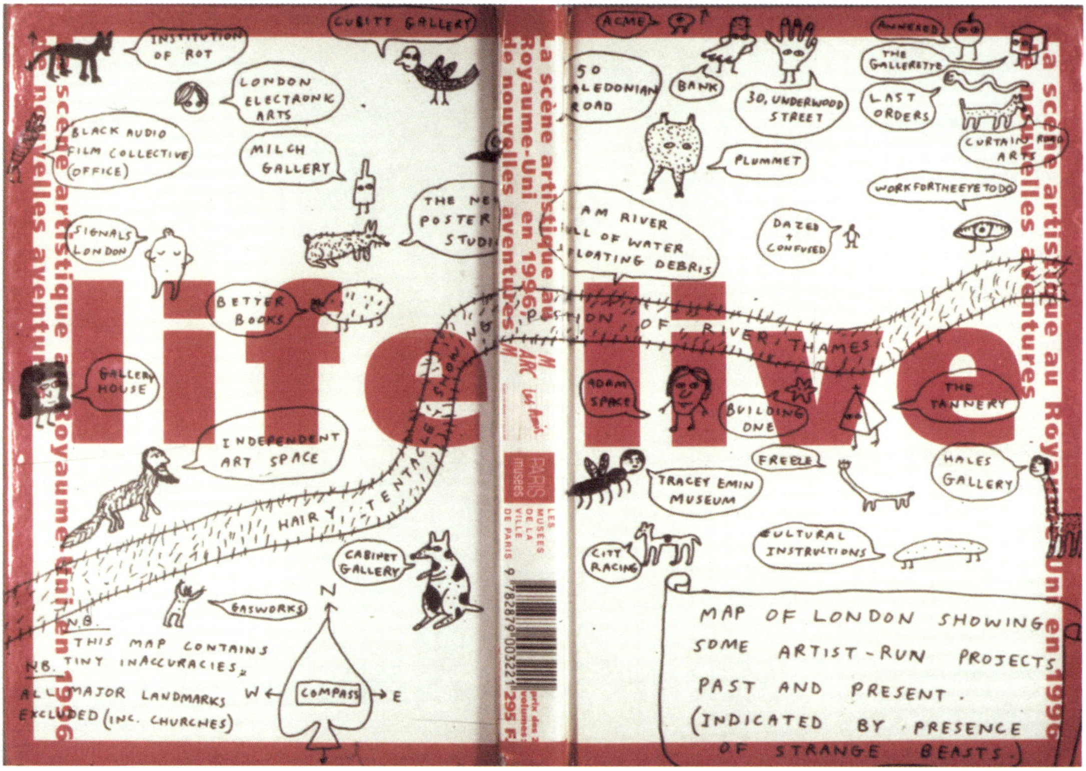

Above: The cover of the 'Life/Live' anthology — drawing by David Shrigley.

Right: 'Life/Live' — Richard Wright at work.

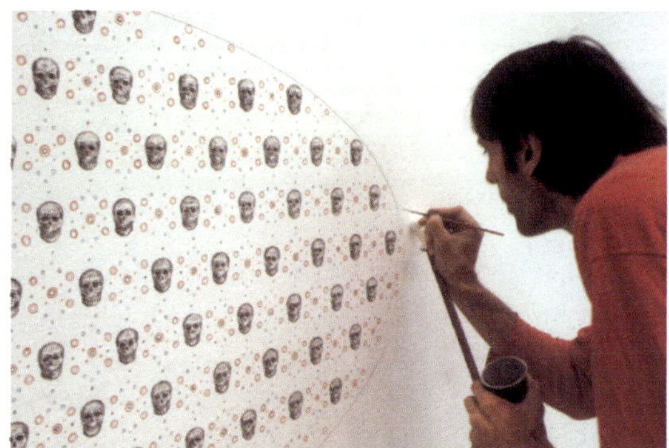

V: Well, I will be working on one painting with the other in mind. Although I work practically on one thing at a time, in a sense there is just that kind of flitting from one thing to another and the ideas are minute. I mean they're just like—what would it be like if I put pink on top of this?"

10 Life/Live: Transmission participated in 'Life/Live', an exhibition which attempted to highlight the diversity of artist-run spaces and projects in Britain. 'Life/Live' was held at the Musée d' Art Moderne de la Ville de Paris. The artists shown by Transmission were Richard Wright, Martin Boyce, Sue Tompkins, Heather Allen and Roderick Buchanan. The show toured to Lisbon in January 1997.

"…where does that leave us now, when it is said that the avant-garde only exists as a myth, or that the avant-garde has become the academy? What is an 'independent' art independent from these days?" David Batchelor (extract from 'Imagine this…', p.18, from the 'Life/Live' anthology)

10 Stay on your own for slightly longer: One of four exhibitions in the UK of Swedish artists which was part of a project called 'I am Curious' curated by Maria Lind. Artists who exhibited at Transmission were Lotta Antonssonn, Henrik Håkansson, Annika von Hausswolff, Anders Widoff.

"The work consisted of ten blackberry bushes in a kind of laboratory set-up. However, the closer one approached this piece, the more disturbing it became— the bushes were covered in stick-insects, and the work emerged as a metaphor for social control and the denial of danger." Mark Sladen (*Art Monthly*, December 1996–January 1997, pp. 40–41. Originally published in *Expressen*)

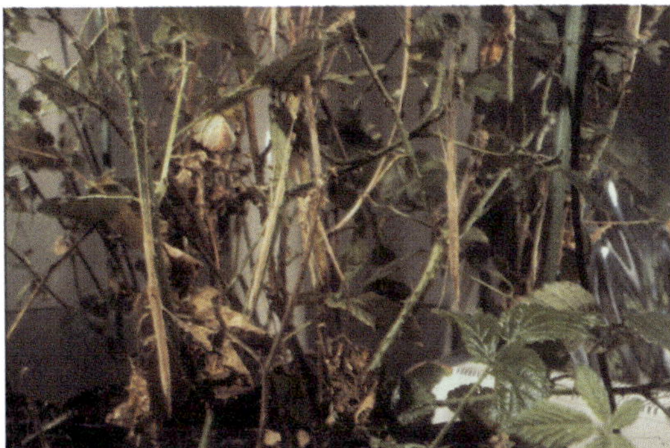

Below and bottom: Henrik Håkansson, *War of the Worlds (Sipyloidea sipylus).*

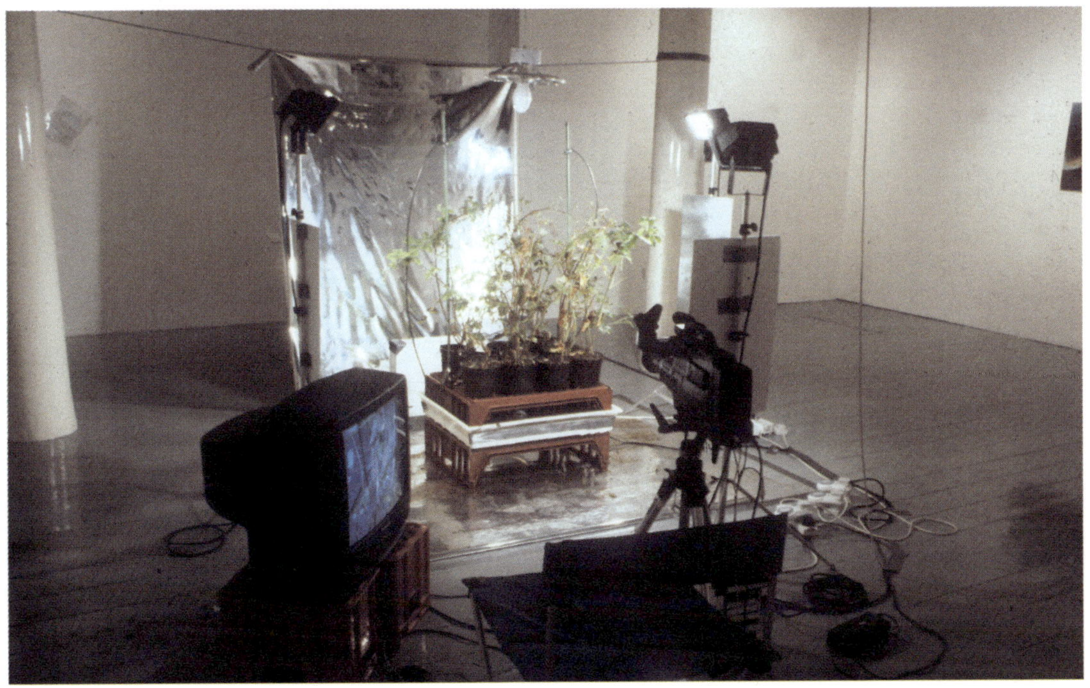

1997

01 Hong Kong Island: A group show based around propositions of unrealisable projects by Alan Currall, Chris Evans, Claire Barclay, Kevin Kelly, Billy Clark, Aoise Farren, Kate Gray, David Wilkinson, Andrew Miller and Simon Polli. The poster was designed by Brendan Sowersby and there was an accompanying archive with proposals and projects by international artists, architects, writers and radicals.

"The impossible dreams of ten artists are being showcased in 'Hong Kong Island', an exhibition at Transmission. Their responses to the question of what constitutes an unrealisable project are found in the political, personal and psychological realms…

Kate Gray is offering you all unconditional love on 0141 552 1577. I advise all male 'members' to ring this number now—it may prove a more rewarding experience than lavishing your own unconditional love on 22 strangers every Saturday. Alan Currall's video documents his parents' instructions on how to survive when the ship literally goes down. In a rare instance of useful parental advice, Mr Currall senior details how to drink the blood of a captured seagull. Beat that.

Elsewhere, Billy Clark takes you about as close as you'll ever get to the front door of Number 10 Downing Street, while Simon Polli exhibits a drawing of a block of flats on wheels—the council could consider this to help solve urban decay. The other pipe dreamers, Chris Evans, Kevin Kelly, Aoise Farren, David Wilkinson, Claire Barclay and Andy Miller, have all doodled away admirably, and with the addition of the unabomber's manifesto, this is a rich stew.

Now I've been in their dreams, so they can be in mine. Waking up in a cold sweat, I saw an exhibition of all the rejected proposals for art shows in Scotland last year. Now that would be interesting, but that's another story…" John Beagles (*The List*, 24 January–6 February 1997, p. 62)

03 JoyJoy: David Burrows, Gary Perkins, Stuart Purdy, Karen Reynolds, Peter Kapos, Gitte Villesen, and Paul McCarthy exhibited work in this show which presented innocence as the harbinger of deception.

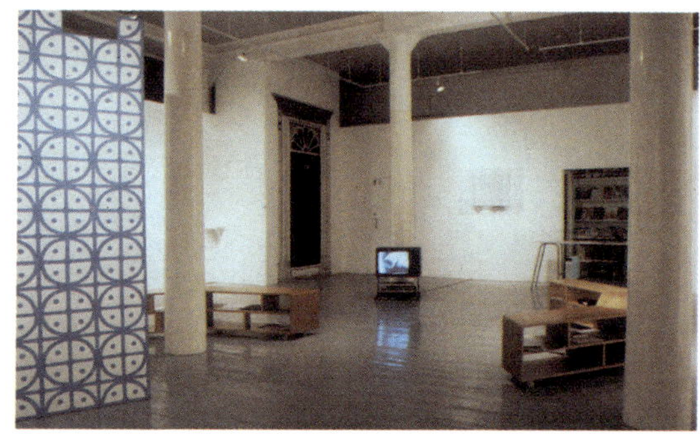

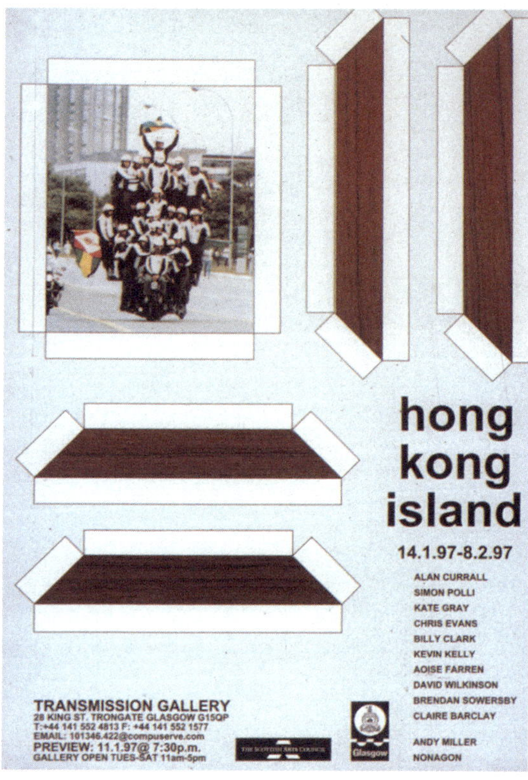

Top: 'Hong Kong Island'—left–right: David Wilkinson, *Black Hole Transmission*; Andrew Miller, *Nonagon* (centre left and right, containing archive); Billy Clark, texts: *Muckraking*, *Prison Privatisation*, *Directors List*, *Glasgow's Dubious Agenda*; Untitled (wall-painting of Number 10 Downing Street); Kevin Kelly *'Paddy's Market'*, *A TV Soap*; Simon Polli, *Just put some multis on it and some low rise II*.

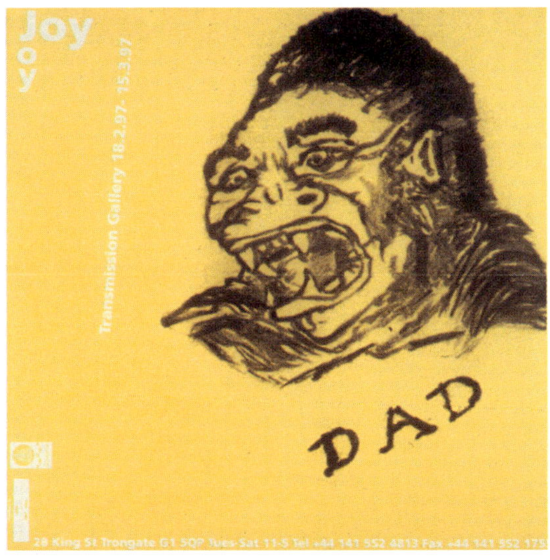

Above: 'JoyJoy' poster — drawing by Hayley Tompkins.

'Young Parents': Transmission participated in an exhibition in Manchester of artists and artist-run spaces with City Racing (London), Three Month Gallery (Liverpool) and hosted by The Annual Programme and Castlefield Gallery. Transmission's contribution was curated by Tom O'Sullivan and Joanne Tatham from proposals by Transmission members and included Amanda Bindley, Jamie Burroughs, Alex Frost, Steve Hollingsworth, Eva Rothschild, Tom O'Sullivan, Joanne Tatham, Beáta Veszely, Toby Webster, David Wilkinson and Caroline Woodley.

03 New York Public Access Experience: Organised by Patterson Beckwith, Alex Bag and Sam Soghor.

"Public Access in New York is a virtually non censored collection of channels on cable television. The channels are open to the public, so that anyone with access to a video camera and a little free time can have a show.

Consequently there is a large variety of shows with different formats including live call-in, interviews, religious propaganda, music videos, experimental shows done by hosts, and artists exploring their work in video media ranging in age from teens to old folk. Public access is much nicer to watch than the government sanctioned channels since it is home-made, commercial free, and created with the least expense possible. If someone has

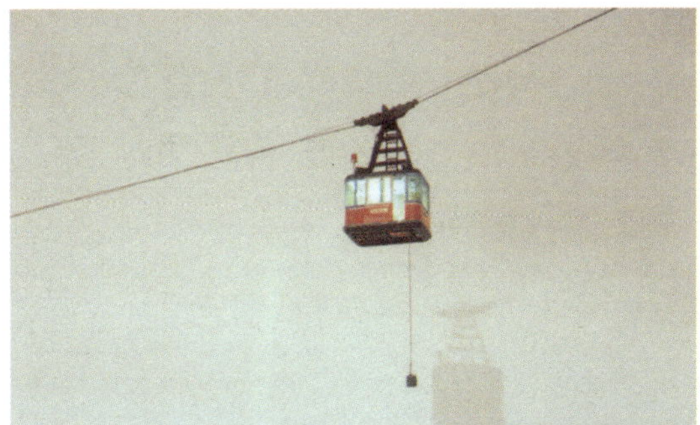

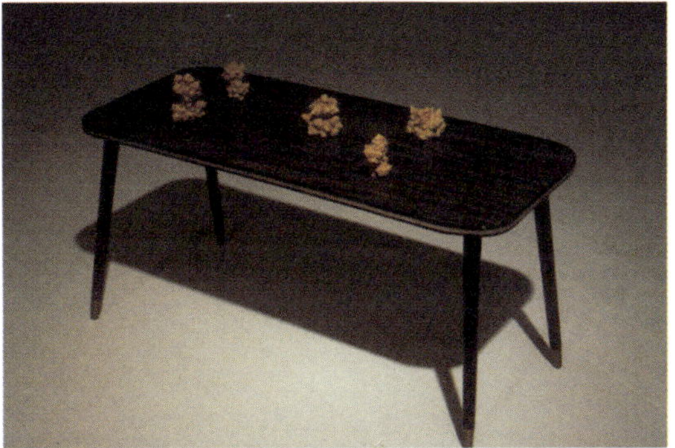

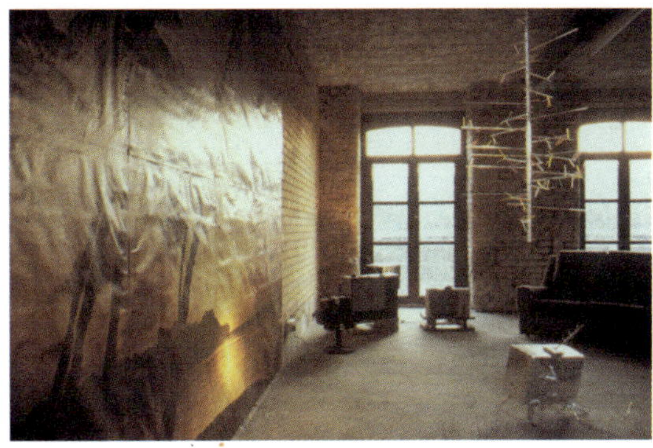

Top: Gary Perkins, *Unless one is born anew, he cannot see the kingdom of God.*

Centre: Stuart Purdy, *Gerunds.*

Above: 'Young Parents', March 1997 — left: Toby Webster, *Photowall* and right: *Loose Reverb* (hanging sculpture); Alex Frost, *Black Box* (sculptures on floor); Amanda Bindley, *Cold Comfort* (couch).

something to say, public access is the most efficient method of talking to the masses." Sam Soghor

"25.3.97–12.4.97 Transmission will be presenting The New York Public Access Experience, with literally hundreds of hours of clips and shows. There will also be recorded interviews with the producers of various NY public access shows." (press release)

06 Jonnie Wilkes/Russell Crotty: "This two person show includes new sculptural work by Jonnie Wilkes and three hand-drawn Planetary Atlases by Russell Crotty.

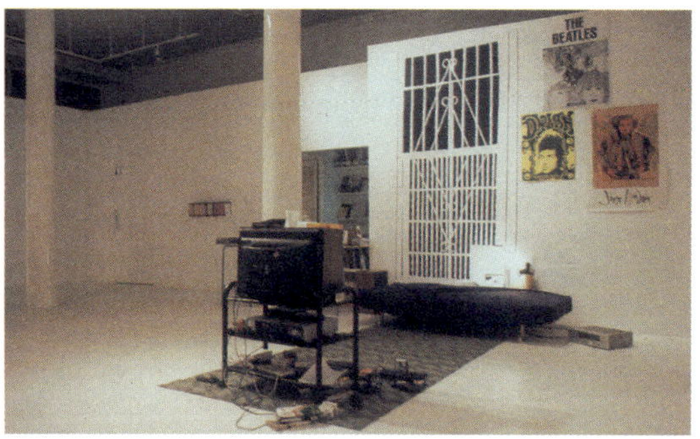

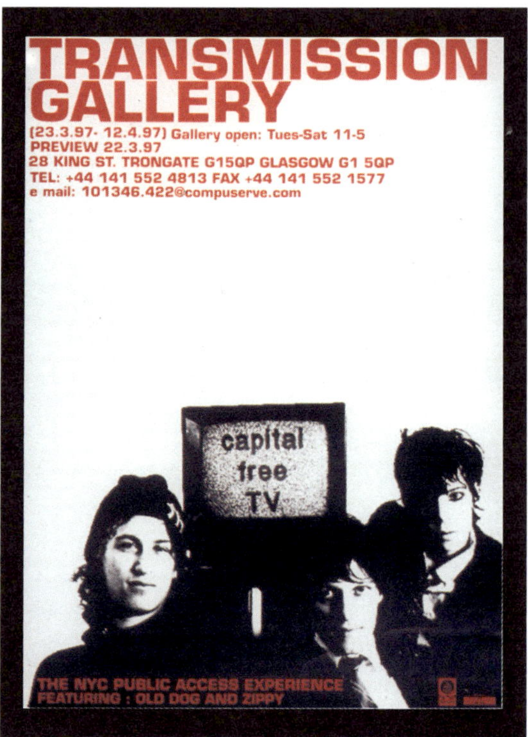

Jonnie Wilkes was born in Belfast in 1967. He now lives and works in Glasgow as a sculptor and a DJ/recording artist.

Russell Crotty lives in Malibu, Los Angeles. His current work includes references to the experiences of surfing and stargazing for NASA." (from press release)

"Wilkes' main installed work, *Sleep*, 1997, included the kind of platform you might overlook at a gig, a light rig or speaker stack scaffolding. Underneath it, a specially designed disc, familiar from club lightshows, sent a spinning, comet-shaped pool to turn eternally in the shadows. A white plastic sheet, hung from a string line, provided the screen for a video projection slowly showing the names of some dance tracks — Washing Machine, Madface, Humanoid — that would be immediately recognisable to a dedicated club audience but very few other people. Yet, at the same time, because it was decontextualised, it was not without interest; the change of space from club to gallery provided a moment of

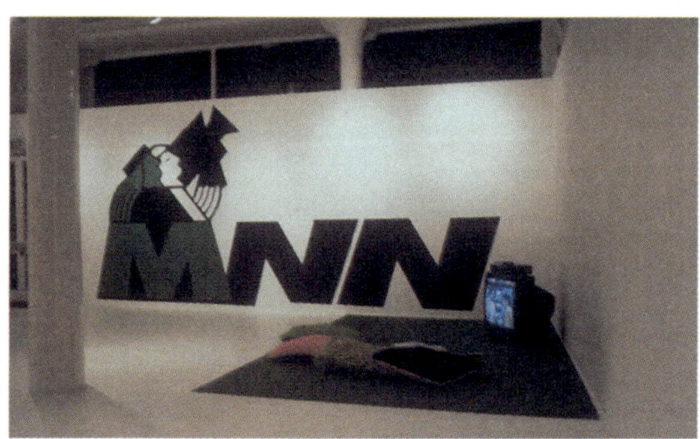

Above and above left: 'New York Public Access Experience', March 1997.

clarification which allowed the set-up to be seen as poetically intended.

One hundred screenprints of the word 'fever' lay stacked on the floor with the printer's packaging around them; club culture has long been adept at finding resonances for its style in flyers and design and *Fever*'s half-buried metaphor of distribution and delirium was concentrated in a seemingly casual setting. It is one of the hardest things to make a deliberate arrangement look totally uncontrived, but Wilkes sidesteps this problem by choosing arrangements that are experienced originally through some form of disorientation, perceptual shift or stream-of-consciousness meditation.

Russell Crotty also displays his lifestyle options but in a way that is immediately apparent as you look at his books of drawings that project an idea of a kind of West Coast casuality and ease of effort alongside a total dedication to the pleasurable, the interesting, and its recording, at the same time. It comes as no surprise to learn that he has made a book of surfing drawings, showing amazing tubes and

indication of Crotty's tireless patience—whole spreads of the night sky, drawings sometimes five feet across and entirely filled in with a black Biro. One of them, *Orion over Piz Gloria*, in following the contours of the alpine slopes, revealed an excerpt from the plot of Crotty's favourite Bond film. Handwritten texts used in the books, like hieroglyphics, emphasised the personal or particular significance of some of the drawn imagery. Looking through a telescope to draw the details for the moon's surface in *Atlas of Lunar Drawings*, Crotty's eye, in a state akin to reverie, has picked out areas of interest. The whiteness of the page became a mirror-image mapping of his diagram of lunar luminescence. The letters, in

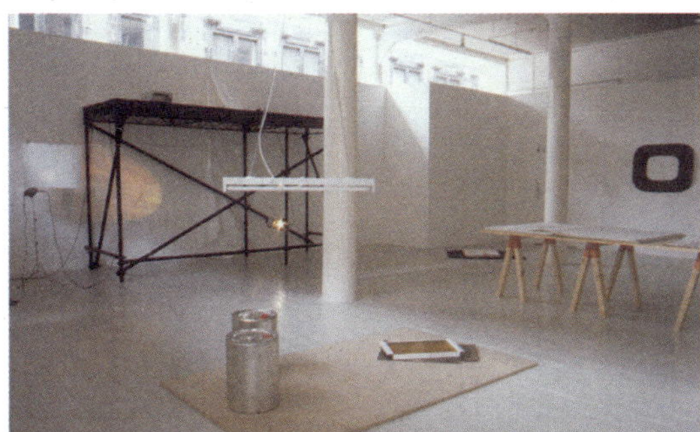

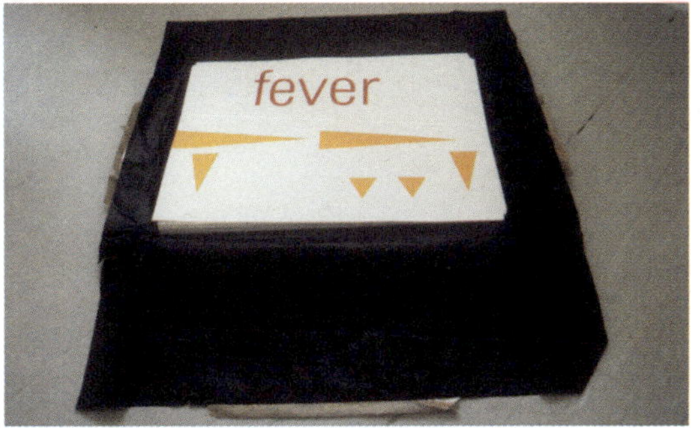

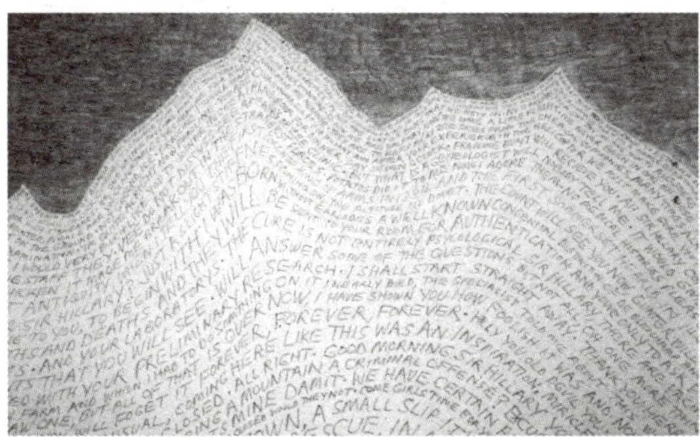

Above left: left–right: Jonnie Wilkes, *Sleep*; *Punishment, Reward*; *Fever*; Russell Crotty, *Atlas of Lunar Drawings*; Jonnie Wilkes, *Fukulator*.

Above right: Jonnie Wilkes, *Fever*.

Left: Russell Crotty, *Five Nocturnes (Orion over Piz Gloria)* [detail].

handwritten capitals that got larger towards the bottom of the page, prompted a strong vertiginous effect. Here Crotty noted 'The Deep Basin Copernicus…evidence of massive impacts under high illuminations…Brings to mind HP Lovecraft's *The Dark Brotherhood*…

For it was an extraterrestrial scene that I witnessed…one of great grandeur in its proportions and yet one completely incomprehensible to me.'"

Padraig Timoney (*Art Monthly*, July–August 1997, p. 208)

always with a perfectly poised little surfer on the board. He did these right on the beach.

On large tables in the Gallery, Crotty showed three gargantuan books, (all 1996) whose pages had to be turned with the help of the gallery invigilator. The pages of the smallest one, a red book, *Jupiter Strip Sketch Book*, portrayed a progression of orbital views around the latitude of the great Red Spot. This was envisaged by Crotty to be seen as a very slow flick book. *Five Nocturnes* was a superb

09 Simon Starling—**Blue Boat Black:** "'Blue Boat Black' is the first solo show in Scotland of work by Glasgow based artist Simon Starling. Transmission Gallery has been altered to create a rhetorical exhibition space in which *Blue Boat Black*, a new work made for Transmission in Marseille and *Work, made-ready, Kunsthalle Bern* are exhibited.

The project began with the transportation of a large vitrine from the National Museum of Scotland to Starling's temporary studio in Marseille. There, the case

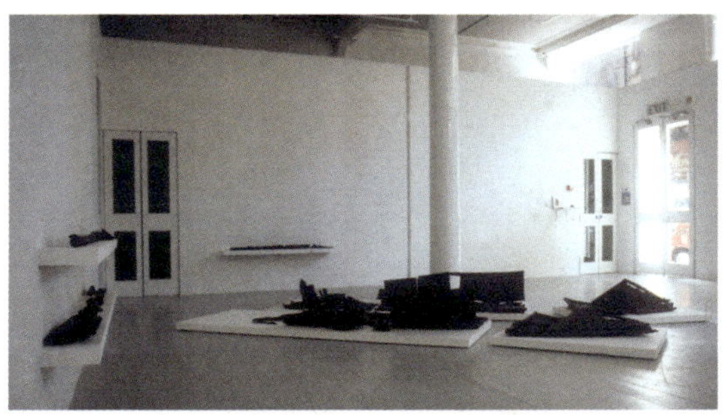

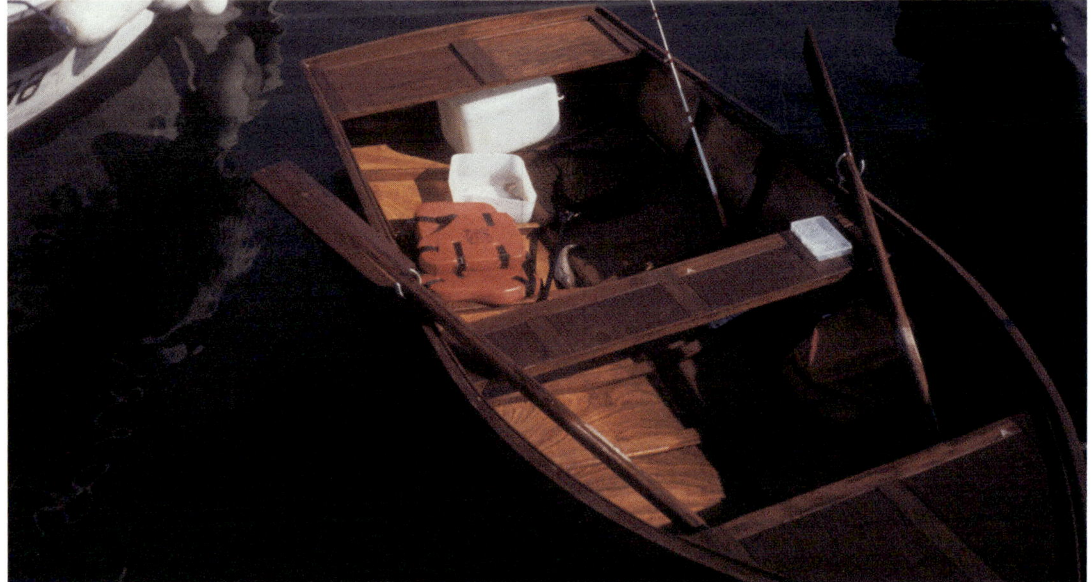

Above: 'Blue Boat Black'—photograph of the 'blue boat' in Marseille.

Top: Installation view showing the reconstructed 'mirrored' interior of the gallery.

Right: At the 'vernissage'.

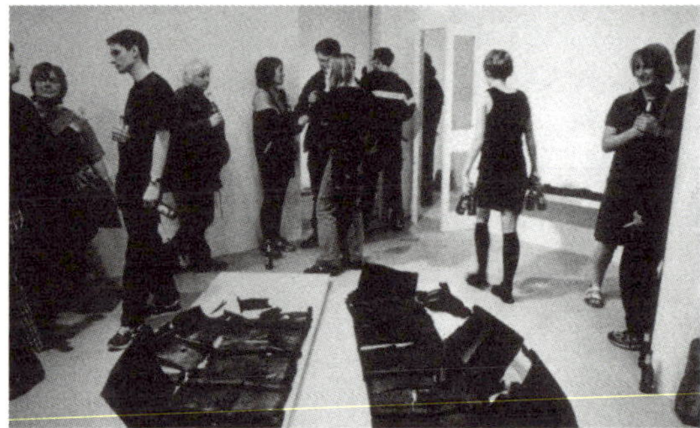

was disassembled and the wood was reshaped to construct a 'barque'—a traditional Marseille fishing boat—which was then painted blue (Bleu de Provence). Oars were made and the boat was put to sea to fish. Amongst the catch were sea bream, pandora, European porgy, rock fish, saddled bream, dorade and red mullet or rouget. The boat was then returned to land and transformed into charcoal. Later, using the charcoal as fuel, the fish were cooked and eaten. Finally, turning full circle, the traces and remains of the project were placed on public display." Francis McKee (from an essay written to accompany the exhibition)

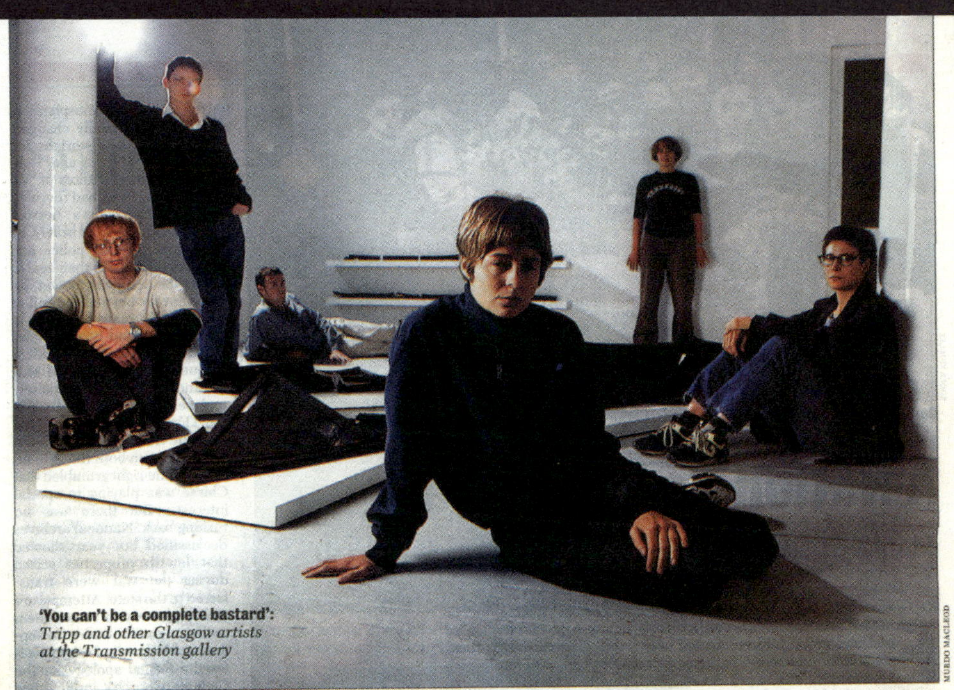

'You can't be a complete bastard':
Tripp and other Glasgow artists at the Transmission gallery

Glasgow Gets Conceptual

The city's new art scene reflects Scotland's spirit of independence—and the world is taking notice

BY PETER PLAGENS

NONE OF THE ARTISTS HELPING fellow conceptualist Simon Starling install his exhibition at Glasgow's publicly funded Transmission gallery is yet 30. And in the inauspicious storefront in Trongate, just off the main shopping avenues, the word that crops up most in their conversation is "practice." No, not rehearsing an artistic skill until it's gotten right, but practice as in a dentist's. These artists constitute the committee that runs Transmission, and *everything* they do—working day jobs as waiters, collecting the dole—is part of their practice as artists. Most of them don't even have studios, preferring to set up cooperative "project rooms" where they work and show, often in groups with such rock-bandish names as Filthy Swan. And they cliquelessly lend each other moral support. As Transmission committee member Sarah Tripp puts it: "You can't be a complete bastard in Glasgow, 'cause your granny's gonna tell your auntie you did that."

This is the new Glasgow art world, and, a month after Scotland's landmark referendum, the scene reflects the same independent spirit that voters displayed when they elected to create a Scottish Parliament.

Young Glaswegian artists reject the shocking sex-and-death installations of such highly publicized London "Britpack" phenoms as Damien Hirst and the Chapman brothers. To artists around Transmission, the tabloidy Londoners merely repackage punk and soft porn for superrich collectors like Charles Saatchi. In Glasgow private patronage is almost nonexistent, and a work of art is likely to be conspicuously modest: say, a bunch of carrots used to swipe orange paint on a wall, then placed on a shelf and titled "18 Carrots." But the art world outside Glasgow is taking notice. Tobey Paterson, another Transmissioner, says, "There's at least one foreign curator a week in town, scouting. And sometimes we get 10 all at once—from Korea."

One of the scene's stars, 31-year-old Douglas Gordon, became the first non-Londoner to win the prestigious £20,000 Turner Prize in 1996. (His work includes Alfred Hitchcock's "Psycho" extended to a running time of 24 hours.) Another Glaswegian, Christine Borland, 32, is considered the favorite to win this year. (For a recent installation piece, she commissioned six traditionally trained sculptors to create bronze portrait heads of Josef Mengele from photographs and verbal descriptions.) The prize will be awarded Oct. 29.

The art boom in Glasgow—historically

1998

01 **Henry VIII's Wives:** "'Henry VIII's Wives' is an international collaborative show made over an intensive three-week period in Glasgow. After working on previous group shows together which were collaboratively curated, the artists felt a more full collaboration would be productive. The process began with a series of mail-art projects to form a basis from which to discover and explore shared concerns, often task-based but open to interpretation.

When the artists regrouped in Glasgow they began by exploring different tactics for collaboration, using only easily available materials. Hence, some of the works are purely documentary, whereas others are obviously more resolved.

Some processes and ideas initiated in the letters, partly originating in previous collaborations, are recognisable in the themes emerging.

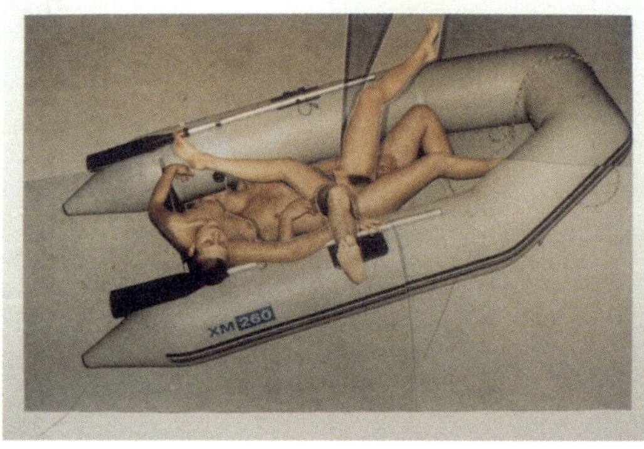

Above and right: Henry VIII's Wives, collaborative work.

The resulting works, which have been devised mostly within the Gallery itself, represent a synthesis of directions that have been pursued over this three-week period." (from press release)

The group, who graduated together from the Enviromental Art Course, Glasgow School of Art in 1997, have since exhibited many times locally and internationally as Henry VIII's Wives.

02 **I love this life:** "The best things in life, and love, are never simple or tidy. The best art can't be described in a few sentences, if at all. Sometimes all you can really grasp is your faith in something, faith that although you don't quite understand it, it's worth something, it's good, and that faith can allow you to cross a line, to go somewhere you've never been before, the artists we've asked to help us make 'I love this life' don't seem to have much in common at first, but

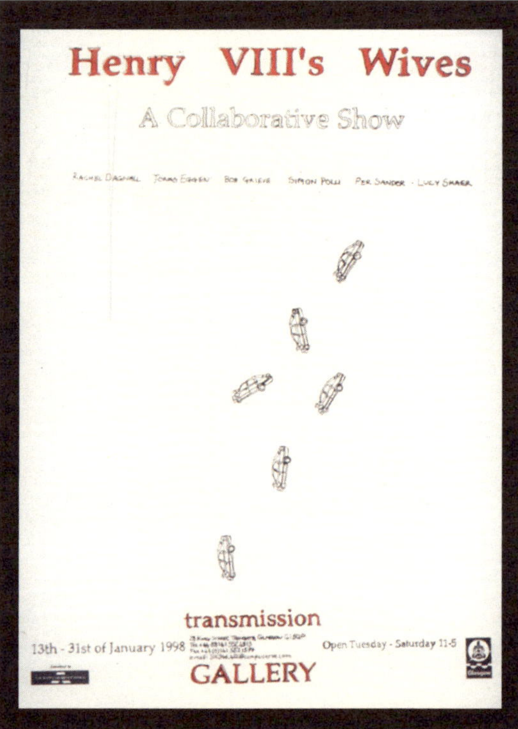

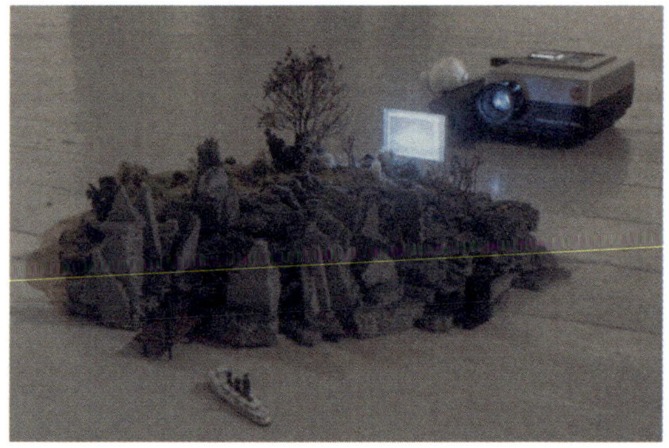

the work that they're making seems to us to be somehow crossing the odd line, being a bit transgressive—some quite loudly and some very quietly.

In a few words then: sad, angry, weird, pretty, ugly, beautiful." (from press release)

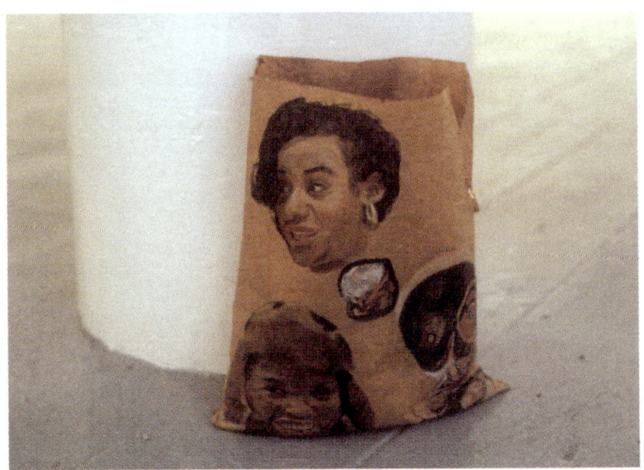

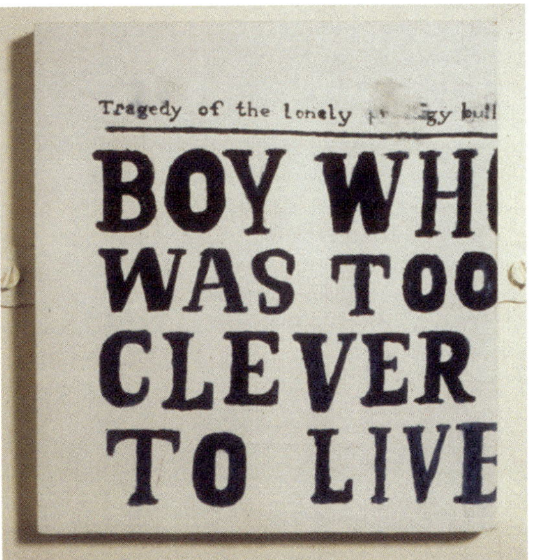

Above: 'I love this life' — Hayley Tompkins, *I am down*; **above right:** Paul Johnson, *Saturday, July, 1997*; **below:** Michael Fullerton, *Siouxsie and the Banshees (porno)*.

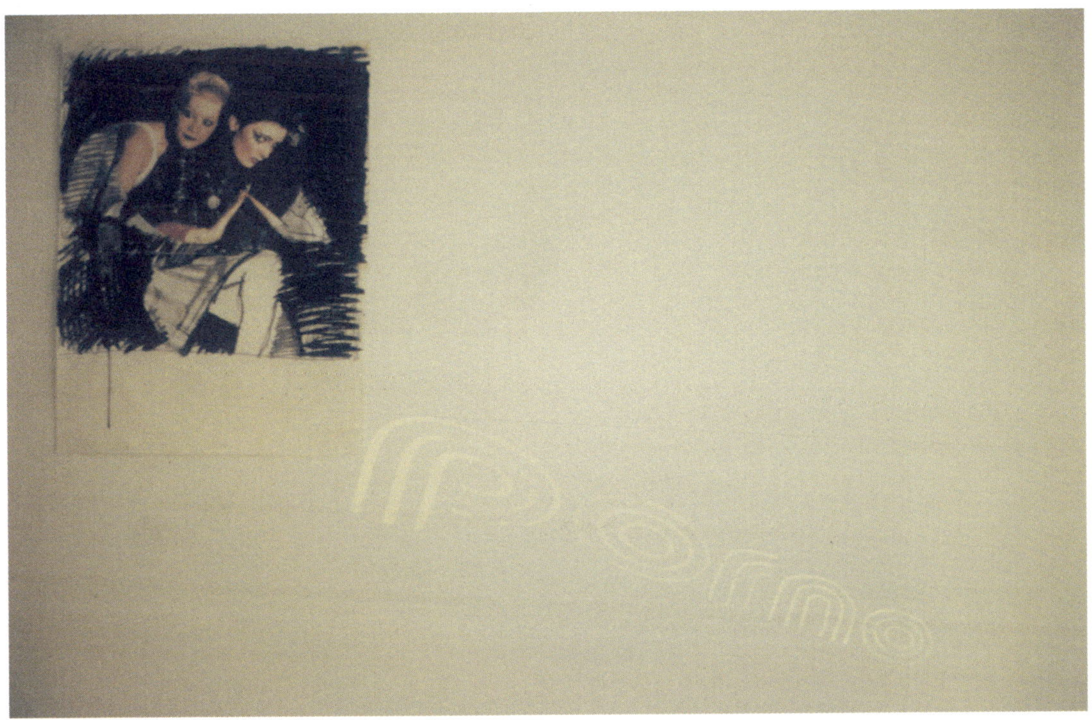

03 Something Ahhh … Nothing: "The Transmission has had an interesting and often chaotic time since the start of this year. The personnel of the ever changing committee have felt it necessary to mess things up in order to demystify the space a little and veer away from a seemingly predictable path. The programme has been a mixture of short projects, research based shows, and a live season with bands and performances where the gallery was filled by noise, dry ice, and 200 people none of us had ever seen before. New people have entered the gallery and hopefully will come back for more." Ewan Imrie (for Konstakuten's FESARS Newsletter, July 1998)

Three weeks of live chaos at Transmission in conjunction with the newly opened 13th Note Bar. This varied and hectic programme of performances, music, readings and talks included Rob Mitchell, Rose Thomas & Sophie Macpherson, The James Orr Complex, Fukuyama, Richard Maddalena, Dario Kavara, Kevin Henderson, Robert McShane, Cut Joey, Cylinder, MCDJ AB-Normal Tupperware, Badgewearer, Gael McDougall, David Hopkins, Ricky Campbell Allen and the DeepFried DJs.

The 13th Note re-located from Glassford Street to King Street (and opened a club venue on Clyde Street) early in 1998. Hosting gigs from local, national and international bands the 13th Note is at the centre of Glasgow's independent and experimental music scene.

Transmission slide talks and other events are often held in the 13th Note basement. Talks also happen at the Mitre Bar, Brunswick Street.

04 Alex Frost—Theme Show: "First, some facts.

During the last government, Michael Portillo and Peter Lilley were well known in Whitehall to be lovers—these are the men that Michael Grade saved from being outed on the final episode of Brass Eye. *Prince Andrew is the illegitimate lovechild of Princess Margaret and Lord Canarvon (photos of Lord C—although he is famously camera shy—are all the proof you need. These can be seen in an issue of* Hello! *Magazine). About five years ago there was an article in* The Spectator *which suggested that Marshal Tito was, in fact, a woman. Mrs Thatcher attended an occult-ish ceremony in the mid 1980s called 'The Cremation of Care' which involved circling a vast*

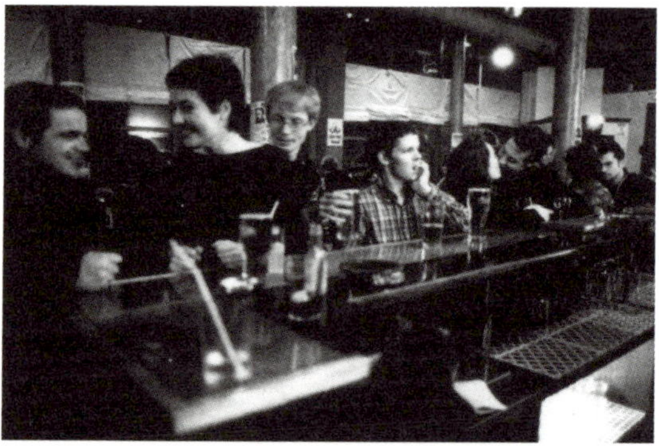

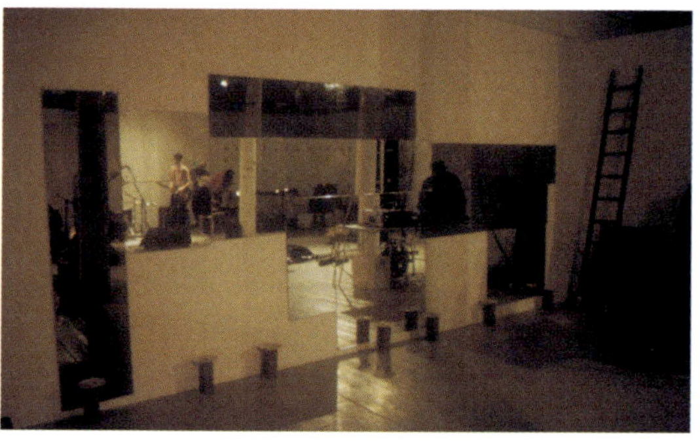

Top: The 13th Note—'performances' arranged by Rose Thomas and Sophie Macpherson took place in the bar for the whole of one night: a couple kissing, a man hogging a table and nursing his pint, a girl sitting on the stairs smoking.

Above: Transmission during 'Something Ahhh … Nothing', Cylinder soundcheck.

bonfire. Ian Fleming suggested to his superiors in British intelligence that the best man for the job of interrogating the captured Rudolph Hess would be Alister Crowley.

The title, 'Drop City', comes from the name of a community of drop-outs in Colorado, USA. Inspired after hearing a lecture by R Buckminster Fuller to build domes for their housing units, the 'droppers' utilised discarded materials from mainstream culture for the construction. They look like a cross between the EPCOT centre and Watts Towers.

Neither classically slack or particularly architecturally faithful, it was reasonably well made and looked like it might be difficult to put together. Despite the adhocism of the materials, the dome looked close to having production values or at least aspiring to them in a way that didn't seem comically unfeasible. I took this as a sign that the dome was meant to be itself and about itself, simultaneously." Alan Michael, extracts from a review of 'Drop City' at the Assembly Gallery, Glasgow School of Art (used as a press release for 'Theme Show')

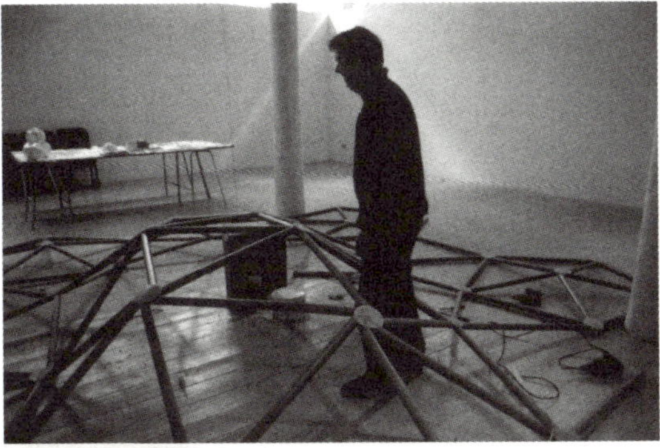

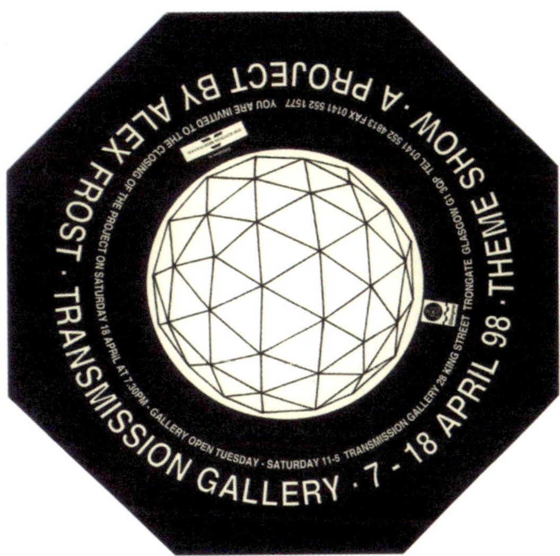

Above: 'Theme Show'—Alex Frost building the geodesic dome; **below:** the dome completed.

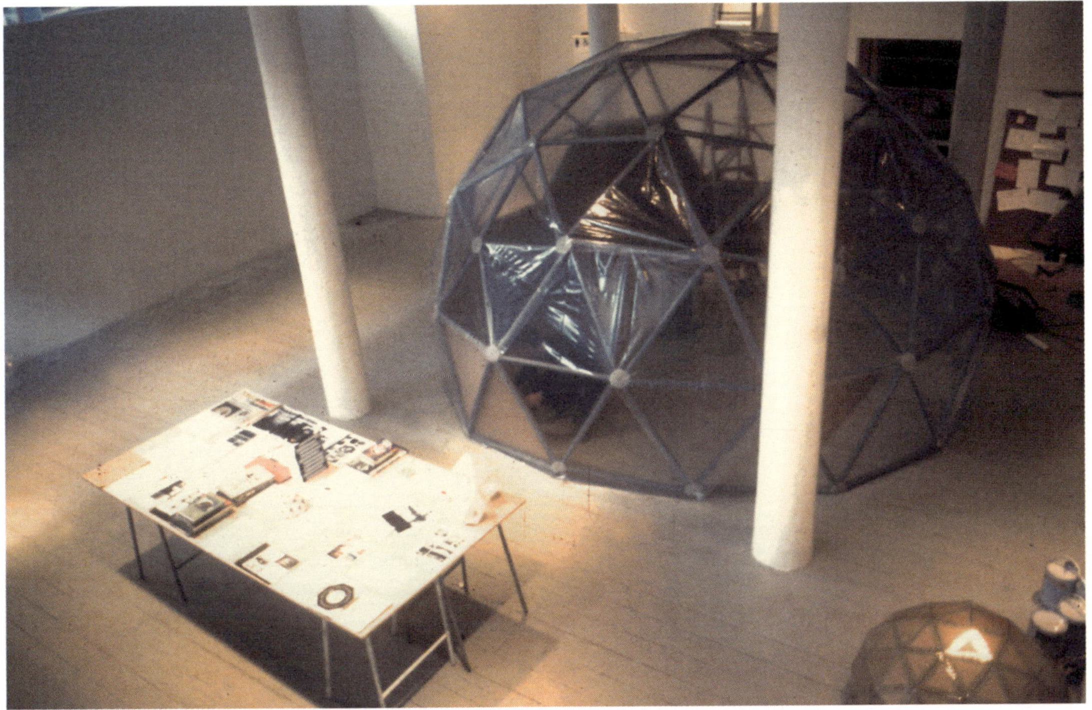

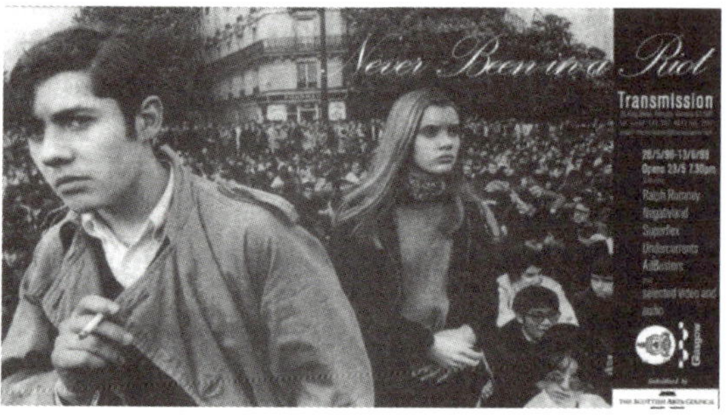

Below 'Never Been in a Riot', May 1998.

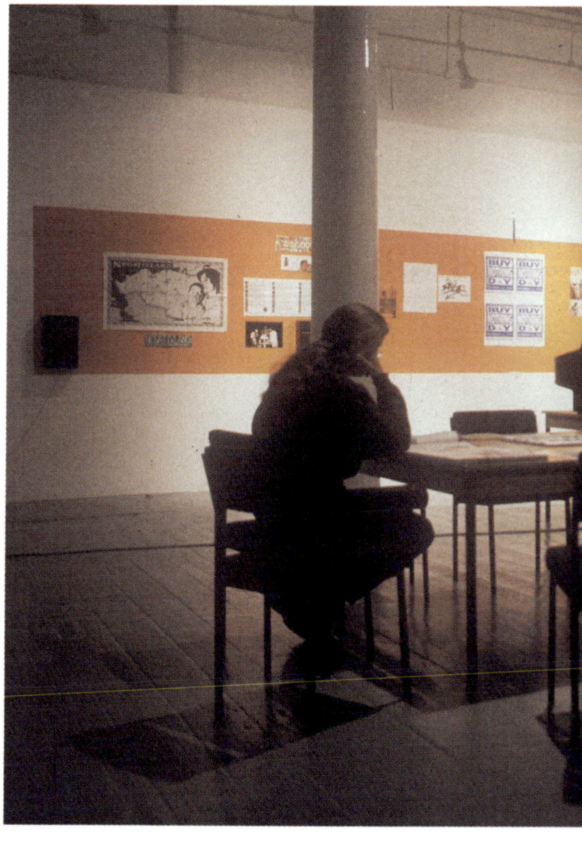

04 Above: 'Philosophical Inquiry', April 1998.

05 Never Been in a Riot: "A chance to examine the ways in which methods of resistance often incline towards art and vice versa. Including Superflex, AdBusters, Ralph Rumney and Undercurrents this exhibition offers a free Negativland compilation tape and screenings from a video library including films such as *Manufacturing Consent: Noam Chomsky and the Media, Hated,* a documentary about GG Allin and *Sonic Outlaws.*" (from press release)

'Never Been in a Riot' referred back to earlier events in and around Transmission. Ralph Rumney was invited back and made a video especially for the show — presented by the writer and art historian Alan Woods. Noam Chomsky spoke at the 'Self-Determination and Power' conference in Govan, Glasgow in 1990 which was described by Malcolm Dickson (former committee member) as "a key event and perhaps the pinnacle of

events that brought together many of the parallel projects operating in Glasgow at that time." The strategies of Negativland recalled the 'Festival of Plagiarism' held at the gallery in 1989 and those of the collaborative exhibition 'Desire in Ruins', 1987.

09 Anne-Marie Copestake — Always Have and Always Will: "Transmission has reopened with a kind of anti-refurbishment, where the partition walls and unappealing carpet which previously defined half of the downstairs area have been ripped out to leave a rough-and-ready basement underground car park-style space now equal in size, and by implication kudos, to the clean, white gallery above. Anne-Marie Copestake has hung a screen in the middle of this now large cellar, and it's back-projected so the image floats in the surrounding darkness, of which there is plenty. The scene is an interior—we see just enough to signify a typical dwelling—carefully lit and shot in a way that moves it out of the genre of amateur video and closer to low-budget TV drama. In turn, three young men describe their feelings for an absent fourth, but all three actors seem to have been given the same script. Start with one standing by a door, apparently talking to someone just out of shot. Cut to another, sat at a table, delivering the same line. Cut to the third, appropriately enough he's stood by the kitchen sink, and the same line again. Continue until a complicated and conflicting picture of an obsessive, emotional relationship emerges, like listening to that guy who you don't really know that well who ends up round your flat one night at 2am and tells you a little more about their life than you actually ever wanted to hear and you wonder why they can't just go home and deal with it but at the same time it's weirdly compelling. Another projection shows the three men sat uncomfortably together on a sofa, in silence. The split performances recall well-known works by Bruce Nauman or Stan Douglas, but the effect is closer to that of minimalist theatre. These strategies—the repetition, the circular cutting, the language which is emotionally precise but short on physical description—aren't being used as deconstruction or for dramatic effect, but as part

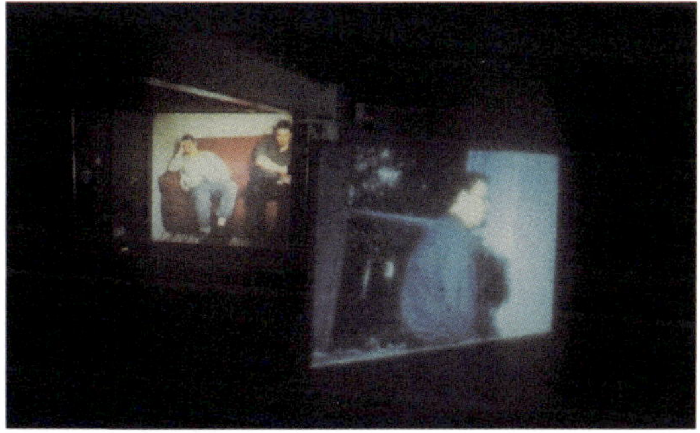

Above: Anne-Marie Copestake, 'Always have and always will', September 1998.

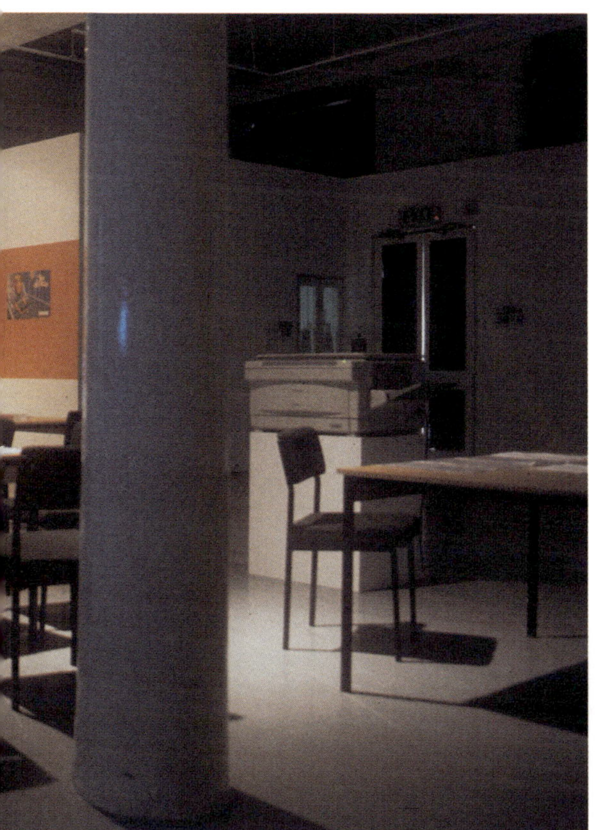

of a drama, and to effect. It could be another contribution to the current mini-genre of audition art, especially as only two of the three characters are totally convincing, but it goes further than that. This is serious, sincere work, in the spirit of Sam Beckett vs Mike Leigh, very different to a lot of what's around at the minute and I guess this is both its strength and its weakness. You need to be in the right state of mind and you need to spend time with it, but it has an intensity that works." Will Bradley (*Untitled*, Autumn 1998, p. 28)

10 Eurocentral: "For many of us the guilty pleasure of industrial architecture is impossible to resist—the pure form-follows-function ethic of freight terminals and grain elevators tantalises neurons that still respond to ultra-modernist starkness. So no apologies for naming this project after the new development off the M8 between Glasgow and Edinburgh. Miles and miles of battleship-grey corrugated steel and stacks of shipping containers blind us to the politics of it all.

The artists participating in 'Eurocentral' assume different positions in relation to the architecture that surrounds them, real or imagined. Manfred Pernice, showing in Scotland for the first time after a riot of continental shows that have generated comparisons with Gordon Matta-Clark, dreams impossible edifices and then maquettes them from found material; Chad McCail has drawn a plan for a troubled ecosystem on the verge of revolution or destruction… We also hope to organise a tour of the Eurocentral development site. Please call the gallery if you would be interested in attending." (from press release)

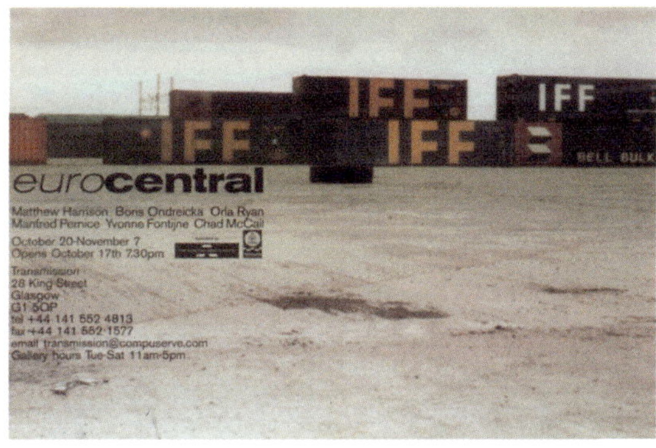

Below: 'Eurocentral'—Manfred Pernice, *Stralau 1.*

Below right: Chad McCail, *Spring* (detail).

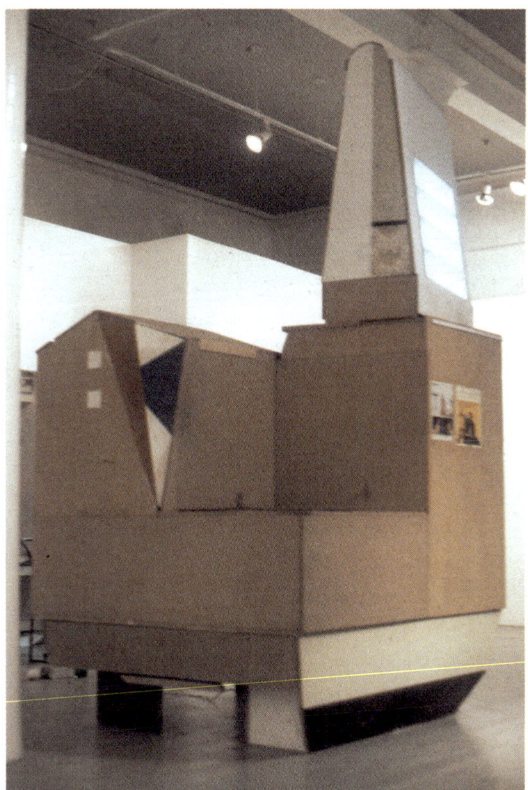

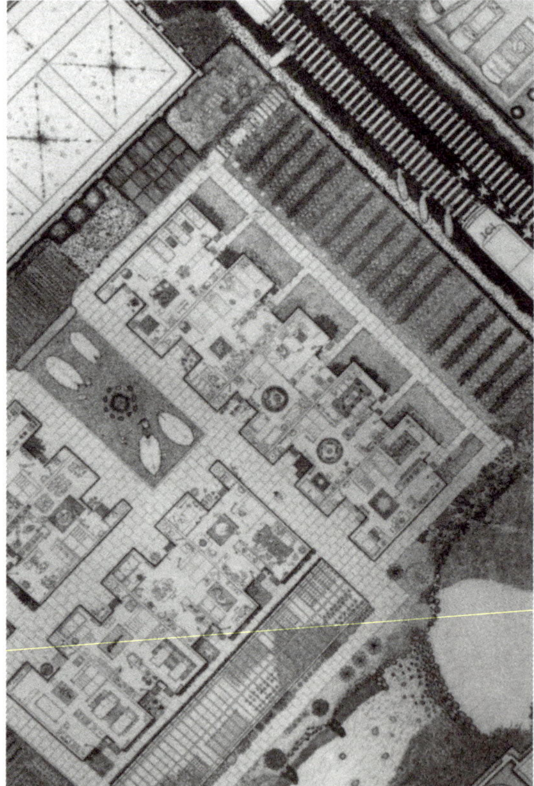

11 **The Janus Programme:** "Transmission has [socially] engineered a group of Glasgow-based artists to take part in The Janus Programme: Meet; discuss; familiarise; establish a strategy; construct and exhibition; dismantle; construct a second." (from press release)

'The Janus Programme' opened and closed twice: two alternate shows; one arranged by the artists, the other mediated according to the rules of Feng Shui.

Below: 'Janus Programme I'—Lyndsey Orr, *The Dragon, the White Bear, the Black Tortoise and the Red Phoenix*.

Below right and bottom right: 'Janus Programme I & II'—Michael Wilkinson, *Work in Progress*. The outdoor construction was moved inside for the second exhibition.

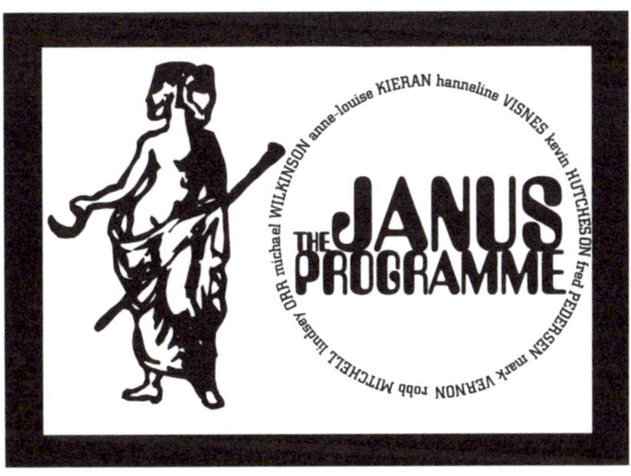

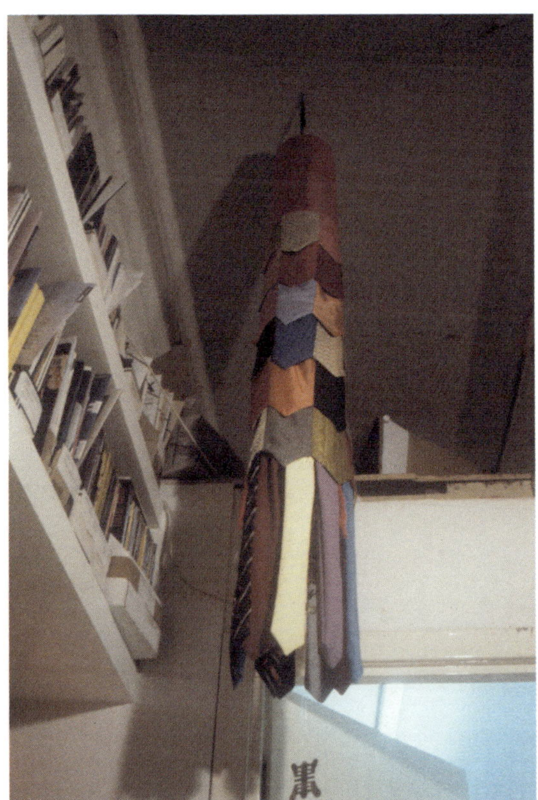

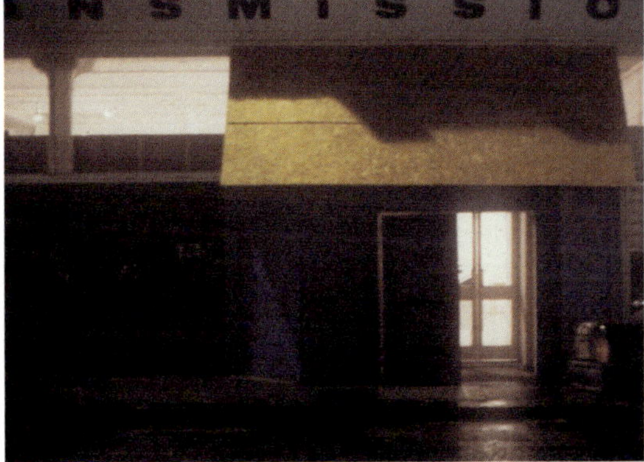

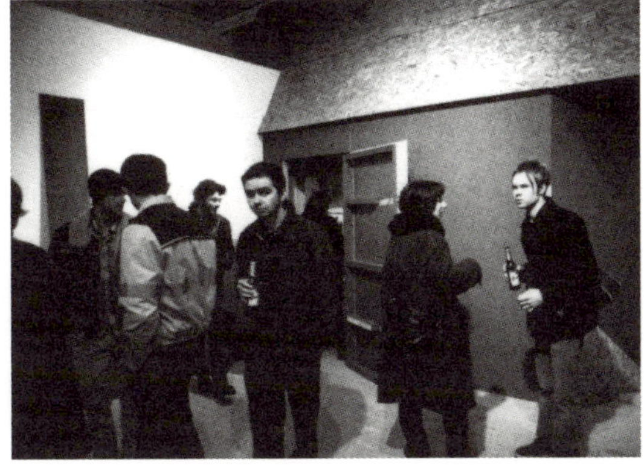

1999

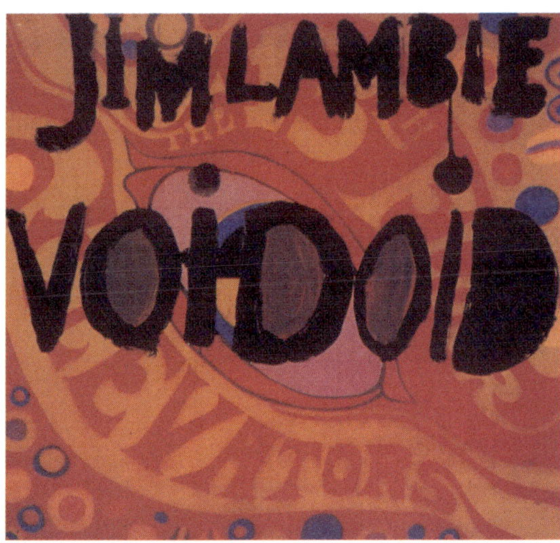

01 Jim Lambie — Voidoid: "After returning to his native Glasgow tanned and urbane from a residency in Marseille, and following a series of successful domestic and overseas projects with The Modern Institute, Lambie has been bursting to stretch out a little.* Transmission are proud to present VOIDOID, Jim's first solo exhibition and an excellent kick-off to spaced 1999: lysergic floorboard alterations will melt into psychedelic soul-

*The Modern Institute was established in 1998 by former Transmission committee members Toby Webster and Will Bradley, along with a former curator at Tramway, Glasgow. The Modern Institute co-ordinates artists' projects and exhibitions in Scotland and abroad.

Below: Jim Lambie, 'Voidoid', January 1999.

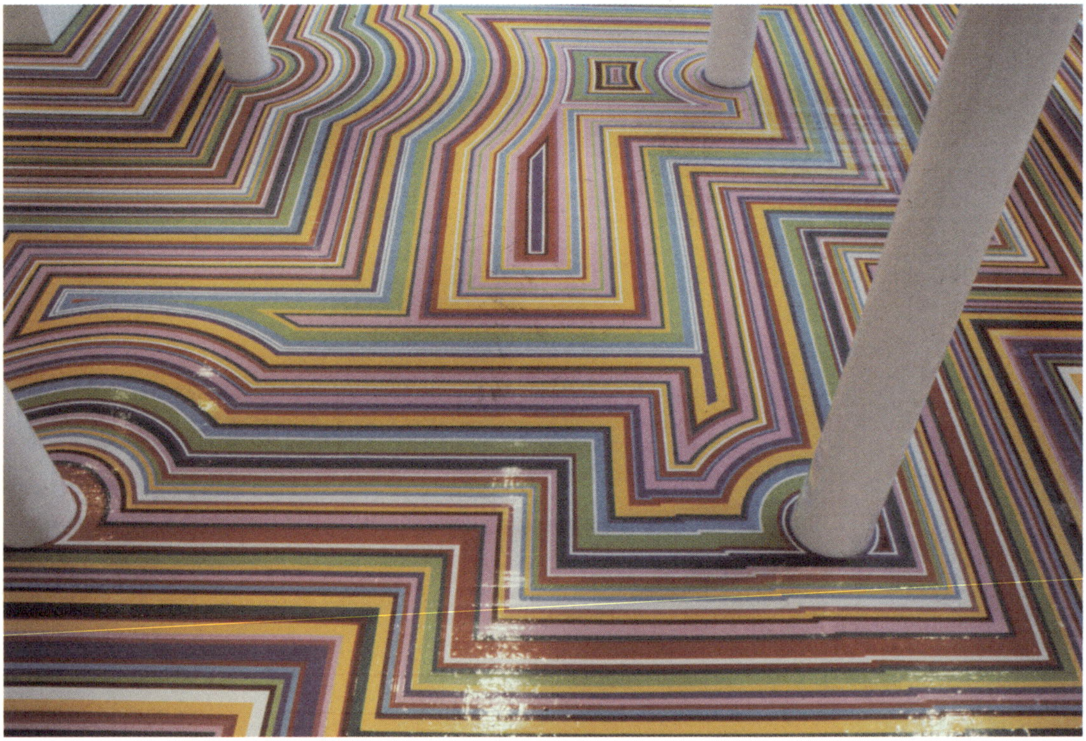

Energetic flower children can follow their second winds to DA CAPO, a night of psychedelic punk-rock soundtracks at the 13th Note Cafe (beginning around 9pm).” (from press release)

02 Tobias Rehberger—Standard Rad: “Pulsating light from paper globes. A scarlet floor. A vaguely ghostly white glow emanating from behind crisp looking furniture-cum-partition hybrids. They’re painted candy oranges, reds, pinks and whites. You’re in Transmission and it’s cosy.

Yes it’s cosy, and that’s because Tobias Rehberger has installed STANDARD RAD and the feel-good factor is here in spades, and unabashedly so as well. The story goes that when asked to design some functional objects for STANDARD RAD LTD (a youthful design partnership with offices in Frankfurt, Rehberger’s home town, and London) he instead deemed to use them as an impetus for this particular show at Transmission. Rehberger’s work has a long history of collaboration with people who might initially appear to be outside the direct process of making that work. Local gardeners in Luxembourg,

Below and botom: Tobias Rehberger, ‘Standard Rad’, February 1999.

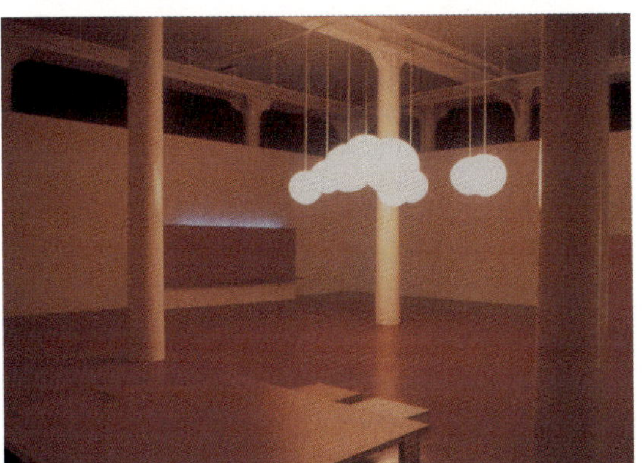

exhibition venue staff in Venice and Berlin, craftsmen in Cameroon, gallery goers in Portikus, his friends and fellow artists. All these groups impact on specific works and it seems to be that which makes it all so, for want of a better word, friendly.

For STANDARD RAD each member of the company discussed films with the artist and a list of those which had apparently scared them as children was utilised in the video element of the exhibition’s final incarnation. *The Incredible Shrinking Man*, *A Man Called Horse*, *Soldier Blue*, *The Invasion of the Body Snatchers* all casting a slightly sinister pale glow from behind colourful objects in what is possibly a reversal of the old hiding-behind-the sofa situation.” Toby Paterson (Transmission Newsletter)

03 Where the Wild Roses Grow: Part of the Scottish leg of the ‘Melbourne, Glasgow, Edinburgh’ cultural exchange project. Transmission’s contribution featured Melbourne based David Noonan and Daniel von Sturmer along with local collaborators Elizabeth go.

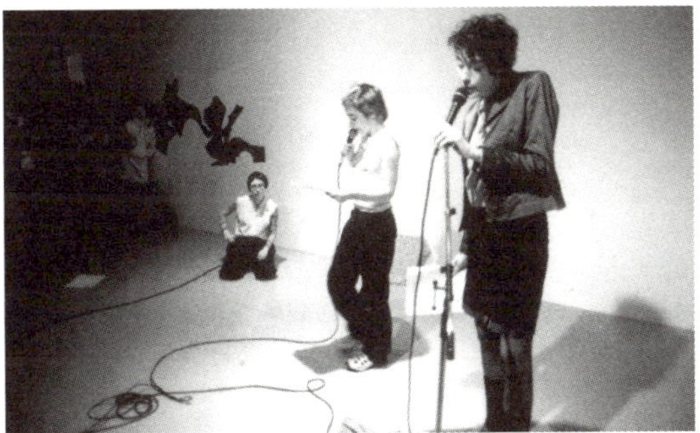

Above: Elizabeth go, *Anti-War You Take It From My Heart*, preview night performance, March 1999.

“With a few acknowledging nods and smiles the Glasgow based Elizabeth go[1] implied that they knew that they were somewhere between friends and a couple of live microphones and that there was only their self esteem and collaborative future at risk. To potentially screw up in front of sympathisers and strangers is some extreme to venture into. Made easier perhaps through the mutual support of collaboration, and with Elizabeth go, the additional freedom claim of not having to fully understand the sum of their original contributions.

This can seem a little naive, harking to avant-garde attitudes of letting things happen with the assumption that what follows will be of definite interest. Elizabeth go therefore focus on presenting their actions and objects as in the creation of what should be a full and intense (and hopefully shared) experience for both themselves and their viewers.[2] Their collaborative work is complex and considered and fragile. They take it seriously but also seem aware of its own brief life in the bigger scheme of things.

The performance was set up in the designated area and designed to begin and end with a pre-recorded bass-line.[3] On its perimeter were objects that initially appeared carefully placed but which were moved between or passed around throughout the performance—more as

The text was read out, repeated and adapted by each performer and became a tuned-in mantra—made more effective, stranger and funnier through repetition. The stage presence of the performers also had an effect—the impressive awkward-sexy confidence of Sue Tompkins and the intense stillness of Cathy Wilkes whose repetitious singing of the words 'Don't Worry' (throughout the performance) brought up the question of sincerity. Sincerity on stage always seems so well—staged. This is something that Elizabeth go artworks never bring into question as they are—firmly or incidentally—exactly as they are.

(For real, for real, contemporary naturalism is about being yourself; it signifies a right and a choice to be who

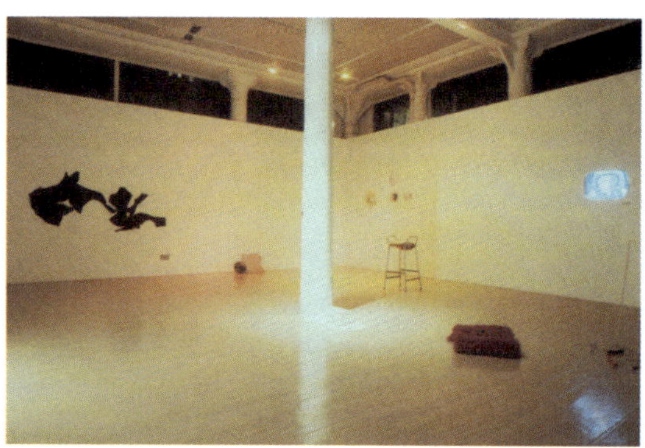

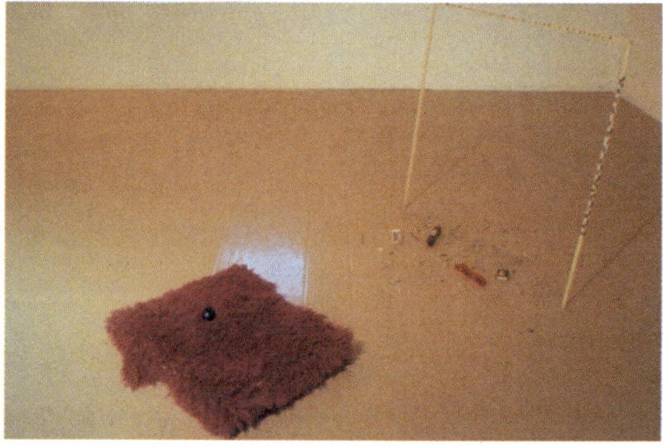

Above and right: Elizabeth go, *Anti-War You Take It From My Heart.*

instruments or props than installed artwork. For example a black egg-shaped shaker passed between hands as did a dictaphone which was rubbed against clothing and then sporadically played back into a microphone. Also a pink sequin-covered bar stool was home to a pile of type-written text which was again handed to each performer.

> …i must be dreaming i must be dreaming immust be dreaming i must be dreaming i must be dreaming house int the valley house oin the valley house in the valley house in the valley house in the valley i must be dreaming from helly hanson from helly hanson take the crescent moon and fly take the crescent moon and flky takae the crescent mommmn and fly the sikhs are in the car the sikhs are in the car the sikhs are in the car the sikhs are in the car and its amazing the sikhs are in the car and its amazing…[4]

you are in all your fullness and to express yourself in your own language.)[5]

Hayley Tompkins' quieter presence was also the most touching, absorbed by the artworks/props she (as was the case with Victoria Morton and—happy behind video camera—Sarah Tripp) was not performing so much as working and thinking. Elizabeth go work with the current time of now. Their methods seem surprisingly traditional, but their intention seems to be an embracing of everything (without judgement) and for that reason, the Elizabeth go action/object could not easily be found elsewhere. It is its own oddly familiar and usually beautiful thing, whether sung, spoken, constructed, painted or tampered with (whatever), it's an uncommon phenomenon."

1. Elizabeth go are: Victoria Morton, Hayley Tompkins, Sue Tompkins, Sarah Tripp and Cathy Wilkes.

2. Other Elizabeth go projects include: *Hit 'em with this, Antoinette*, in 'Satellite City' at Catalyst Arts, Belfast (1997) and *Floatina Happiness*, in 'Host' at Tramway, Glasgow (1998).

3. Pre-recorded bass-line by Victoria Morton.

4. Excerpt from performance text for 'ANTI WAR YOU TAKE IT FROM MY HEART' written by Sue Tompkins.

5. Excerpt from 'The Lion for Real', written by Cathy Wilkes and published in STOPSTOP (1997). In writing on the cultural and commercial phenomena of 'keepin' it real' Wilkes discusses the strategies of repetition and refers to the rap dialogues of Sun Ra, the poet Paul

Below: David Noonan, *Saturn Return; the Mishap*.

Beatty, early Funkadelic, Patti Smith, Allen Ginsberg and Schooly D.

Caroline Woodley (for Transmission Newsletter)

05 Neal Beggs — **Dead Flat Vertical:** " 'Dead Flat Vertical', an interactive installation in the basement, consists of a climbing wall suspended from the ceiling, several second-hand mattresses, and hair-raising scenes from four Hollywood films, Hitchcock's *Vertigo* and *North by Northwest*, Stallone's *Cliffhanger*, and Eastwood's *The Eiger Sanction*. Neal Beggs sees climbing as a primary investigative human activity — something that as children we all used to do. As adults, for the most part it has become redundant, being replaced by other more useful activities." (from press release)

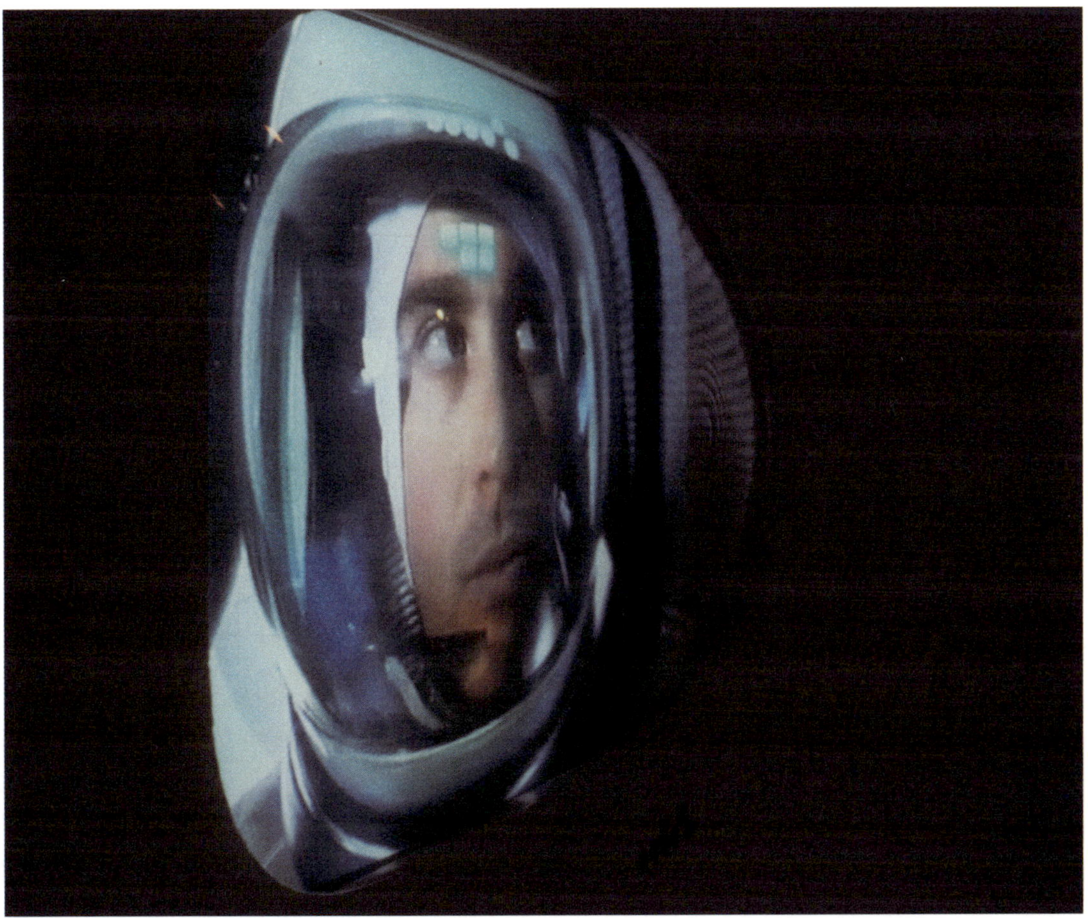

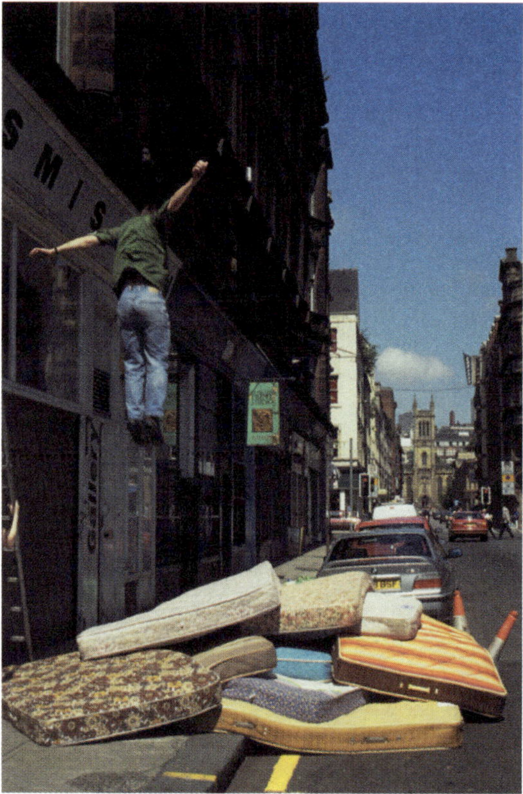

Above: 'Dead Flat Vertical' — Neal Beggs in a post-exhibition performance.

06 Right: 'Hundred Years Egg' review from Transmission Newsletter, July 1999. Photos clockwise from top: Simon McAuley, Untitled, Michael Fullerton, *Padraig Murphy Conversation as a Feedback Loop*, Magnus Wassburg, *Plan B*, Mats Adelman, Untitled.

09 Atelier van Lieshout — AVL Equipment: "If you can call Joep van Lieshout's irremediably crafty production from 1983 to 1987 his first-generation work, and the Atelier van Lieshout's utilitarian or architectural applications that of the second generation, then AVL Equipment's recent show at Transmission Gallery in Glasgow outlines the parameters of van Lieshout's third generation of artistic practice. Since 1998, when the Atelier van Lieshout mounted a homemade, 57 millimeter cannon on a Mercedes

HUNDRED YEARS EGG 15/6 - 3/7

SIN

Mats Adelman seemed quite pleased when I told him that his mis-spelling
DOME") was actually the way it was spelled in old English (viz. the Domesday
manic scrawls have a definite sense of spell-casting: "I GIVE TO YOU THE T
/ THE SUN THE MONE THE STARS / ALL UNDER MY SIGILL" (I looked s
meaning would be 'seal' or something - in fact top of the definition list is "a s
these things reminded me oddly of Raushenberg's early stuff, in their super
stinky old goat and the stuffed eagle on the bit of paint-dripping plank), alt
on the constructions have an Anselm Keifer-ish thing going on. Which I gue
from - a kind of backwoods Nordic Romanticism. Walk anywhere near them a
ghost train lurch into life: owls stare at you with slowly flashing eyes; a ha
you; a turntable with mutant copper cartridges whirls. One of the murky,
flashes "DROPP OUT" and "HAND OF DOME" next to a flaming skull and a He
which wants to hex you, although to what end I'm not sure. Maybe he wants t
creepy (counter) cult (ure). In any case the seriousness of his intent seems e
of the pieces have loony carved text on them too: "RAIDERS IN THE SK
DEVIL". Shiver.

NEXT

Next paragraph, next artiste. Michael Fullerton presents Padraig Murphy, 'A
guy in Ireland and was impressed and confused by his unorthodox approac
anything and apparently was none too keen on Fullerton telling the youth o
(which aren't really anything out of the fluxus-ordinary - he would "tell somebody to dig a hole" or freeze his sperm in mountain snow). As I've come to expect from Michael this is elegant and graciously presented work, exhibiting some of what are coming to be motifs: paintings made from hair and an interest in the processes of recording sound.   PADRAIG MURPHY CONVERSATION AS A FEEDBACK LOOP is a microphone an unenclosed speaker on a glass shelf, the one hissing into the other. It feels like it might illustrate the way Michael is thinking about Murphy and the relationship between artist and art. I have an intuition that Fullerton's admiration for Murphy pivots on that nagging doubt shared by earnest artists everywhere that you're doing what you're doing *for the right reasons* - "aarrgh, am I just doing this painting so that people will like me/want to buy it?". A doubt easily got around by never telling anyone what you're up to, ever. It's a toughy, and I don't think there's a simple answer - a dilemma which goes to the heart of the whole shebang. Why do you

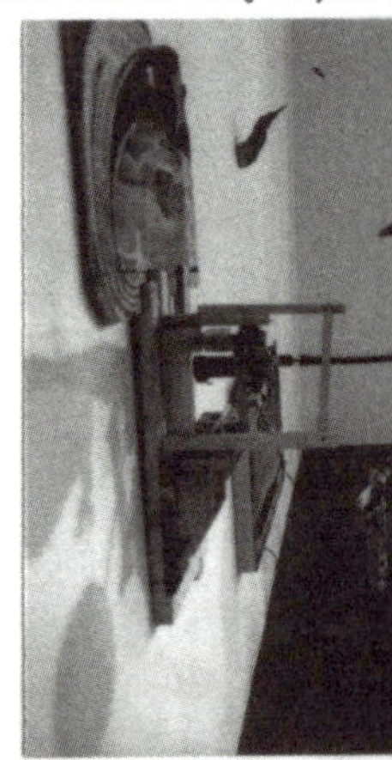

think those French 'intellectuals' invented that old convenient get-out called
"I didn't really do it. How could I have? I was dead at the time")? There are m
make, devious and daft. I guess anyway the fact that Mike's made this stuf
common sense and just owned up. This is an Author who is happily alive and

PEEK

It's interesting for me to watch the baby-boomers' societal locus be filled by
Ceefax, Prestel and the ZX Spectrum. Hence the phenomena of nu-electro in
Internet swells with programs that emulate old arcade machines, games cons
enough to contain the old many times over. Those of you who are technologica
Alan Turing concept of the Universal Machine (mention this text next time y
head off for you, but not here).

See, that's what it's all about. The early-to mid-eighties were the last time
Computers did computery things and made your telly look computery, instead
recent movies (go see *The Matrix*), when they want to show you the future th

pippity-pip typing noises. And nobody really knew what they were for; they were just *computers*. They couldn't be a typewriter or a piano or a camera. All they could be was a computer. Then there were synthesisers, which sounded like nothing but . . . synthesisers. Nothing wanted to be anything except new. For all the talk about genetic engineering, nanotechnology, concept cars and digital telly, I think those of us who care feel like our future has been stolen. It's not going to be shiny and sleek, blocky and bleeby. It's not even going to be like *Bladerunner* (except if you live in Tokyo). It's probably going to be just like now: underwhelming. The year 2000 approaches and the future is running scared. And that doesn't mean go and read *The End of History*. It means that it befalls us, the microchip generation (when was the last time you heard anyone use the word 'microchip'?) to have a pretty serious re-imagine, and if that means retracing a few steps, then OK.

So Magnus Wassborg uses under-powered workhorses for courses: his art wouldn't work properly if he had to use today's Mhz machines, so he employs old Macs and archaically beautiful screensavers to interfere with radio frequencies and make his modern noise. It smacks of New York schollkids buying up obsolete Roland drum machines in 1983 to make music too modern for anyone else to have thought of. It also makes me think of the word 'artefact': this is a word which programmers and techies use to describe unexpected behaviour arising from properties inherent in a machine, for example the spirograph patterns that emerged when your told your Spectrum to draw loads of circles because it couldn't do it properly. 'Artefact'. Hmmm. I leave it to you.

IF L

I've always really liked Simon McAuley's work, and I felt a bit embarrassed at the opening of *Hundred Years Egg* because after sitting in front of his untitled video for about 10 minutes I just couldn't figure it out . . . what it was all about. I sat there anyway and gradually it cast it's spell, though. I started, weirdly, to kind of feel a *presence* in what seemed to be a long tripod-mounted shot of a lane during the dawn chorus. Then I noticed that the tripod wasn't too steady. I was spooked before I found out that the sot was hand-held and the bird song was produced spontaneously by the artist. It's a funny, chilly, brave piece of work, documenting one of those urges to go out and do something inexplicabe. Mkes me think of Robert Smith talking about how the song *Hanging Garden* came about: "When I was at home, listening to the noises of cats outside . . . it made me go strange . . . I wanted to go out in the garden . . . so I did . . . stark naked . . . stupid . . ." It's strange how when you feel wrong you want to go out and just be with the birds and the trees. The outside always feels bigger and stronger and more dignified than you do. In a funny way it civilises you. You feel like, in the presence of this, you just have to behave yourself. It also makes me think of that Oasis ad where the guy says "Kaaa . . . kaaa . . . !" like the dolphins.

RANDOMIZE

This is a strong, coherent show, full of rich and serious work. It's good to see the Gallery capitalising on the promise that Fullerton and McAuley have been showing, and continuing the valuable process of introduction amongst peers here and abroad. If the show has been properly publicised, and if McAuley and Fullerton make the most of their opportunity, they should find some doors opening for them. I understand better than most that Transmission can't be all things to all people, but as a mere bog standard member now, I'd like to see more of this kind of continued support for local artists who have the dedication and talent to keep up such solid pactices. Artists living here need this kind of support, and, vice versa. Transmission needs the support of a healthy community of artists. It's a neat little ecosystem, which has made Glasgow into a world-class city to be an artist in. And my (probably unwelcome) Baz Luhrmann-esque advice to all is to remember that, whichever side of the fence you think you're on. See you all at the member's show.

Robert Johnston

pickup truck for a show in Rabastens in France, its utilitarian aspects have opened to a certain brand of socially illegitimate behaviour, that is to say, counter-violence in the face of authorities who have the monopoly on violence, but don't administer their responsibility in a satisfactory manner.

This jibes with Atelier van Lieshout's distinctly bad-boy attitude, but may also be a reaction to the group's international success. In any case, notions of collectivism and self-institutionalisation inherent in AVL's previous production inform a body of new work whose ultimate goal is the construction of a completely self-sufficient village for the Atelier's members, to be produced in Rotterdam in 2001. The Atelier plans to build houses made of materials they have themselves manufactured, to produce their own food in its entirety, and to perform otherwise illegal tasks including but not limited to fabricating weapons for personal consumption.

Accordingly, Transmission was equipped with a machine for producing alcohol from hog feed, a sawmill for cutting timber from logs, and three mortars, all presented in their naked functionality, along with a series of drawings relating to the larger project. The AVL camp will apparently not take the form of some cozy hippie utopia, but rather culturally approved, active resistance to straight society. As Dave Hickey emphasises in his essay 'Rebel housing: Architecture as Rock-and-Roll' (1999), it is not so much from the look of its product, or even its utility that the primary value of the project derives, but from the fact 'that the Atelier van Lieshout, in its shaggy democracy, its bad fashion and devotion to primary values, functions less like a "design group" than a rock band. For both, it's the noise and joy that matter, the sex and drugs, the democracy and mobility.'" Lars Bang Larsen (*Art & Text*, February–April 2000, p. 88)

Below: Atelier van Lieshout, 'AVL Equipment', September 1999.

Bottom: Joep van Lieshout preparing to produce alcohol from hog feed.

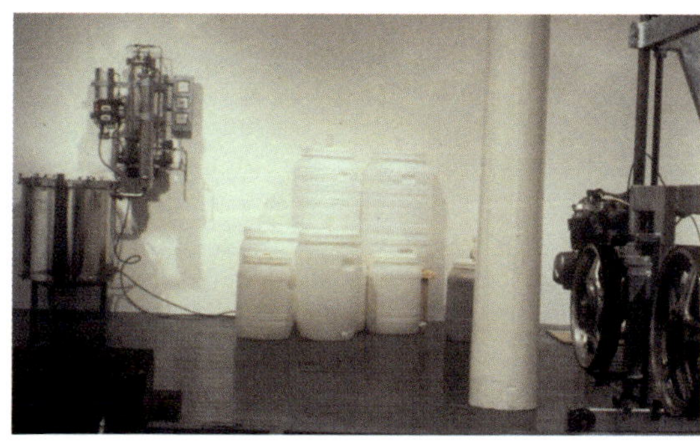

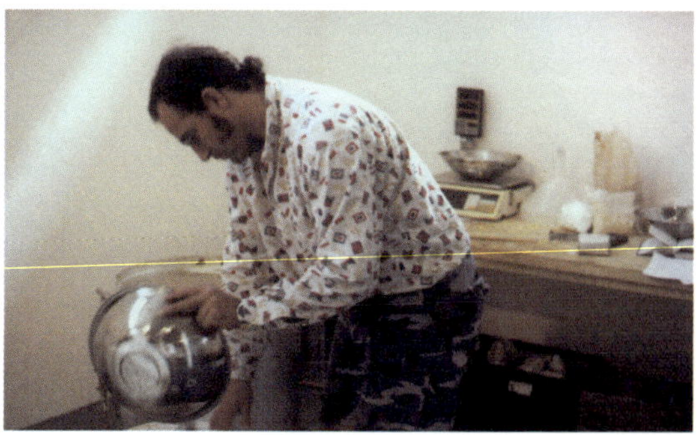

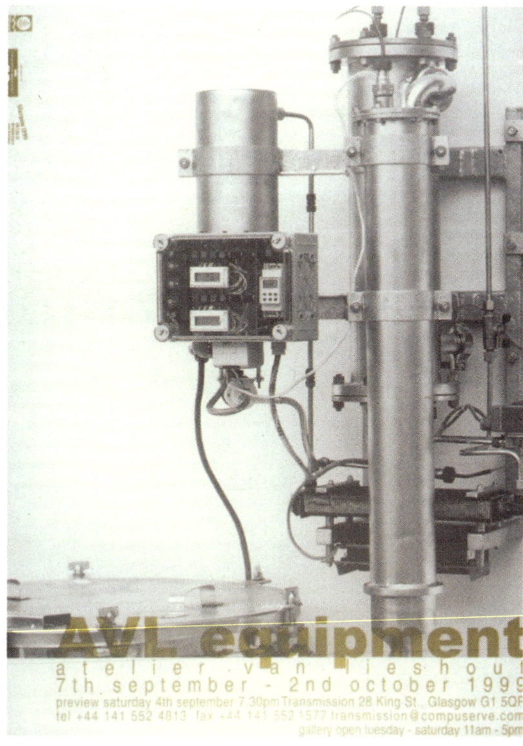

2000

02 Complecity (11) and The Social Engineer: two one-week projects by young artists.

For the second of the projects, Luke Fowler created his own social experiment situation where active, vocal members of the local community from different lifestyles could engage in personal, theoretical or sceptical debate over the issue of social control within their lives. 'The Social Engineer' utilised and referenced methods of social experimentation from key periods of ground breaking research completed in the 60s and 70s — from experiments quantifying obedience to authority, role-playing, power relations, anti-social behaviour to the effects of social housing. The conversations were documented and became the basis of a series of sound collages created live in the gallery.

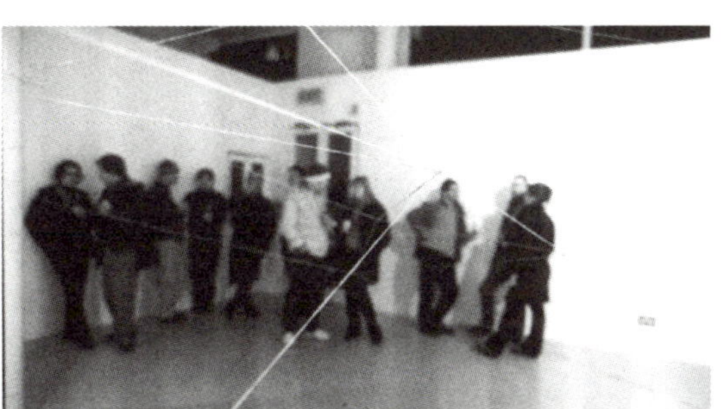

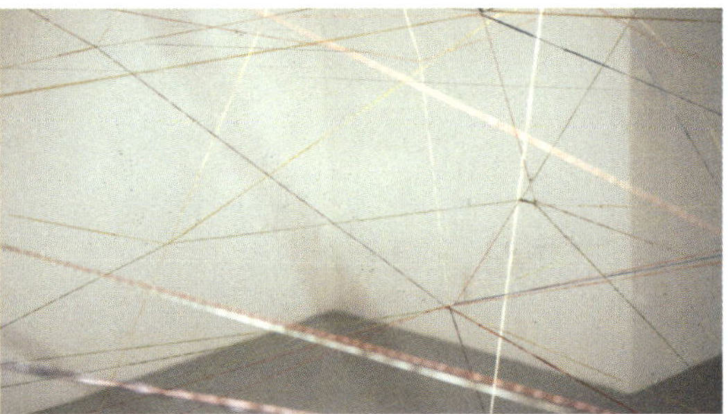

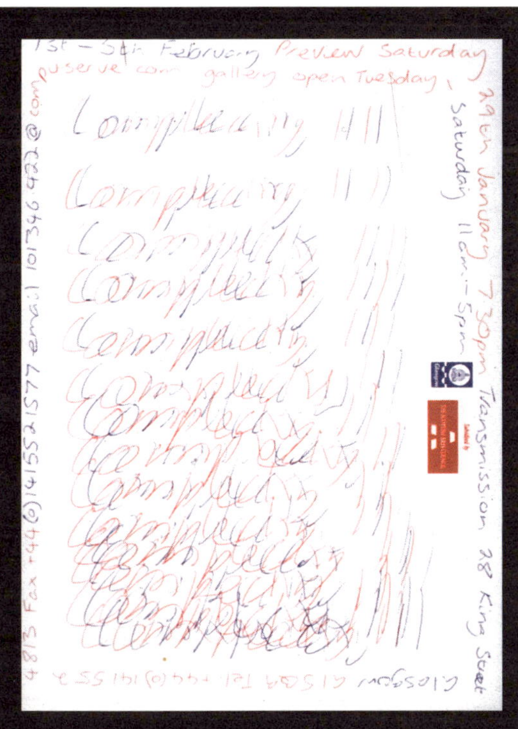

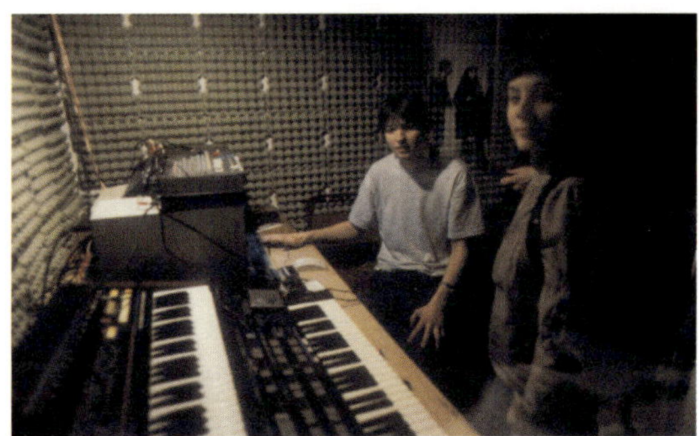

Above: Luke Fowler, 'The Social Engineer', February 2000.

Top left and top right: 'Complecity (11)' was part of a series of collaborative site-specific projects by Neil Bickerton and Lorna Macintyre which used a wide variety of lo-fi materials. Existing fixtures were used to anchor a 'web' of elastic bands across the gallery space.

The project also included contributions from the artists Jakob Kolding (Copenhagen, and designer of the poster for this project), Chad McCail (Edinburgh) and Scanner (London). Scanner gave a talk in the gallery and in collaboration with the 13th Note Club, Glasgow, performed live.

02 Knut Åsdam: "Knut Åsdam designs and constructs optimal viewing areas for the presentation of his video and sound works. For his project with Transmission he is presenting *Legendary Psychasthenia 1999 reedit*, which 'seeks to deal with an idea of the urban unconsciousness through the conventions of the radio play, experimental audio and a reference to beat poetry. The piece reveals architecture or space as embedded with fantasy and sexuality, and functions as a sort of audio-collage of topical monologues, a love story and a narratively textured audio'.

Knut Åsdam is from Norway and lives in New York." (from press release)

Below: Knut Åsdam, *Legendary Psychasthenia 1999 reedit*, February 2000.

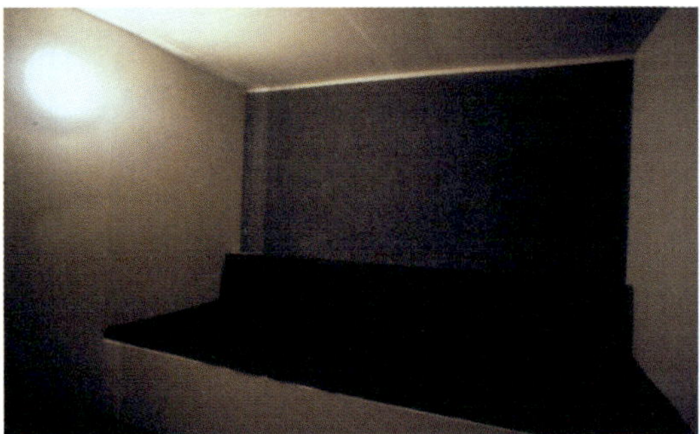

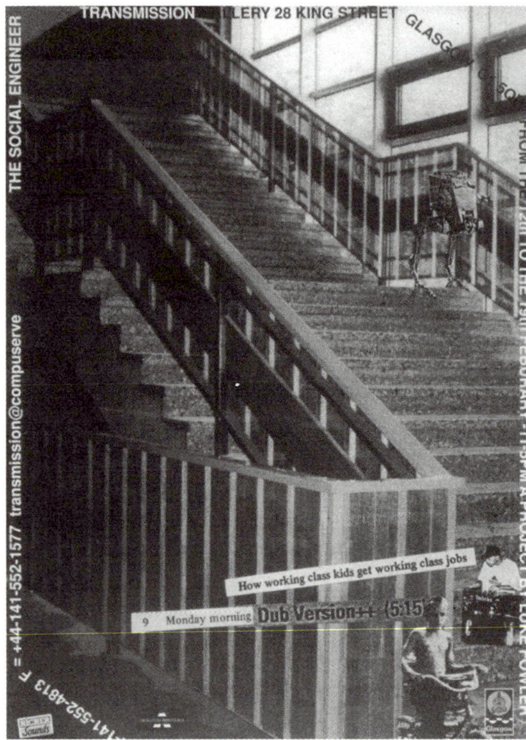

03 radiotuesday — e.g. Sometime Instant: "A project built around a series of unofficial FM broadcasts, 'e.g. Sometime Instant' brought sound works, performance and the potential of freedom of thought not only to the local airwaves, but also to a variety of Glasgow venues. A follow-up to a previous project, 'Wide General Vicinity' by radiotuesday, where for four Tuesdays in June 1999 artworks and ideas were broadcast from roadsides and rooftops. 'e.g. Sometime Instant' based radiotuesday at bars, clubs and Transmission Gallery. The latter provided a sound studio, a stage, and a couple of weeks focused upon making noise. This led to a prolific presentation of work.

Making sense of the specific content of 'e.g. Sometime Instant' seems an irrelevant task. There was no apparent order, no clear or chronological relationships—many of the events were not art. Not that this is uncommon, but

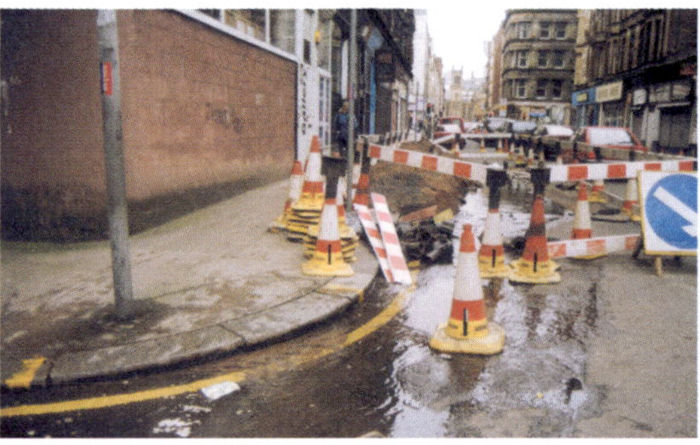

Above and opposite: "Shit happens … just as we were about to welcome radiotuesday into the warm bosom of Transmission we found that the basement had a complete coverage of two feet. of extra water—surplus to our requirements—and courtesy of those crazy bloods at West of Scotland Water. They were getting a bit carried away carving up King Street with their pneumatic drills and struck a rich seam of pure mains water which seeped into our premises overnight (see photo). We're still in the process of drying out 15 years of files, posters etc. Ha Ha Boo hoo." (Transmission Newsletter)

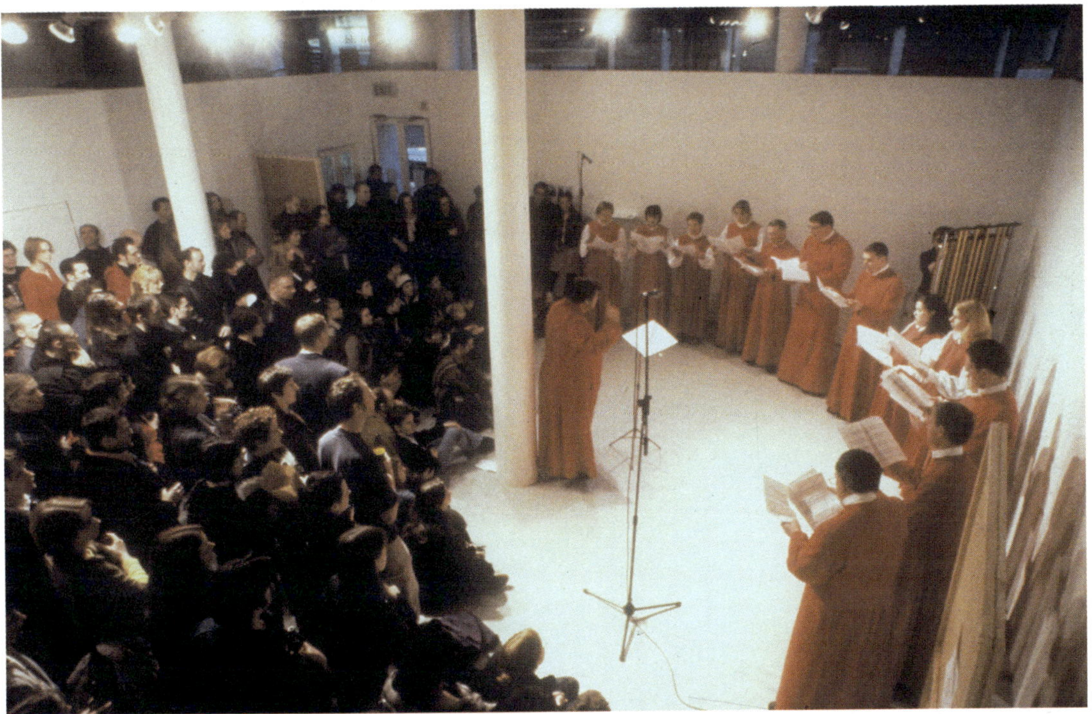

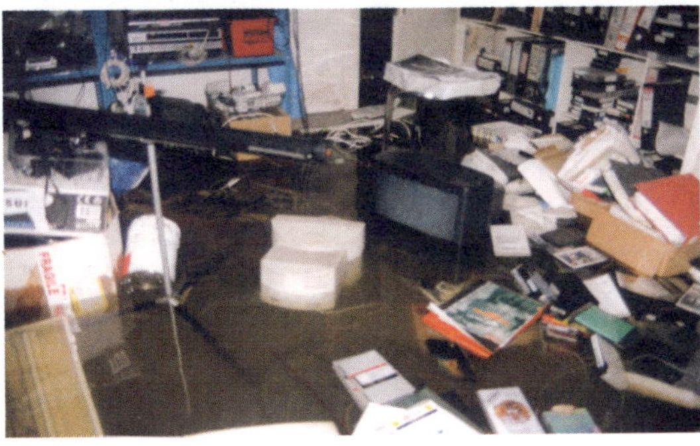

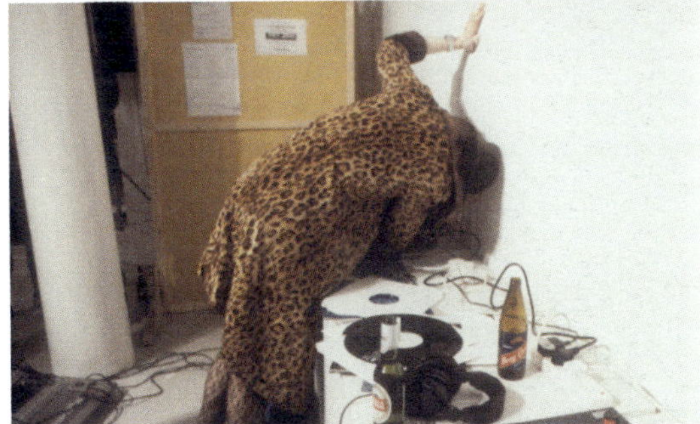

perhaps more fun than the usual not-art-project-in-an-art-gallery. 'e.g. Sometime Instant' appeared more like an encamped contemporary media-and-culture course, where the gallery location might just as well have been a student union bar/common room or small-town hall. The result was a magazine-like assemblage of exhibits and events: something boyish—like *NME* meets *eye* meets *Which PC*. Erratic publicity meant that events and broadcasts were happened upon randomly, through persistent curiosity, or through visiting the gallery

Above: Diskono—'Doktor Barnes Advocaat' performs on the closing night.

Top: Ian Balch presents *Gift*, a new choral artwork in collaboration with composer Stephen Davismoon, chorus master Frikki Walker and the choir of Saint Mary's Cathedral—April 1.

website. Plus a sense of 'point me towards the project please' pervaded the gallery, substantiated by a displaced gallery office (replaced by the sound-proof studio) and a more than moderate display of exhibits pinned to the walls or laid out on the tables." Caroline Woodley (*Circa*, Summer 2000, pp. 58–59)

'radiotuesday' is run by Duncan Campbell, Alex Frost and Mark Vernon.

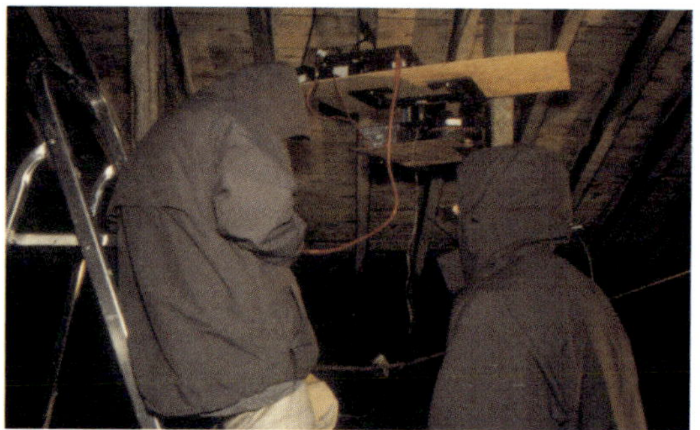

Above right: Life Without Buildings performing in Transmission.

Above: Installation of radiotuesday broadcast mast.

Right: Foreground: Mutti Geld recording in the gallery; background: installation of *Touch* audio magazine archive, presented by Anne-Marie Copestake.

04 Ellen Cantor: A solo exhibition by the American-born London-based artist. The upstairs gallery was split into two distinct exhibition spaces. One was used to exhibit drawings and photographic works; the other for the video installation *Within Heaven and Hell*.

"… 'You sound like a movie'

Ellen Cantor has done something remarkable with this film (*The Texas Chainsaw Massacre*). Matching it to another fairy/fantasy/horror story, another culturally defined and important film, *The Sound of Music*, she reveals something about what cinema means for us. It is the mirror from which we learn about ourselves. *The Sound of Music* is a film about a fascist territory, about a personal revelation, about sexual maturity and investigation, about the terror of the family (dead mother, pained, bullying father, string of idiot siblings), about patriarchy, about who we look up to and take our cues from. It's also about the countryside. And like *Chainsaw* is about how the countryside is a stupid

place, free of urbanism and thus dumb, uncivilised, uncultured. It's about thick people who don't know any better. But more importantly the film is about Maria/Julie Andrews, nun, singer, 'mother', pure and lovely. And what she eventually becomes. (The critic Lee Hudson describes Julie Andrews as a "nun with a switchblade.") *Chainsaw* is

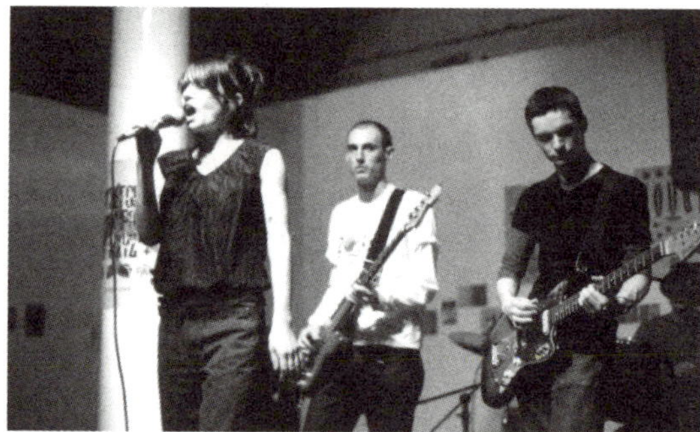

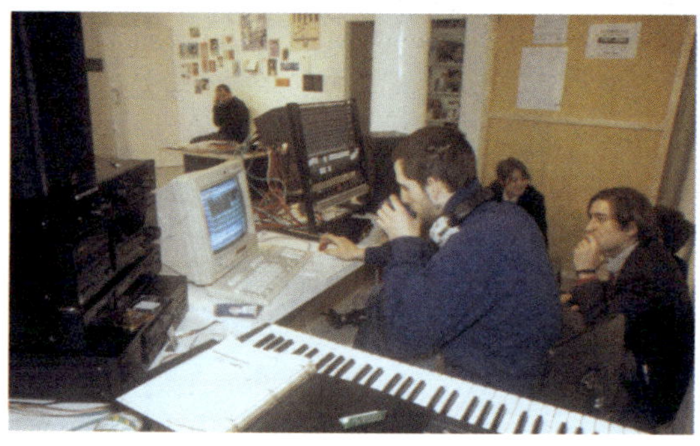

about Sally/Marilyn, daytripper, 70s hippy chick, young, liberal American, candy girl and what she becomes and has to survive. They both represent what American film/cultural critic Carol J Clover calls the final girl. The set up is the same, the film's name doesn't matter, but as the cast get hacked, shot and butchered one by one, the last survivor is always a woman. She's the one who sees the killer for what he really is—dumb, sexually absent, culturally dead, morally dilapidated, only about destruction and mutilation…

Ellen/Marilyn/Sally/Julie/Maria

Cantor's video *Within Heaven and Hell* is like a terrible dream. And then waking up. It shows what it is like to get processed or manufactured. By film, cinema, image, representation, performance, by narrative. Cantor shows us what's going on behind the cinema fantasy, what we know exists but would rather not see. Watching the video, these films become more honest, more real, more complete. She stops them from existing as little dramatic pleasures in our head, and makes us see what they really are. It shows us what it means to be represented in a specific, constraining way: Marilyn/Sally/ Julie/Maria, victim and survivor, mother and whore, replacement, girl to woman…. The work shows us how these cinematic definitions of identity work and how they can become so seductive. And as the voice-over to the work demonstrates, there is a personality,

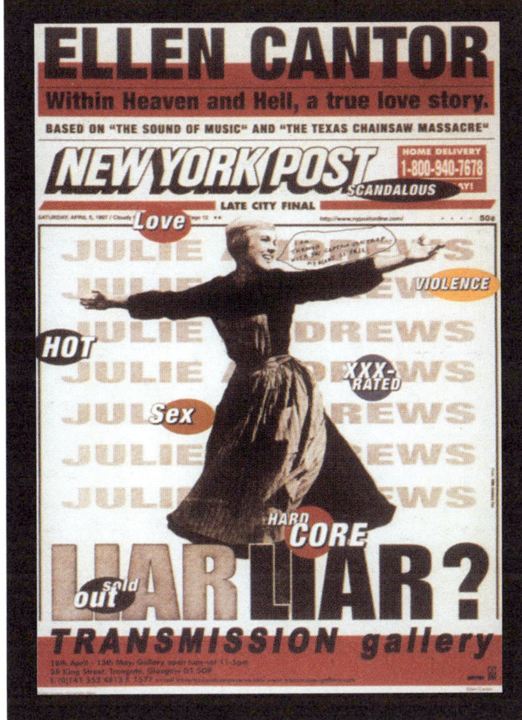

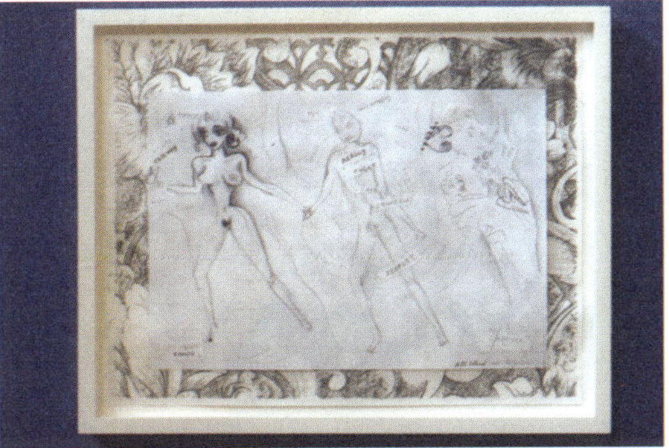

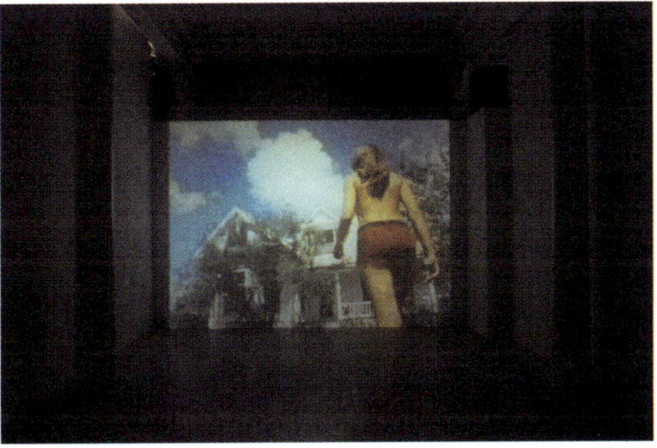

Above: Ellen Cantor, *Within Heaven and Hell*, video installation, April 2000.

Top: Ellen Cantor, from the series *Snow White S+M*.

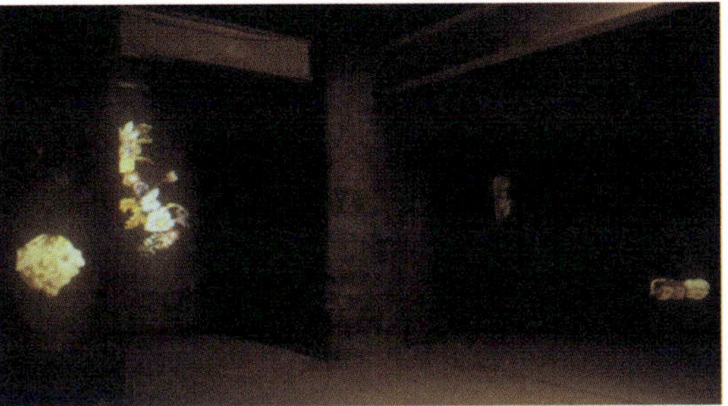

Above: 'Fragile Paradise' by Claudine Hartzel consisted of slides of paintings of friends and their partners interspersed with images from Mills and Boon romance novels projected onto the basement walls.

an individual intimacy at work that is not fragmented or dispersed by easy classification. Cantor sees and shows us what this 'killer' is all about. You can see it in Cantor's drawings. Honest, direct, tender, real. Actually real, not a slim, titillating slice of reality, fragmented memory, or passive, shallow or supposedly appealing depiction. She presents the illicit and goes for the throat." Alex Hetherington (extracts from 'The Mad, the Macabre & the Final Girl', written for Transmission Newsletter)

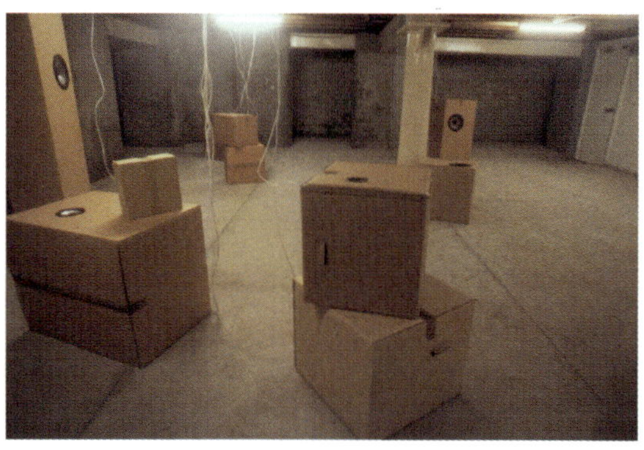

Above: 'Movers & Shakers', an installation by Rob Kennedy (cardboard boxes, loudspeakers, 3 CD players, 3 amplifiers).

05 Rob Kennedy — Movers and Shakers:

"contents

fast flowing air
moving stairways
pokemon
sing song

refrigerate
king of rock'n'roll
www.
round gong

at the junction
crowded pub
underground strings
hailing loud

drunk and orderly
street cleaning
night surfing"

(accompanying text)

06 Joanne Tatham and Tom O'Sullivan — The Glamour: Joanne Tatham and Tom O'Sullivan live in Glasgow and have worked collaboratively since 1995.

"Joanne Tatham and Tom O'Sullivan produce objects, images and installations where aesthetics and attitudes from moments in cultural history are recovered and re-staged in new ways. Their work often encourages viewers to combine a spatial experience with shared memories of representation. For this project at Transmission they will use rubble, mirrored surfaces and fluorescent lighting to create a new installation for both the main and basement spaces." (from press release)

Below and far right, top: Joanne Tatham and Tom O'Sullivan 'The Glamour', June 2000.

Far right, centre: 'The Glamour'—the basement of Transmission.

Right: "On the opening night, Glasgow's art crowd has never looked more glamorous, the bright reflections of their clothes swimming across the distorted silver background of the room dividers." Sarah Lowndes (*Metro*)

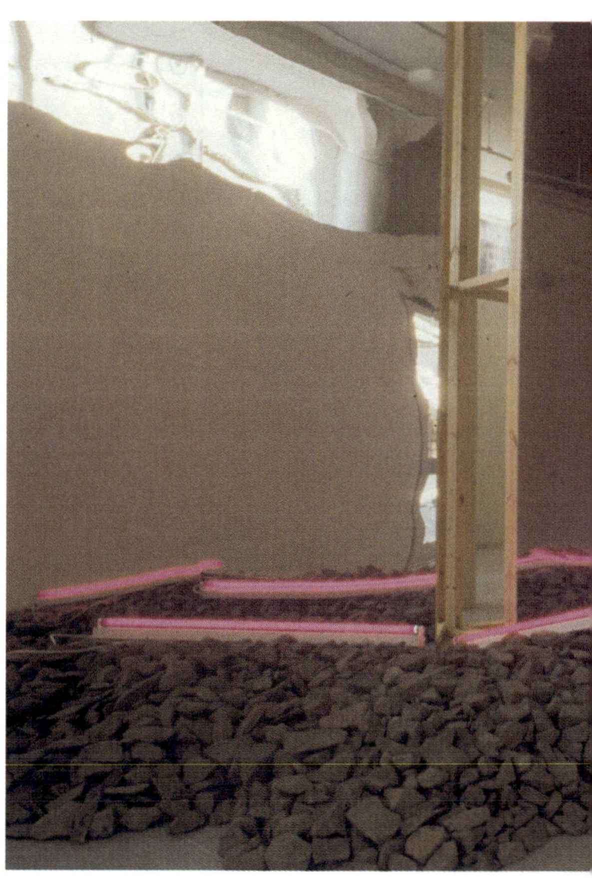

 It May Be a Year of Thirteen Moons But It's Still the Year of Culture: "When a year has thirteen full moons it is said to affect the mental balance of people suffering from depression. In 1990, Glasgow was the

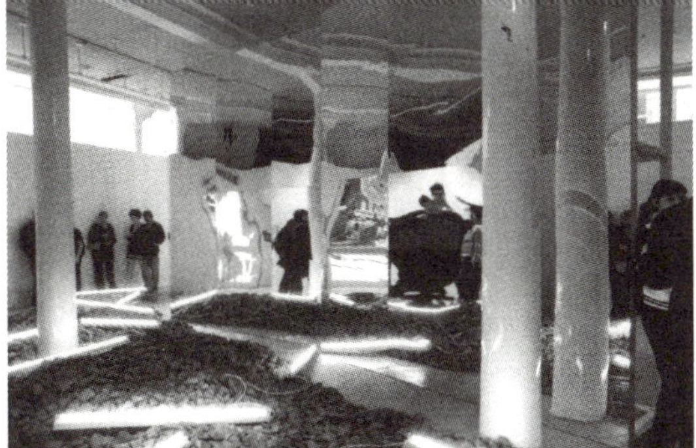

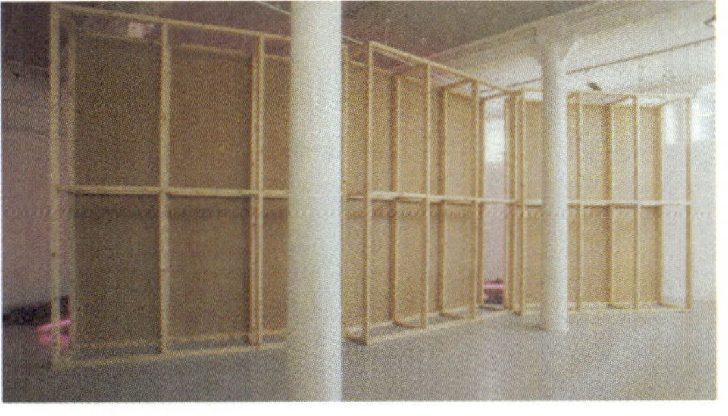

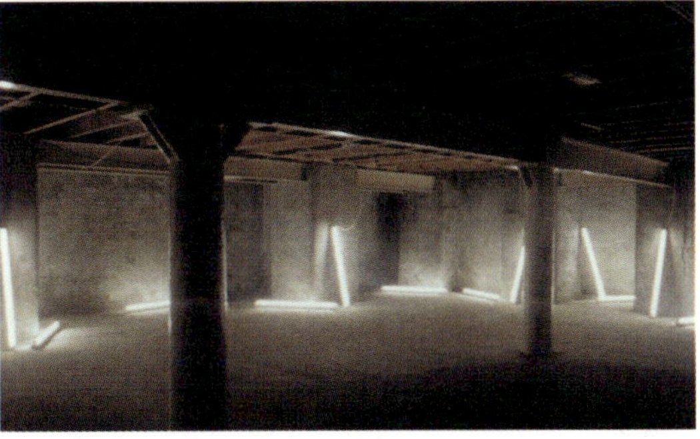

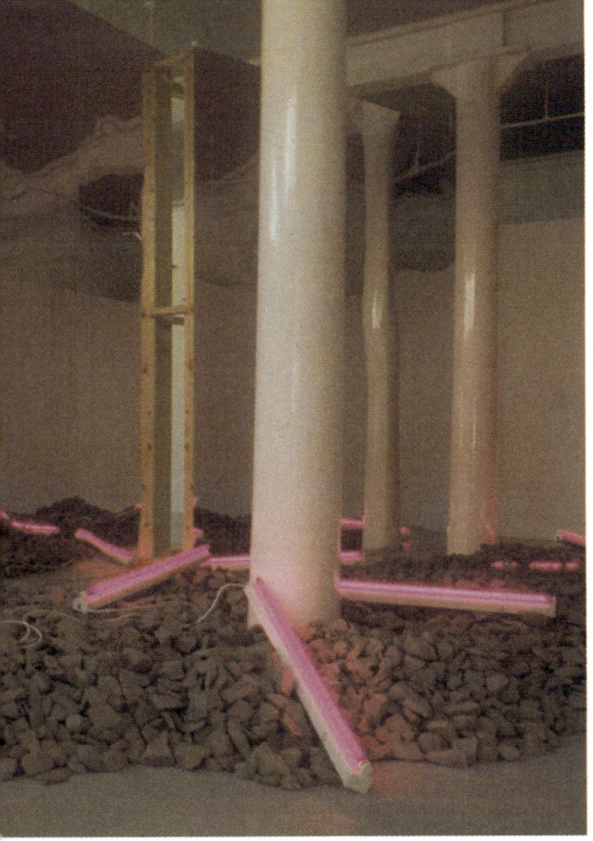

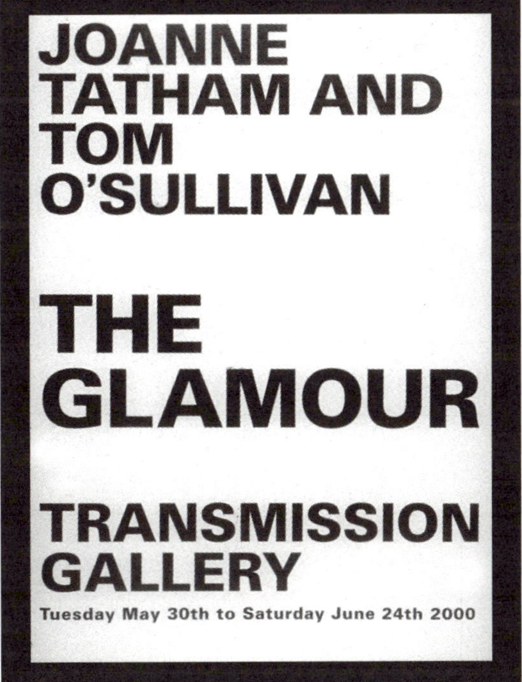

European Capital of Culture, and 1999 saw Glasgow as the European City of Architecture and Design. It also had thirteen moons.

Charisma is the collaborative partnership of Keith Farquhar and Lucy McKenzie, who both moved to Glasgow in 1999 from London and Dundee respectively. They approach curation as an extension of their practice as artists, with subjectivity clearly stated, in no way least by the inclusion of their own work in the contexts they create. Looking to models such as Konrad Fischer, they show work by themselves, their friends, and people they want to be friends with.

'It May Be a Year of Thirteen Moons But It's Still the Year of Culture' takes on themes relating to the value system and constructions of taste which surround contemporary art in Scotland. The work of the artists involved is from disparate political and aesthetic

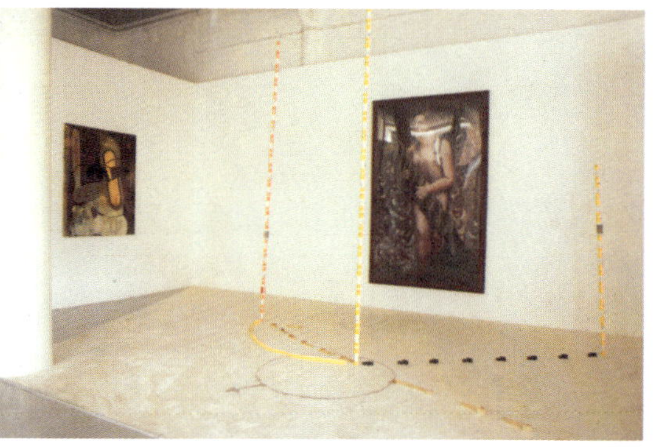

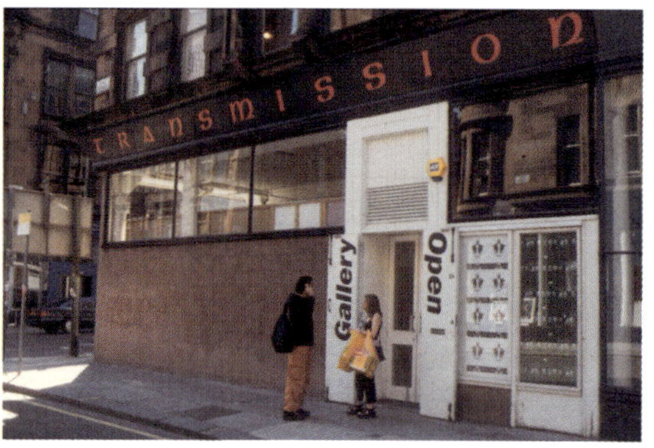

Above: Lucy McKenzie and Keith Farquhar, *How Long Can We Keep This Up?* (2000)—altered gallery sign.

Right: Lucy McKenzie, *Force The Hand of Chance 1900* (2000)—'a welcoming vestibule in the style of Glasgow's heritage industry patron saint Charles Rennie Mackintosh'.

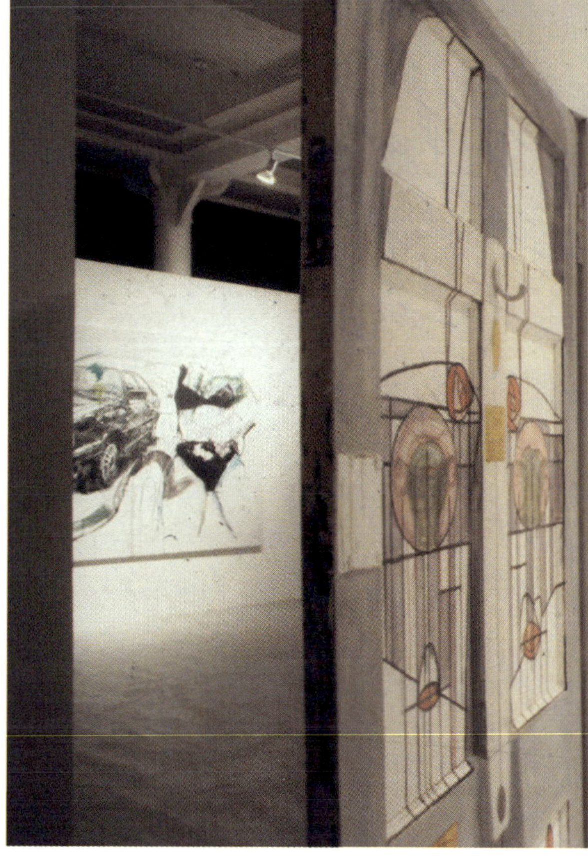

standpoints, with varying levels of irony, but together they explore the gulf between commercial and contemporary art—its presentation, its subsidisation/patronage, and the desensitisation towards heritage. One way in which this is done is by the inclusion of artists outside Scotland, to act as a mirror to our parochial experience." (from press release)

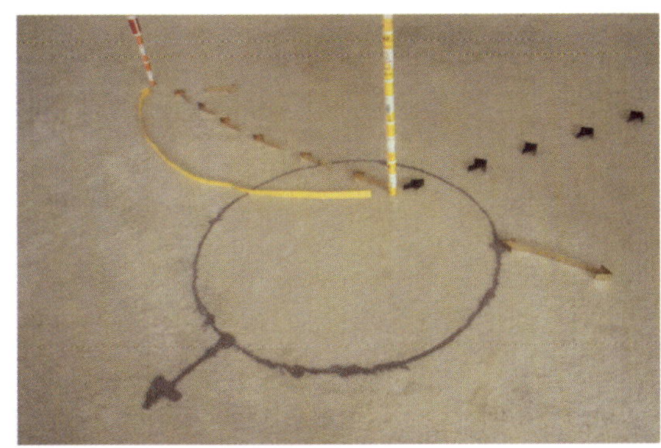

Far left: foreground: Keith Farquhar, *Polymorph Moderne: Sex in Scotland* (2000); left: Albert Oehlen, Untitled (1990); right: Stephen Campbell, *Man With Spiral Tree* (1983). Stephen Campbell is one of the so-called 'Glasgow Boys' of the early 1980s, who featured in the exhibition 'New Image Glasgow at the Third Eye Centre, 1985 (see pp. 10–11).

Left: Keith Farquhar, *Polymorph Moderne: Sex in Scotland* (2000)— 'paper, arrows, multi-vitamin tubes and red-wine stain on carpet'.

Below: Reverse of poster for 'It May Be a Year of Thirteen Moons But It's Still the Year of Culture', curated by Charisma, July 2000.

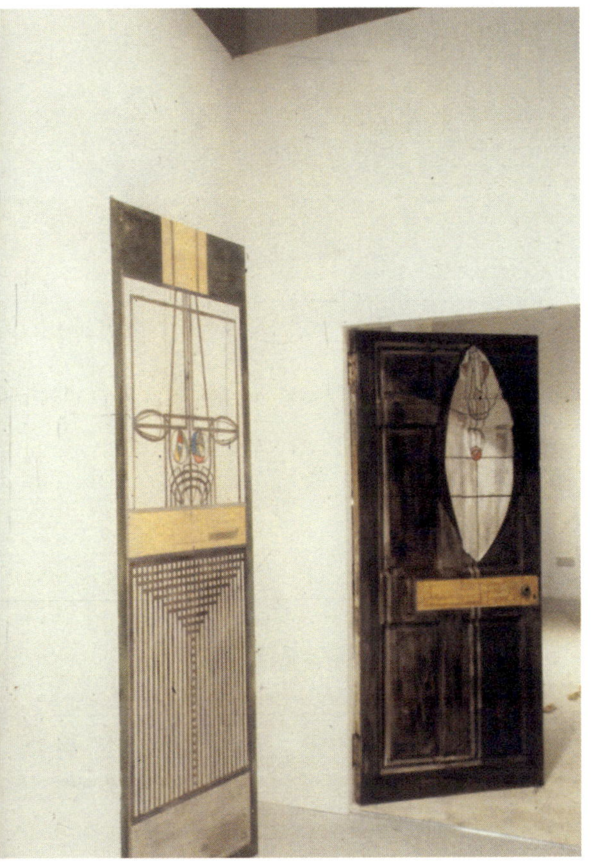

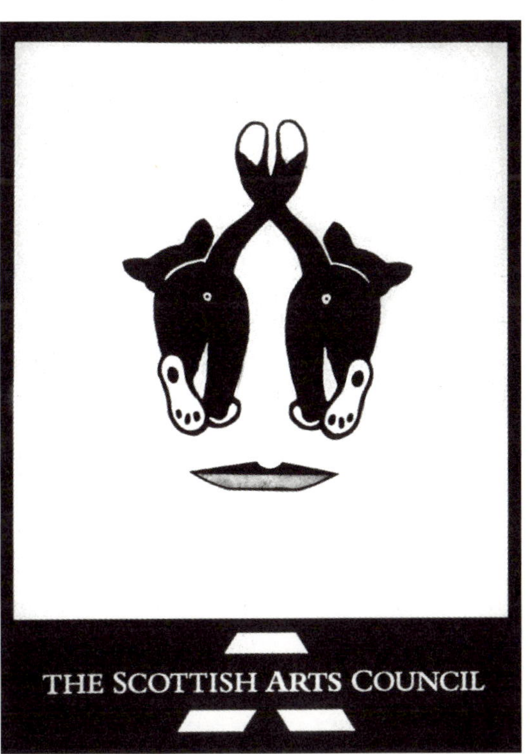

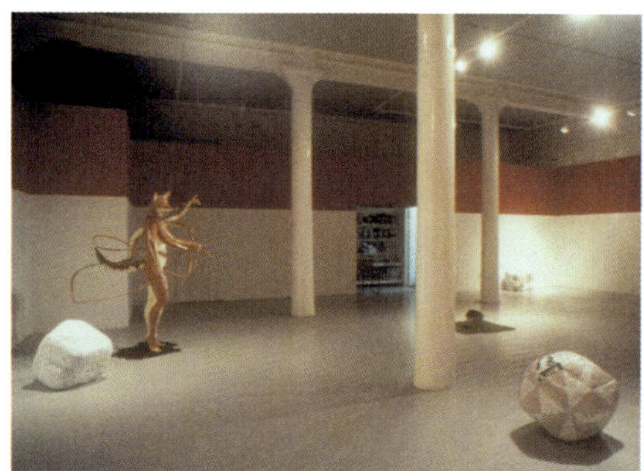
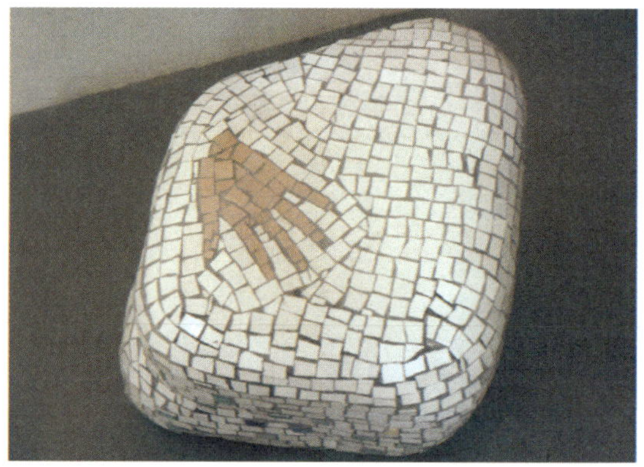

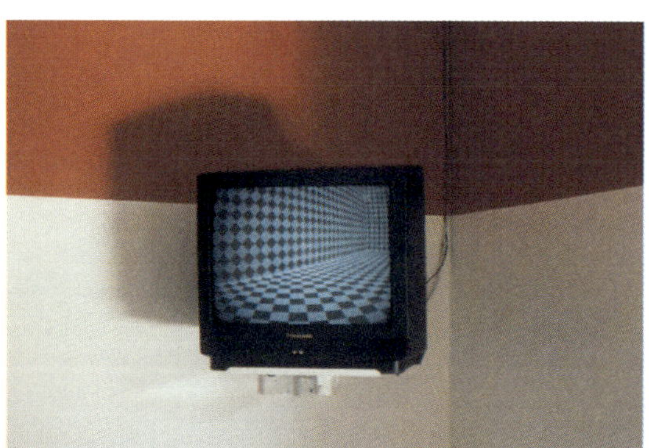
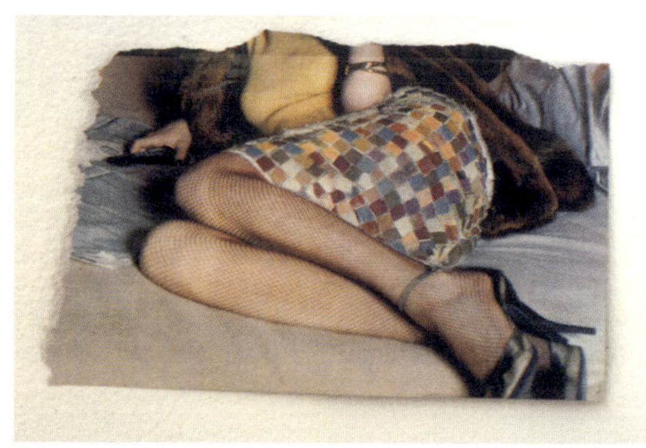

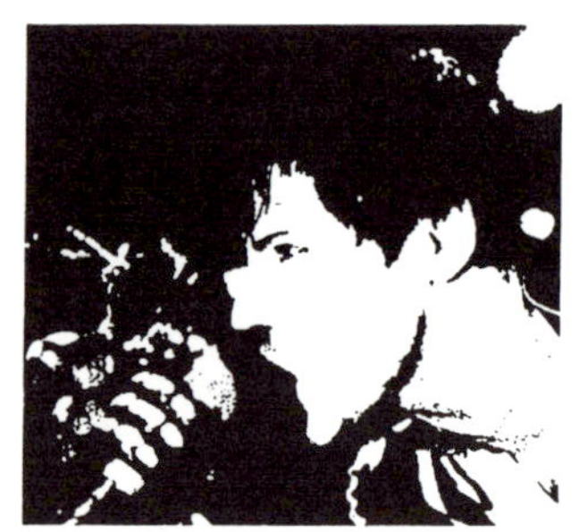

Good Luck for You

09 September-07 October 2000
Preview:Saturday 9 September at 7:30pm

"Ancient formulas of exorcisms and excommunications
that witches and those made wolves believe
I maim now the demon clothed in wolfskin
Having to hide in the hollow of a tree
I believe that they so can be changed"

From 'Halloween II' by the Misfits,
original lyric in nonstandard latin by Glenn Danzig

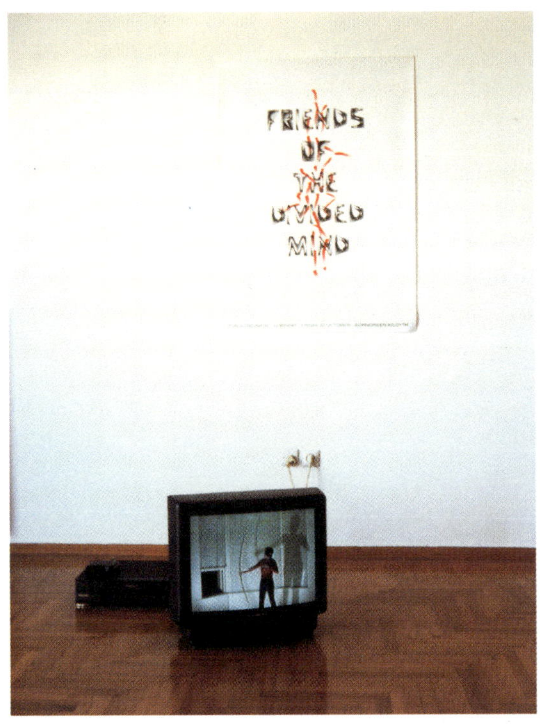

Left: 'Me, We', Chris Evans, *Friends of the Divided Mind* (poster), Michelle Naismith, *Rock My Prehistory* (video).

Below: Chris Evans, Friends of the Divided Mind—poster flyposted around Kilsyth, a small, infamous town outside of Glasgow, advertising the public reunion of a fictitious and undetermined organisation. This poster was shown as part of the exhibition 'Day of the Donkey Day' at Transmission, October 1999.

Bottom right: Duncan Campbell, *The Material History of Glasgow*.

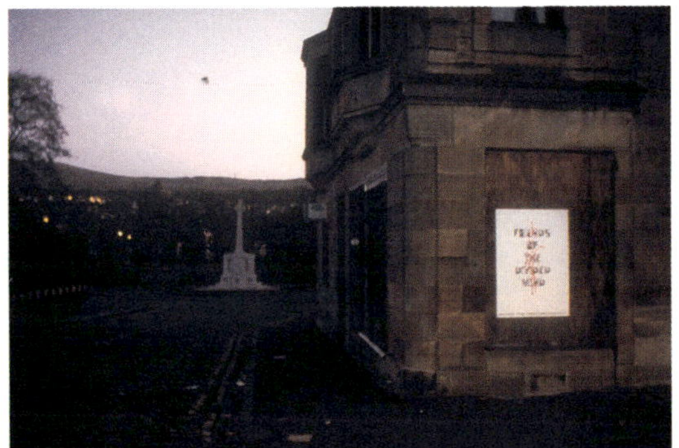

09 **Opposite, top left:** 'Good Luck For You'—from left: Alex Frost, *Necking and Spooning*; Liz Craft, *Foxy Lady*; Peter Wüthrich, *Literary Model IV*.

Opposite, top right: Alex Frost, *Necking and Spooning*.

Opposite, centre right: Julia Schmidt, *Pause*.

Opposite, centre left: Elizabeth Kent, *Pattern*.

Opposite, bottom: from press release.

11 **Me, We—Transmission at Project Space, Athens:** Project Space is a new artist-run initiative in Athens, Greece. Transmission were invited by Dimitra Barba and Vangelis Vlahos to curate an exhibition of Glasgow based artists—'Me, We' brought together the work of Duncan Campbell, Chris Evans, Luke Fowler, Michael Fullerton, Andrew Kerr, Michelle Naismith, Clare Stephenson and Cathy Wilkes.

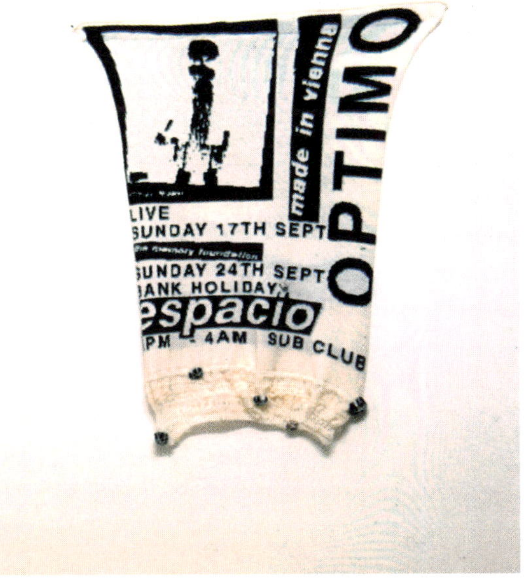

01 Lucy Skaer—Like a circle in a spiral
or
The cotton was high and the corn was growing fine, but that was another place and another time.
or
A modern pig of Iron age type: A one week project by Lucy Skaer featuring a series of drawings and hand painted objects.

"Through Lucy's work we recognise the importance of objects or artefacts that have lost their historical context" Ben Greenman (Transmission Newsletter)

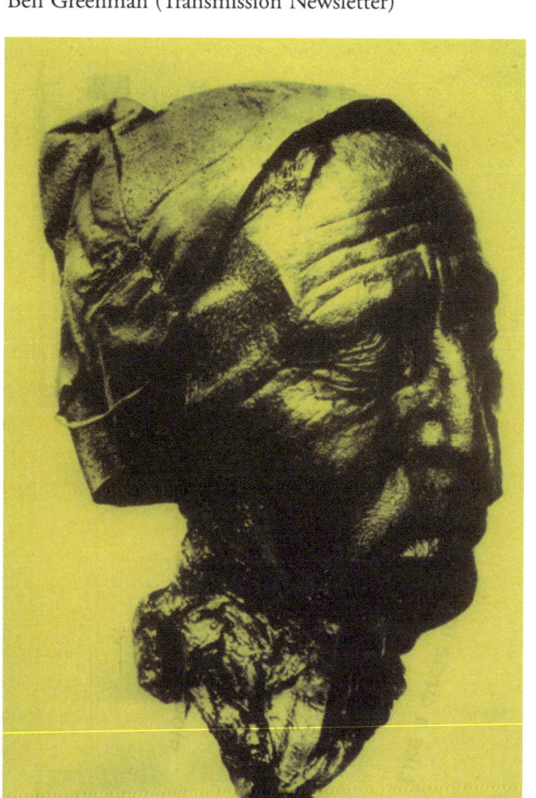

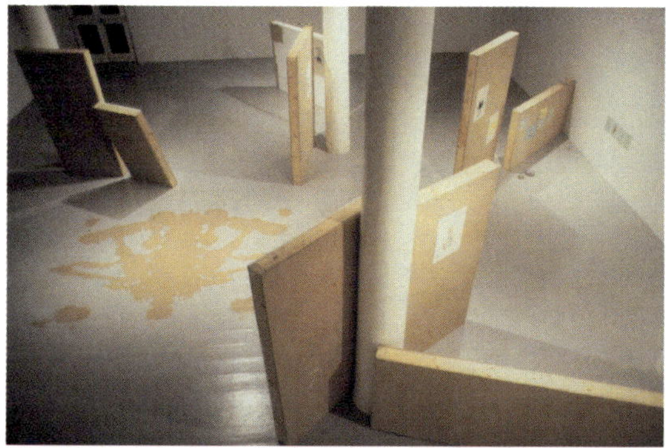

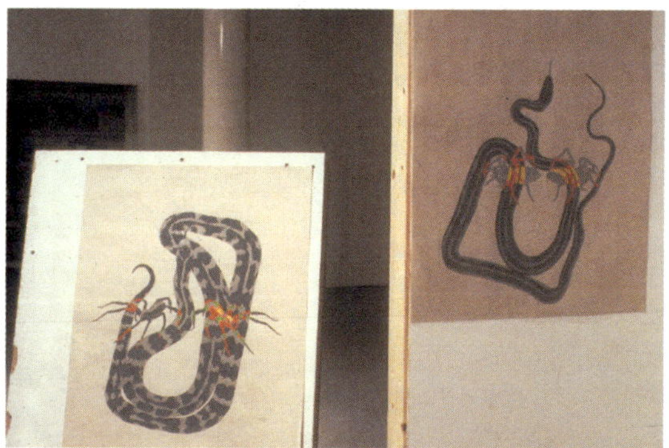

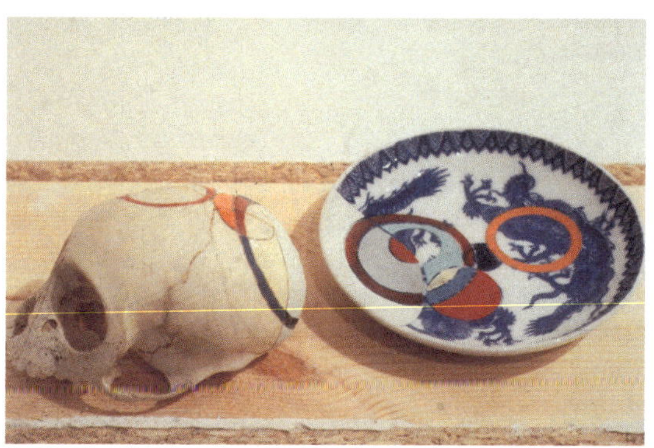

01 Best Eagle: A three person show featuring two Glasgow based artists, Michelle Naismith and Duncan MacQuarrie, and Mark Titchner from London.

Below: Michelle Naismith, *Fever in Fever Out*—a girl rocks precariously back and forth on her chair. The film is punctuated with rhythmic purple flashes.

Bottom: 'Best Eagle', January 2001—Mark Titchner, foreground and right: nails driven into the gallery floor, highlighted with coloured wool to form the words *Consciousness is Artificial Daylight*, and a 26 pointed circular form *The Universe is the Interior Lightcone of Creation*, making reference to the 26 letters of the alphabet and all of their possible permutations. Duncan MacQuarrie, background left: *Anonymous Wash*—art school-style partitions isolating arranged debris—empty lager cans, sports stickers, a potentially functional welding kit—along with framed drawings.; *Andrew W Security*.

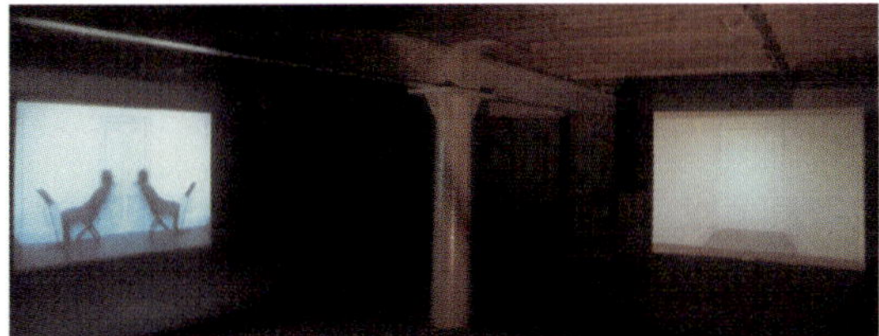

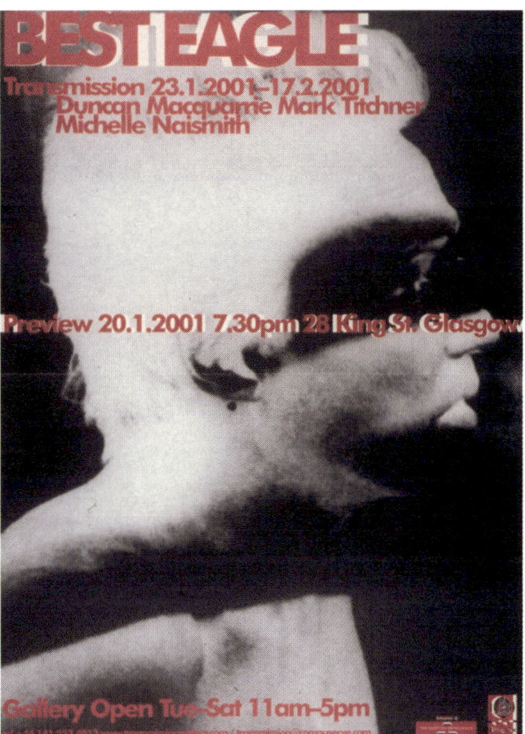

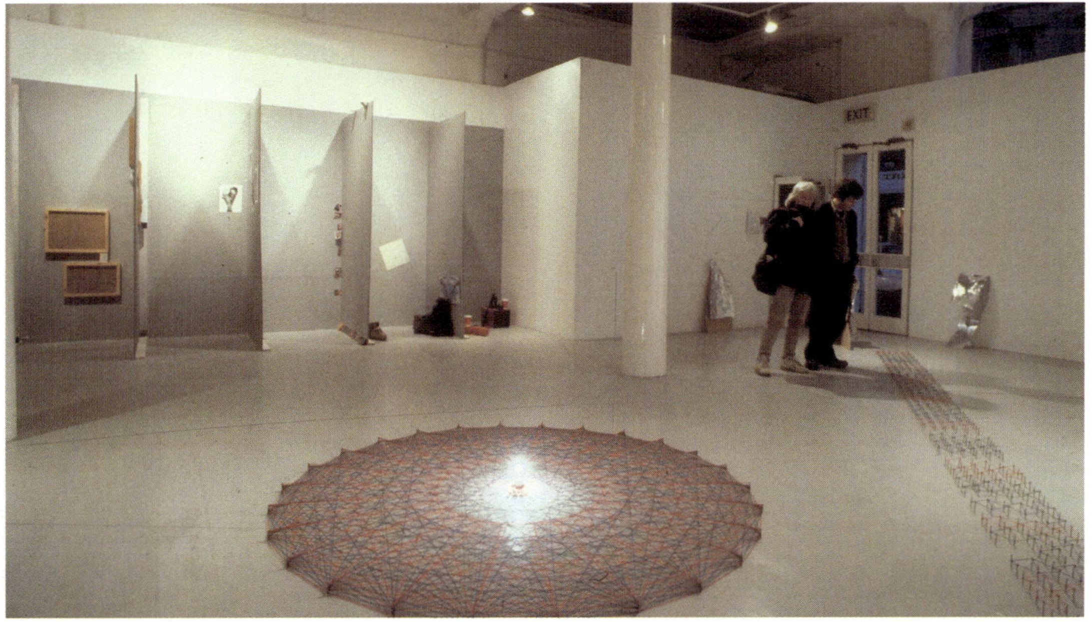

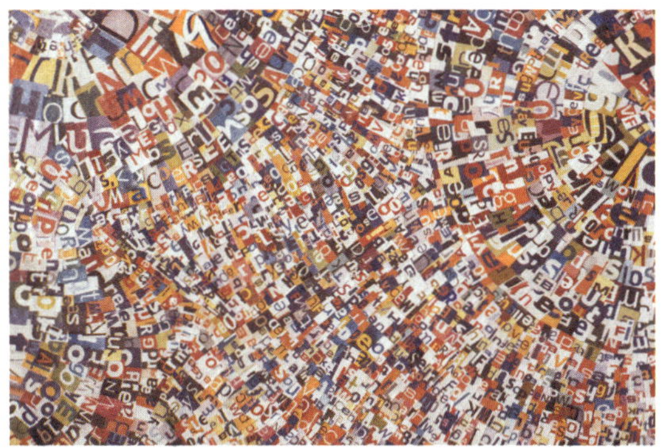

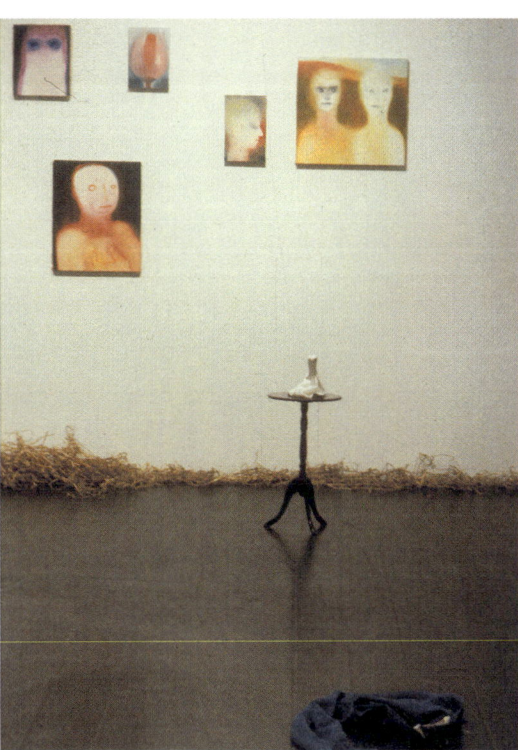

05 hair on one side is swept back: 'hair on one side is swept back' brought together Swiss artist Miriam Cahn; Mary Chong from Hong Kong; final year student at Glasgow School of Art, Laurence Figgis; and Dundee based Michael Mallett.

07 Cathy Wilkes: "Wilkes' concept is not delicate in the whimsical sense; but more in the way of engineering, of precarious physical laws of gravity and tension. She has the power to locate and draw out a feeling of quiet instability, a feeling like vertigo, despite the close intimacy of the space. Her powers to disquiet are an intricate matter of form, of manipulation of light and tone, of objects and materials so that the tableau alters subtly, (shivers, bends, 'flickers') as the spectator moves through it.

There is echo too of theatre, especially naturalistic stage, where fragments of rooms with real furniture

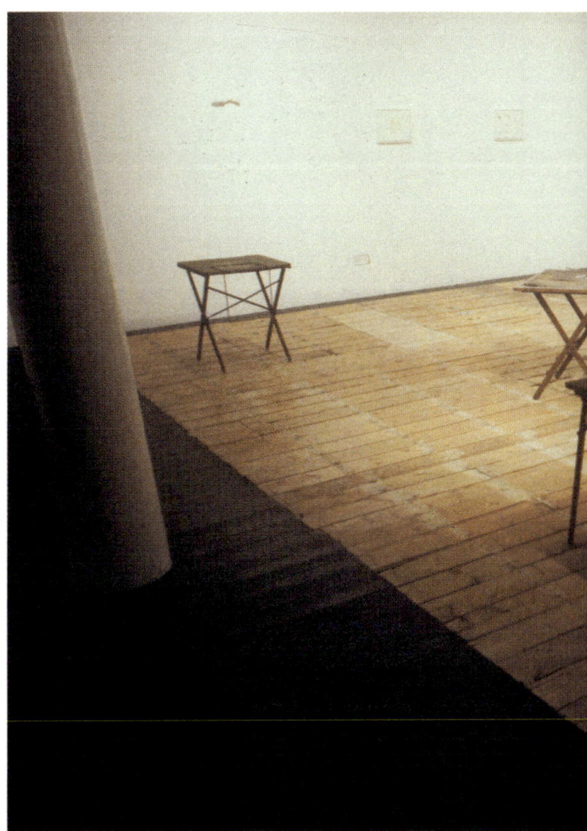

provide the setting for fictional enactment of familial and domestic conflict. An aspect of realism emerges in memory of domestic dis-order, from the jewel-like cosmetics of mess and decay, as with the dilapidated card-table where the covering (ripped off or worn away)

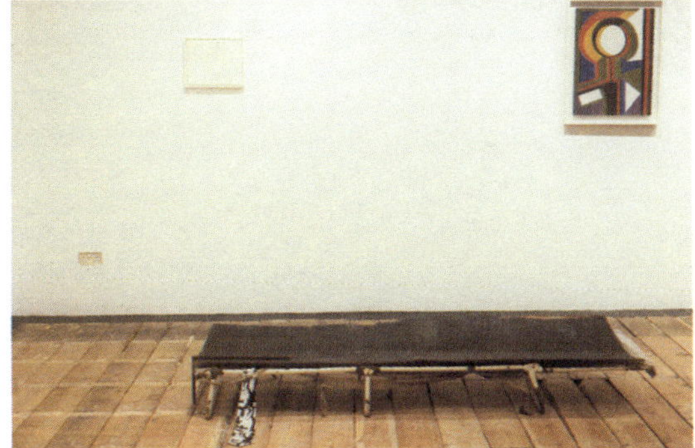

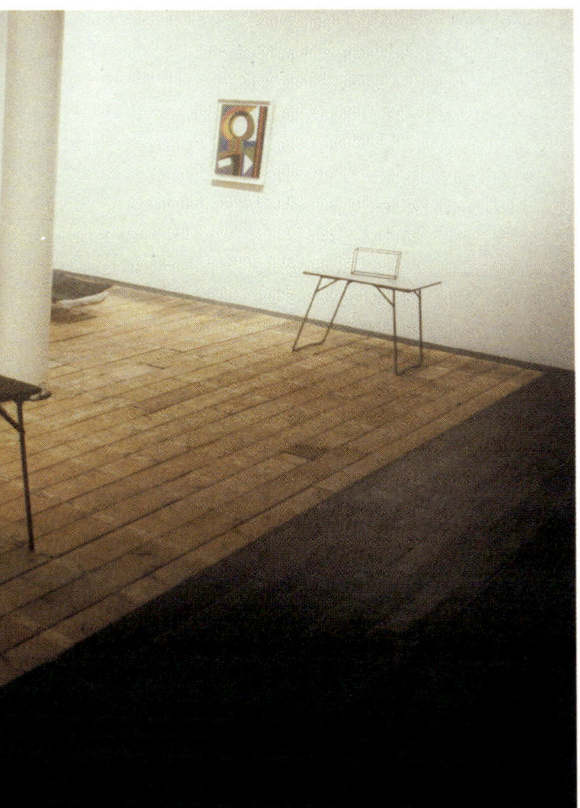

has left tiny fragments of green felt pinned to the greying wood. Her own interventions, sometimes echo the colourings and physicality of the worn props, and more often than not simulate the process of damage related to time, the ghost of the absent human presence. At other moments they seem cruder, as with the bright fabric collages, odd touches of lunacy and vulgarity against the otherwise sepulchral mood.

The resultant discord is quizzical, invites discourse, as opposed to cowed, credulous hypnotism. Wilkes of course invites a permeation of the fabricated space, allowing closer scrutiny of its elements than a stage set would allow. The frame provided by the tampered gallery floor (where some of the black boards have been hewn and overturned to make a stark yellow square) exaggerates this sense of intrusion, demanding that we invade the work in order to view it." Laurence Figgis (Transmission Newsletter)

This page: *Our Misfortune* by Cathy Wilkes. A large tableau of furniture, still life, fabric collage, linear wood sculptures and paintings.

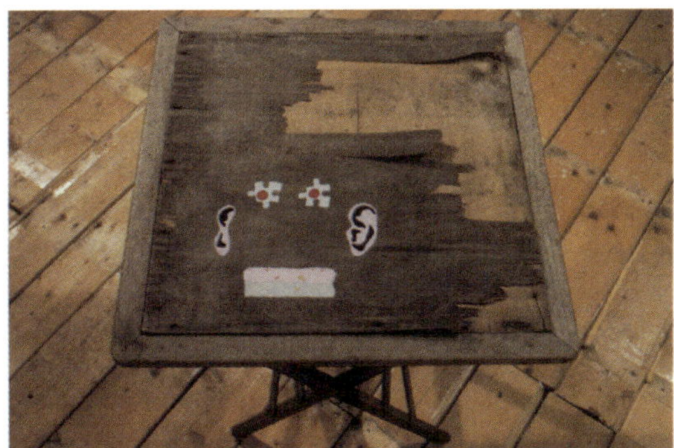

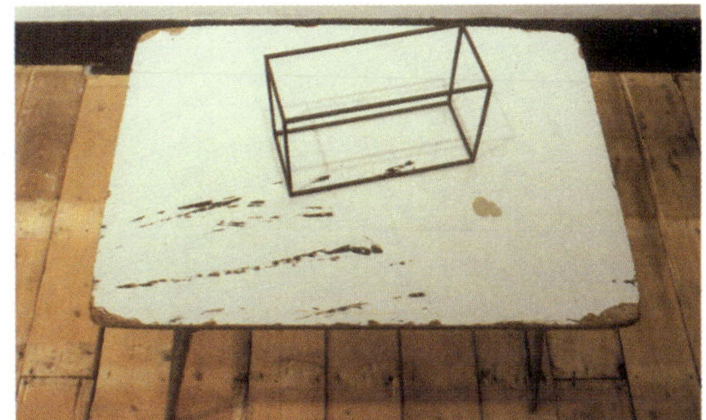

Members' Shows

The gallery hosts an annual open submission 'Members' Show'. The first was 'Art for People' in 1996. This was a development from earlier large group shows such as 'Contact 552-4813' and 'Modern Art' where contributions were invited from members and artists associated with the gallery.

96/05 Art For People: "The exhibition 'Art for People' is the result of an open invitation from Transmission to the gallery's membership to show anything they'd like to for two weeks in May. 'Art for People' is also the title of a book by Julian Spalding, the director of Glasgow's new Gallery of Modern Art, in which he sets out his highly personal vision of art for the masses. Transmission Gallery is a non-profit artist-run space and membership is open to anyone with an interest in contemporary art." (from press release)

97/07 European Couples and Others: "This year's Transmission Gallery members' show has a special twist; to

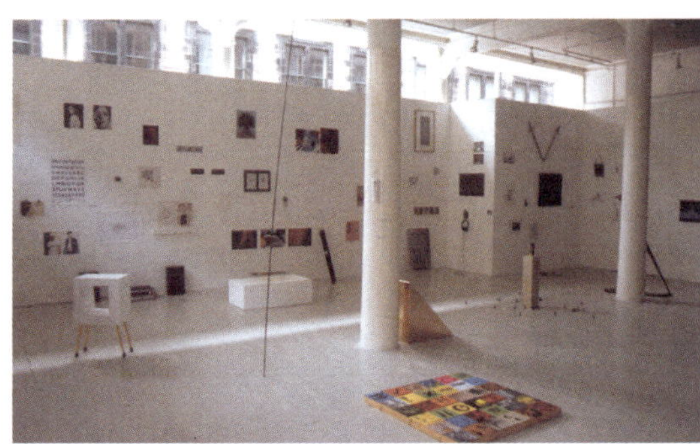

Below: 'European Couples and Others', July 1997.

guarantee a really wide spectrum of artwork, each participating artist has been asked to invite a non-member to submit a piece. Furthermore, to give this show added dimension, each exhibited work is dedicated by the artist to someone or something…

Panel, from left: 'Art For People' poster by Tom O'Sullivan; (bottom) 'Art For People' installation, May 1996; (top) 'European Couples and Others' poster by Ewan café; (top) 'Transmission Open', July 1999; (bottom) 'Members' Show', October 2000.

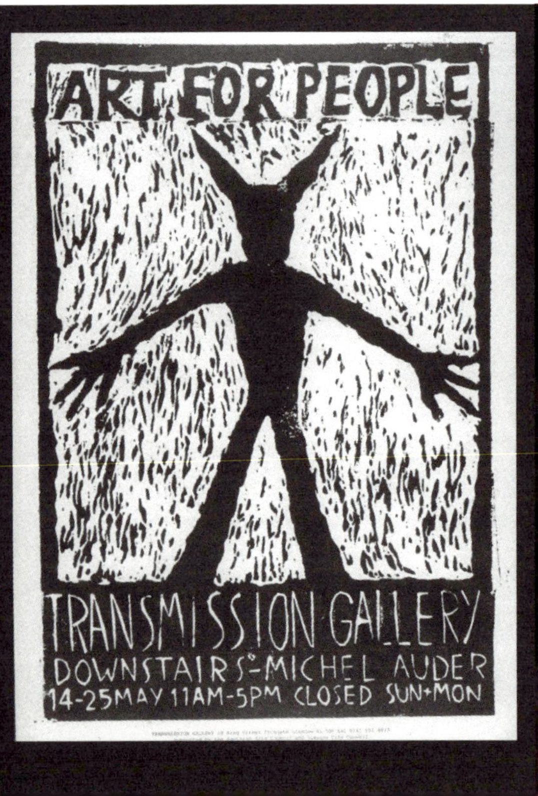

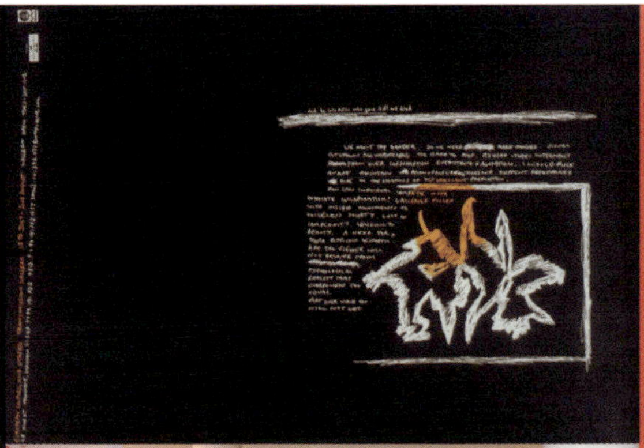

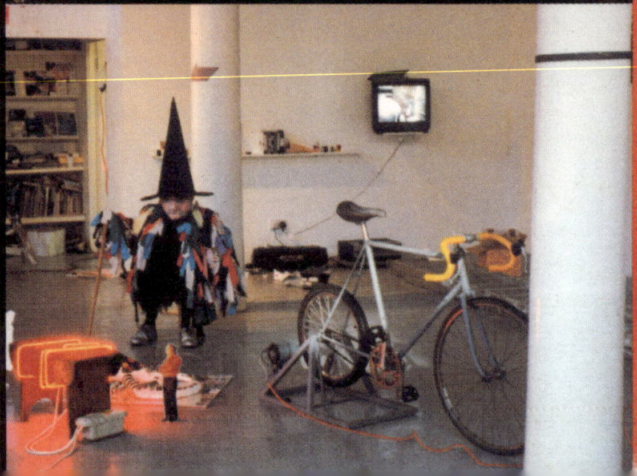

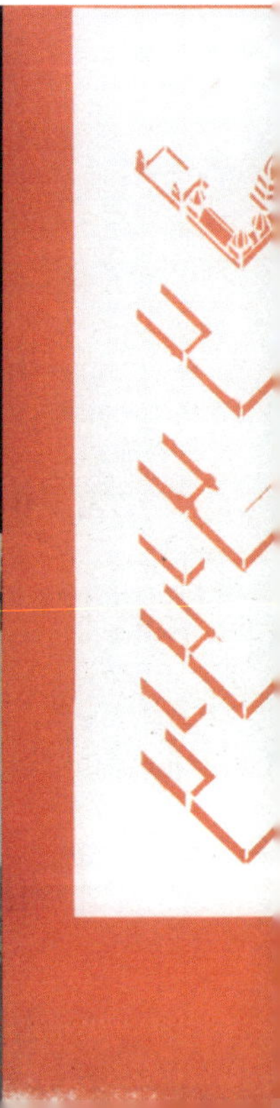

1996–2001

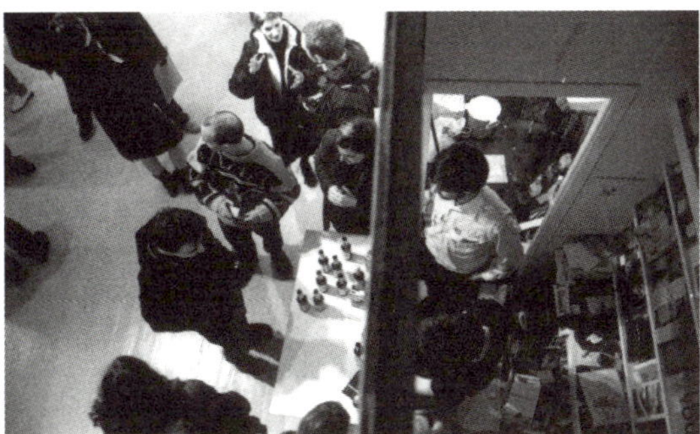 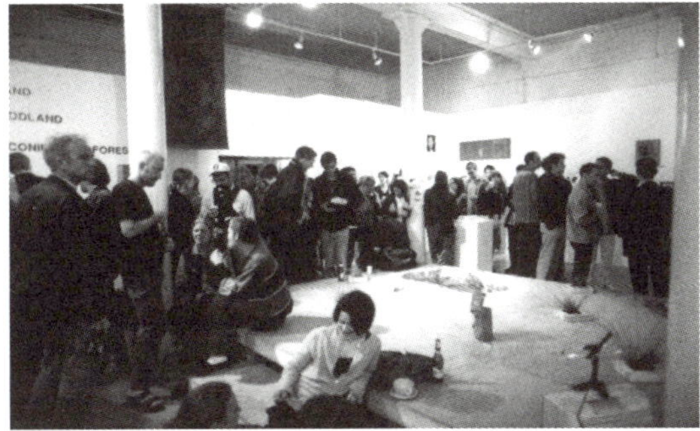

Members' shows are an important part of Transmission; they enable artists to get a direct chance to show work, and bring into the open a whole lot of fresh ideas which are very valuable for our future programming." (from press release)

98/07 Tronway Arts Centre: "The 1998 Transmission Members' Show will see the gallery transformed into an all-purpose arts centre complete with café, sculpture garden and gallery tour, to suit the needs of any modern art-goer." (from press release)

ay Arts Centre' poster by Clare Stephenson; (top) 'Tronway Arts Centre'—sculpture garden created by Caroline Woodley; (bottom) 'Tronway Arts Centre'

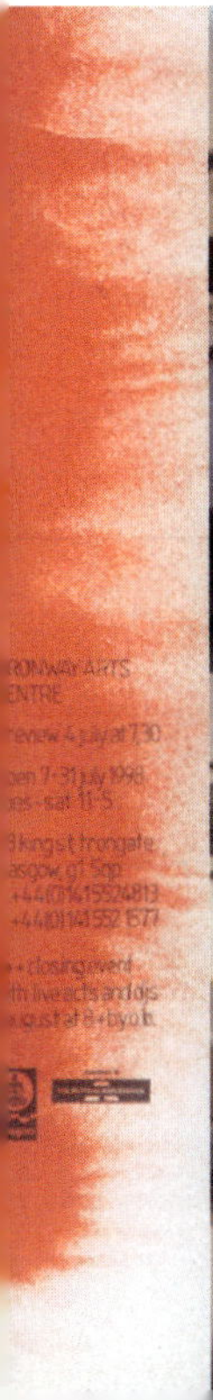

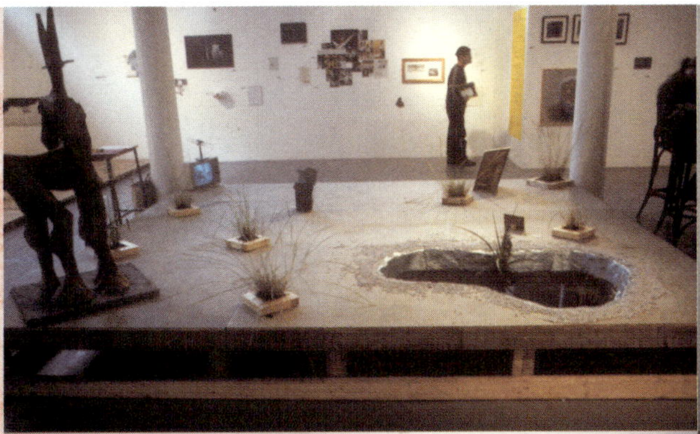

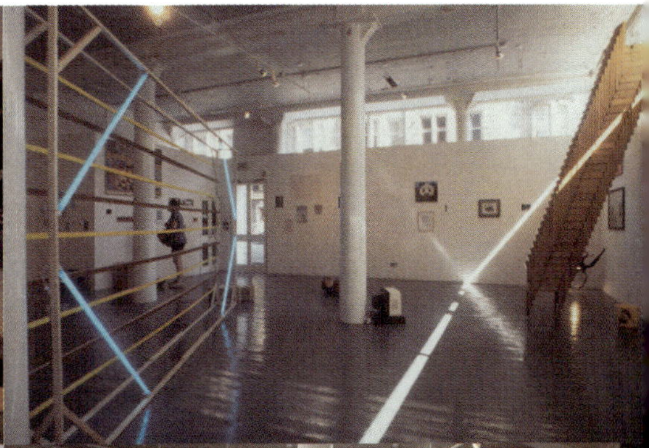

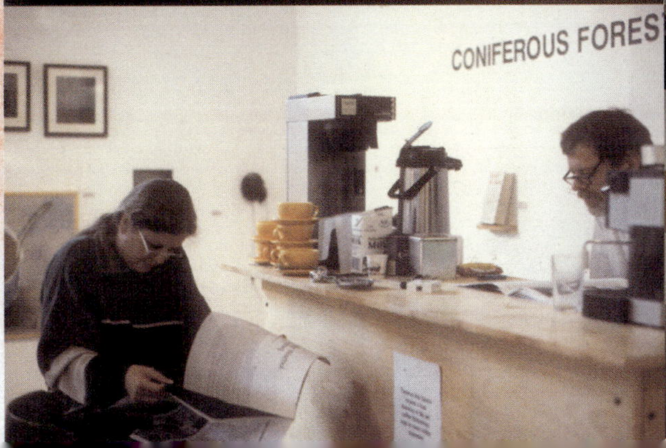

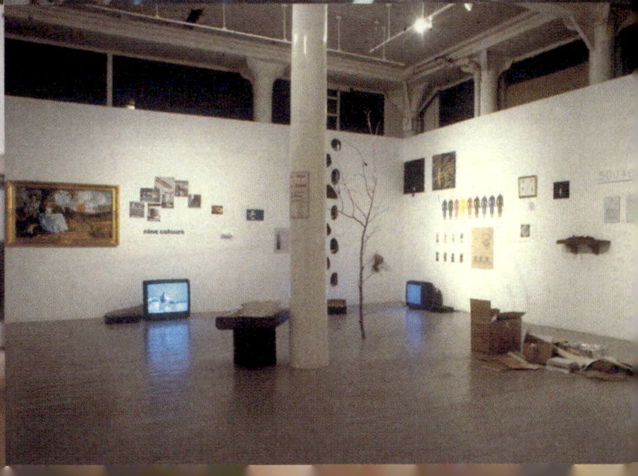

Transmission Gallery Programme 1983–2001

Transmission: 13–15 Chisholm Street, Trongate, Glasgow, G1 HA

02/12/83–08/01/84 Urban Life
Painting, sculpture and photography on the theme of urban life by Tunde Cockshott, John Rogan, Ken Currie, Douglas Thomson, Andrew Squire, Peter Howson, Lesley Raeside, Alistair Magee, Michelle Baucke, Andy Walker, Arlene Stewart, Gordon Brennan, Alastair Strachan, Dominic Snyder, Adrian Wiszniewski, Matthew Inglis, Liz Martin, Jayne Taylor, John Doherty and David Linley.

04/12/83 Benefit Dance at the Mayfair
"The top reggae band 'Man at the Window' will be providing the live music on Sunday and the tickets for the event are available from leading record stores." (*Evening Times*)

14/01/84–12/02/84 Construction Painting
Three-dimensional paintings and reliefs by Alistair Magee, Alastair Strachan, Matthew Inglis, Gordon Brennan and David Heale.

17/02/84–18/03/84 Blunt Image
An exhibition of figurative painting and sculpture by Tunde Cockshott, Allan Ewing, Chris Taylor and Andy Walker.

24/03/84–20/04/84 Winning Hearts and Minds
Drawing and painting by Lesley Raeside, John Rogan, Peter Howson, Helen Gibson, Andrew Squire, Alison Stirling, Stephen Barclay, Gordon Muir and Arlene Stewart.

07/08/84–01/09/84 Recent Work
David Linley, Ian Kane, Linda Taylor and Ian Macpherson.

"In asking these four artists to exhibit together I had three specific criteria. One, I find their work stimulating and interesting, two, I like the varied sources each individual has for their work, three, it is the policy of 'The Committee for the Visual Arts' to promote a wide range of types of art produced by young artists." (Matthew Inglis, press release)

09/10/84–27/10/84 Three Artists at Transmission
Carol Rhodes, Wendy Halstead and Jayne Taylor.

04/11/84–24/11/84 Artists Collectives
Exchange project with Peter Howson, Alastair Strachan, Richard Wright, John Rogan and The Artists Collective, The High Street, Edinburgh.

"Young Scottish artists in Glasgow and Edinburgh are currently sowing their expressionist New Image seeds in two self-run galleries, Transmission in Glasgow and The Artists Collective, Edinburgh. It has to be said that the one in the West is, so far, 10 times better than the one in the East." (Clare Henry, the Glasgow *Herald*, 2 November 1984, p. 4)

Gallery Closed Dec 1984–April 1985

04/05/85–25/05/85 Iconoclasm: Art from the War of Ideas
Paintings and drawings by Peter Thomson, Gordon Muir and Malcolm Dickson.

03/06/85–20/06/85 Very, Very Cyprus
Paintings and drawings by students from the Cyprus School of Art including Elise V. Allan, Lynne Mack, Lesley Finlayson, Anne Campbell and Pierre Turton.

10/07/85–10/08/85 Cornice Hat
Paintings, drawings and sculpture by Tommy Lydon and Alistair Dickson.

17/08/85 Being and Doing and Arbeit Macht Frei
Films by Ken McMullen and Stuart Brisley presented by Transmission at the Third Eye Centre's studio theatre (also shown later at Transmission).

"A collaboration between Stuart Brisley, Britain's leading performance artist, and major independent filmmaker Ken McMullen…. Image manipulation, jagged editing and a powerful soundtrack give it the immediacy of newsreel footage." (press release)

17/08/85–14/09/85 Works on Paper
Paintings and drawings by Graham Magee and Richard Wright.

24/09/85–19/10/85 The Map is not the Territory
Photographs, text, sculpture and reliefs by Ralph Rumney.

09/11/85–30/11/85 The Black Bastard as a Cultural Icon
Mixed media works by Eddie Chambers.

"The exhibition aims to illustrate ways in which the golliwog acts as one of the most widespread negative images of Black people, embodying and unconsciously encouraging racism." (press release)

07/12/85–04/01/86 Transmission Drawing Show
Thirty artists—Transmission members and students from Glasgow School of Art.

"Over the festival period Transmission Gallery will be staging a mixed drawing show. It is open to anyone living/working in Scotland, of any age. Each entrant may submit up to three works, of any size, but preferably in monochrome." (from the call for submissions)

13/01/86–31/01/86 War of Images: Art and the Battle of Ideas
Artists from London, Liverpool and Glasgow in an exhibition at Transmission and the Mackintosh Museum, Glasgow School of Art.

Mark Cardwell, Eric Marwick, Helen Flockhart, Sandra Goldbacher & Kim Flitcroft, Trevor Coombs, Mick Duffield, Ian Hughes, Peter Dunn & Lorraine Leeson, The Intolerants, Mouse Katz, Billy Clark, Tony Rickaby, Peter Seddon, Simon Brown, Peter Thomson, Alison Mcleod, Graham Johnstone, Ian Killen, Carol Rhodes, Ralph Rumney, Malcolm Dickson, Gordon Muir, Crass Graphics/Existencil Music.

03/02/86–28/02/86 Glasgow Event Space
Video, film, performance and installation by Steve Littman, Zoe Redman, Stephen Partridge, Pictorial Heroes, Alister McDonald, Jane Rigby, Ian Haddow, Duncan's Duo, Tony Judge, Joj Goslan/Cammy Galt, Tom McGrath & Friends, Kevin Atherton, David Hall and Michael O'Pray.

11/03/86–30/03/86 Community and Art
Exhibition of and about the work of Community Arts Projects around Glasgow with Kate Thomson, Katie Lorimer and Jayne Taylor.

05/04/86–26/04/86 Richard Walker, Louise Lyons
Exhibition of paintings.

03/05/86–30/05/86 The Shining City on the Hill
Drawings and paintings by John Yeadon.

08/07/86–02/08/86 Oladele Bamgboye, Debbie Coombes
Photographic works by Nigerian artist Oladele Bamgboye and Debbie Coombes from Ireland.

02/08/86 Transmission Goes Verbal
Readings by Tom Leonard and James Kelman in association with the *Edinburgh Review*.

11,12,13/08/86 Stuart Brisley
Performance and seminar.

19/08/86–13/09/86 Lesley Raeside, Matthew Inglis
Paintings, drawings and constructions.

"The artist-run Transmission Gallery in recent months has established itself as Glasgow's premier progressive gallery with a string of enterprising shows many of which come from outside Scotland. This show represents therefore another side of the gallery, showing young artists working in the city and around the Transmission collective. The paintings of Raeside and Inglis seem to be involved with the idea of crowds, history and the individual." (Pete Seddon, 1986)

04/10/86–25/10/86 Glasgow Event Space 2

04/10: Video Art from Germany: A selection of twenty years of video art from the Federal Republic, organised in association with the Goethe Institute, Glasgow; 10/10: 'Super 8, A Storm of Images: Recent Scottish Films'; 11/10: 'A Camera of One's Own', a selection of 16mm films by women, with an introductory lecture by film critic Cordelia Swann; 17/10: Richard Layzell—performance, video and lecture; 25/10: Charlie Hooker—'White Lining', performance and music; 25/10: Chris Rowlands and Stephen Partridge—'The Cover Up, Rutwork and Videvoce: Video work by Pictorial Heroes'.

08/11/86–29/11/86 Helen Flockhart, Alison Stirling, Anne Elliot
Paintings and drawings.

04/12/86–12/12/86 Dead Ending
Installation by Iain Robertson.

15/12/86–20/12/86 Dis-Place-Ment
Performance and installation by Karen Strang.

"Strang changed from figurative painting to installation and performance work when she found that oils and turpentine were impossible to get hold of in Warsaw. Plus the fact that the anticipated Academy of Fine Arts studio turned out to be a corner in a room shared by 40 others. Other experiences, including Chernobyl, May Day rallies, and the boycott of the first so-called democratic election, are incorporated into her work." Clare Henry (the Glasgow *Herald*, 15 December 1986, p. 4)

07/02/87–28/02/87 How To Read Comics
Works by Graham Johnstone, John Rogan, Billy Clark, Gordon Muir, Ed Pinsent, Iain Irving & Judith Findlay, Battle of the Eyes—Savage Pencil, Chris Long and Andy Dog.

"The exhibition discusses the language of Comics, using examples with explanatory text. In addition to this we will be presenting a selection of original artwork from comics, and have commissioned new work from artists not normally working in the medium." (from catalogue)

10/03/87–28/03/87 John Ferry, Martin Banks
New paintings.

07/04/87–25/04/87 Iconoclasm
Gordon Muir and Malcolm Dickson.

05/05/87–30/05/87 Desire in Ruins: No Transmission
An installation of work by Ed Baxter, Andy Hopton, Simon Dickason, Karen Elliot, Stefan Szczelkun, Glyn Banks and Hannah Vowles.

+ 02/05/87 How to Explain Glasgow Painting to a Dead Mackerel: Stefan Szczelkun—performance after Joseph Beuys.

06/06/87–27/06/87 Characterisation
New paintings and drawings by Chris Taylor.

"Chris Taylor, ex-Glasgow School of Art, obviously has an admiration for Egon Schiele, but unlike that unhappy fin-de-siecle Austrian not all his draughtsmanship is angst-ridden." Clare Henry (the Glasgow *Herald*, 19 June 1987, p. 4)

21/06/87 Fangoria Gore and The Golden Dawn
Transmission at Fury Murray's. Performance by Fangoria Gore and The Golden Dawn.

14/07/87–31/07/87 Transmission Group Show
Carolyn Angus, Peter Russell, Alan Wilson, Martin Banks, Wendy Bibby, Tommy Lydon, Fiona Robertson, The Paul Chambers Experience, Gillian Farmer, David Palmer, Mark Campbell, Karen Strang, Paula Stephenson, Craig Peacock and Ian Mackechnie.

14/07/87–31/07/87 Transmission Goes Verbal 2
Readings by Janice Galloway, Ian Brotherhood and Jim Ferguson.

10/08/87–29/08/87 Zoo
Paintings by Gillian Steel and Ken Waldron.

08/09/87–30/09/87 The Secruity of Belief and The Promise of Tradition
An exhibition by Adam Geary consisting of "two installations which collectively transform the gallery into a site where the audience can confront and question the dominant value structures of society." (press release)

03/10/87 Performance/Action Art
'Three women artists, three performances': *Fragments*, Jane Barlett; *Marilyn*, Louise Crawford; *A Prayer for England*, Sabine Burger

18/10/87 Transmission Goes Verbal 3
Reading at Transmission from the newly published collection 'Tower of Babble' by 'Itinerant poets'—Graham Fulton, Bobby Christie, Ronald McNeil and Jim Ferguson. In association with the *Edinburgh Review*.

27/10/87 Transmission Fine Art Auction
Work by Transmission members and supporters auctioned at the Green Room, RAC, Blythswood Square.

Mick Scott, Paul Chambers, Sandie Gardner, Peter Graham, Bob Finnie, John Gilmour, Chris Bramble, Dominic Snyder, Tommy Lydon, Jock Macinnis, Alisdair Gray, Billy Clark, John MacKechnie, Irene Bell, Barry Atherton, David Pratt, Jim Holden, Frank Higgins, Jimmy Cosgrove, Paul Ewing, Jack Knox, Peter Russell, Linda Green, Steven Campbell, Alistair McCallum, Kenny Waldron, Alan Wilson, Janka Malkowska, Peter Bevan, Stuart Duffin, Ricky Walker, Kelvin Guy, Ronald Thompson Fulton, Kenny Hunter, George Wyllie, Chris Taylor, Brian Kelly, Robert Reid, Ian Jamieson, Jayne Taylor, Adrian Wiszniewski, Daphne M Gamble, Francis Law, Alistair Dixon, John Main, Ricky Walker, Robert Stewart, Adam Steiner, Robert Paul, Ian Ramsay, Tom Hutchison, Sandra Oakes, Sam Ainsley, Andrew W Adair, Philip Reeves, Dougie Thompson, Kay Scott, Marian Thompson.

12/11/87 Meta…Trips…Arts…III
Performance by Andrzej Dudek-Dürer.

"Last week the Transmission Gallery was host to a strange visitation. Stopping off on a European tour, the Polish artist Andrzej Dudek-Dürer enshrined the place in echoes of the sixties." Alice Bain (the Glasgow *Herald*, 20 November 1987, p. 4)

17/11/87–15/12/87 Kevin Hannah
New painting and prints by Kevin Hannah.

16/12/87–17/12/87 <<aNTEHYPERAESTHESIa>>
Performance by Puberty Institution: Douglas Gordon, Craig Richardson.

"Their installation work has progressively adapted and evolved Scottish motifs which evoke an atmosphere of a forgotten past and hidden present. The installation utilizes a variety of materials and media and is enhanced by the physical presence of the durational performance." (press release)

12/01/88–30/01/88 Oladele Bamgboye, Stephen Birrell, Stephen Dunlop, Stan Shepherd
Photographs.

09/02/88–27/02/88 The Nicaragua Show
Organised by the Nicaraguan Solidarity Campaign of Glasgow School of Art.

12/03/88–02/04/88 A Conspiracy of Feeling
Mixed media works by Billy Clark.

11/04/88–23/04/88 Events Space 3
Continuous video screenings and special events including an open forum and debate on time-based work.

J D Kelly, Chris Rowland, Cavin Convery, Pictorial Heroes, Liz Power, Richard Cousins, Sandra Christie, Jim Henry, Malcolm Dickson, Lei Cox, Margaret Warwick, Catherine Elwes, David Hall, Mike Stubbs, Mike Hartney, Tina Keane, Lydia Shouten, Sankofn, Sven Harding, Paul Richards & Michael Nyman, John Latham, Rose Garrard, Ian Breakwell, Nicola Percy, Martin Thompson & Dean Stockton, Steve Littman and Jeremy Peyton-Jones.

07/05/88–28/05/88 Residue Septik Activity
Performance, video, installation, film by Ivan Unwin.

+ a selection of IKON videos featuring music from The Fall, Joy Division, Big Flame, etc..

07/06/88–02/07/88 a green-er evolution
Postal Art Show sponsored by the Scottish Post Office and organised by Jayne Taylor.

13/06/88 Puberty Institution
4pm–10pm: Durational performance by Puberty Institution—Craig Richardson and Douglas Gordon—at Midland Street, Glasgow.

09/07/88 Party in a railway tunnel under Glasgow's Botanic Gardens with performance by American Neoist Tentatively a Convenience.

09/07/88–30/07/88 Photography Works
David Allen, Clive Jachnik and Gerlinde Salentin.

06/08/88–07/08/88 Dark Side Operations
Performance by Shaun Caton.

23/08/88–27/08/88 Cut Out 2
30/08/88–03/09/88 Restricted Movement
Two performance based installations by Euan Sutherland.

07/09/88 Paul Wong
Video work and a talk by the Canadian artist.

10/09/88–13/10/88 Work
Graphic works by Graham Harwood.

+ in the basement: Metamorphosis—Photographs by Ivan Sladek.

15/10/88 Transmission Jumble Sale

07/11/88–30/11/88 Land of Opportunity
A five year retrospective featuring documentation of past exhibitions and artwork including 'Events Space', 'Desire in Ruins', Stuart Brisley, 'Iconoclasm', 'Winning Hearts and Minds', Helen Flockhart, Karen Strang, Alastair Strachan, David Linley, Oladele Bamgboye, Lesley Raeside, Alison Stirling, Peter Thomson and Alistair Magee.

03/12/88 Physical Minimum
Tim Brennan performance between 9am and 9pm.

10/12/88–17/12/88 Apocalypse Culture
An audio visual exhibition of provocative statements—views and propaganda presented by Cathexis Recordings (Robert H King).

"Two thousand years have passed since the assassination of the Radical Jesus and the World is going mad. Religious cults, Nihilists and occult prophets are united in their belief of an imminent global catastrophe. Fix your microscope on the tumors of mass delirium." (press release)

06/89 Gallery moves to 28 King Street, Trongate, Glasgow, G1 5QP

07/89 Transmission re-opens

10/07/89–29/07/89 Helen Flockhart & Kay McLean
Portraits based on Polish icons by Helen Flockhart and paintings produced by Kay McLean as Millport artist-in-residence.

04/08/89–26/08/89 Fifth International Festival of Plagarism: Slogans of Reversal/Reversal of Slogans
Mixed media works, lectures and discussions with Mark Bloch, Wendy Lanxtner, The Tape-Beatles, Billy Clark, The Mudguards, AC Acoustics, King Mob, We Are Men, Kola Itch, Jayne Taylor, Stewart Home and Mark Pawson.

06/08: Jamie Reid—Xerox Workshop; 06/08: Jorg Buttigereit—Experimental video work; 07/08: Anarcho/Situationist Videos; 08/08: The Temple of Psychik Youth—Video Installation; 09/08: Fluxday; 10/08: Klaus Maeke—*Decoder* (film screening); 11/08: Florian Cramer—'Night of the Slack' (music and performance); plus numerous spontaneous events and parties.

04/09/89–23/09/89 Scrap-Shot
Sculptural installation produced by Hubertus Hess after a three month residency at Glasgow Sculpture Workshops.

07/10/89–28/10/89 Glasgow School of Art MA Show
Alexander Dempster, James Hamlyn, Rachel Harris, Peter McCaughey, Donna Rae, Craig Richardson, Julie Roberts, Andrew Sneddon, Edward Stewart, Catherine Whippey

26/10/89 The Midnight of the Decade
Screenings and discussions with *Variant Video*, a new magazine produced as an extension of the printed issue documenting areas of artistic endeavour.

Frustration Game; *Mud and Stars*; *Workers City, the Subversive Past*; *De-Classed Elements*—Drumchapel Community Centre; *First Strike, Portrait of an Activist*—Doug Dibble.

28/10/89 Transmission/Oceaan Exchange
David Allen, Karen Vaughan, Billy Clark, Louise Crawford and Stephen Harty in Arnhem, The Netherlands.

06/11/89–25/11/89 Present Histories
Installation by the collaborative group 'Order Out of Chaos'.

"Present Histories will be a continuation of the concerns developed by those exhibiting as 'Order Out of Chaos', the title does not act as a brief but as a means of focussing a content, that has, in the past acted to 'voice silences', to discover the social mechanisms and technocratic dogma of our times, to re-examine the open ended question of our history." (press release)

09/12/89–20/12/89 Four Dutch Artists — Transmission/Oceaan Exchange
Hester Oerlemans, René Roeten, An Van Roosmalen, Wilma Sommers.

13/01/90–02/02/90 Installation Work
David Allen and Peter Gilmour.

+ in the basement: 'The Thatcher Legacy', an installation by Sean Taylor.

24/01/90 *Conversation 2, The Birth of Venus, Poisoned Idyll*
Video by Miklos Peternak and Bonta Zoltan from Balazs Studio, Hungary.

10/02/90–03/03/90 Ivan Sladek & Milos Novy
Photography from Czechoslovakia.

+ in the basement: 'A Model Idea' — collaborative installation by Jean Gavin, Alistair Keddie and Paul Chambers.

12/03/90–31/03/90 Last Look
An installation made specially for the gallery by Sue Brind and Jim Harold.

"The installation is a collaborative work which uses slide projections and texts which argue for a reading for death and its relations to life beyond that of the institution, through the suspension of 'the body' between sites of the hospital and the individual. The images used are drawn from medical archives and photographs of a disused hospital. The text used is a quotation from J K Huysman." (from press release)

+ video screening organised by Scottish Mozambique Aid.

+ slide talk by Chris Taylor.

09/04/90–28/04/90 Dependants
Nathan Coley, Heather Allen, Iain Kettles, Evelyn Jardine, Susan Montford.

05/05/90–30/05/90 Wols: Photographs, watercolours, etchings
"Transmission in King Street is the venue for some of the most fascinating work to be seen in the city at present. 'Wols: Photographs, Watercolours, Etchings' is an exhibition of work made in the 1930s and 1940s by the

outstanding artist Wolfgang Schulze, who is best known under the pseudonym 'Wols' which he adopted in 1937."
Murdo MacDonald (*The Scotsman*, 2 July 1990, p.11)

With weekly talks on the work by Billy Clark.

16/05/90 Technologies and Black Wheel of Anger
Launch of a book by Gerry Fellow and Peter Plate, in association with Polydor.

18/05/90 Outward Gaze
Video screenings of *Eat the Kimono, Compromised* and *Immunity & Ostia*.

(18/05/90–02/06/90 Anne Quinn, Euan Sutherland: Transmission-assisted installation project at 25 Queen Street, Glasgow)

11/06/90–07/07/90 Peter Thomson
Paintings and drawings.

"In images which range from a surreal view of the baroque arsenal of the Holy Loch to dreamlike definitions of the religious flaws within Scottish identity and a reminder that democracy on the UK model will not necessarily make Eastern Europe 'free', Thomson develops a density of symbolism which resonates with the sixteenth century painters of Holland, Flanders and Germany, above all Mathias Grünewald." (Murdo MacDonald, *The Scotsman*)

14/06/90 Experimental films from Manila
"Berlin film maker Christoph Janetzko will introduce and discuss a number of films made during an experimental workshop in Manila, the Philippines." (from press release)

16/07/90–04/08/90 Mark Pawson, Ben Allen
Copy art show including photocopies, T-shirts, books, postcards, badges, collages, etc..

+ in the basement: 18/07/90 Randy Anderson—performance, installation and video by the Canadian artist.

09/08/90–24/08/90 Film and Video Festival
With screenings from an international video collection compiled by the London Film & Video Umbrella.

09/08: *The Body in Extremis*, with a talk by Moira Sweeney; 11/08: Elsie Mitchell—*If the Eyes are Coloured*; Sarah Puchill—*You Be Mother* and *Iron In*; Sue Brind—*Remember Your Womb* and *Luminous Shadows*; 16/08: Ann Vance—*Mortal Signs* and Super 8 Selection; 18/08: Ivan Unwin—*Toxic* and *Eclipse*; 24/08: *Welcome to Glasgow* and *Variant Video*, introduced by Malcolm Dickson, and *Re-action*, film/installation work by Ewan Morrison.

(18/08/90–31/08/90 'Saltoun Arts Project': organised by and including works by Transmission Members)

08/09/90–28/09/90 The Devil Finds Work
Three part exhibition by Keith Piper.

08/09/90–29/09/90 Transmission/Glasgow School of Art collaboration
Julie Roberts, Angus Hood, Raymond Lee.

The exhibiton took place at the Newberry Gallery, Glasgow School of Art. Transmission also presented a video and bookshop.

22/09/90–14/10/90 Fem Fra Glasgow
Norwegian Exchange at Hordaland Kunstnersentrum with Claire Barclay, Malcolm Dickson, Nathan Coley, Ross Sinclair and Martin Boyce.

"Five young artists, all recently educated at Glasgow School of Art, are being shown in the new exhibition at the Hordaland Kunstnersentrum. There is a recognisable unity about the show, which bears witness to the exhibitors' familiarity with each other's artistic ideas and expressions." (*Bergens Tidende*, 14 October 1990)

08/10/90–20/10/90 Belfast MA Show
Roderick Buchanan, Mary McIntyre, Kenneth Parker, David Wilkinson, Belinda Hale, Carol McFarlane, Lindsay P Dumas, John Johnston, Nicola Burrell.

02/11/90–25/11/90 Norwegian Exchange at Transmission
Kurt Johannessen, Jørgen Knudsen, Suvi Nieminen, Torill Nøst.

(01/11/90–31/11/90 Sub Social: Work in Glasgow Underground carriages)

15/12/90–27/12/90 Wishful Thinking
Jacqueline Donachie, Karen Vaughan, Rachel Mimiec, Jacqueline Byrne.

31/01/91 The Reckoning
Workers City book launch.

25/02/91–23/03/91 Silence Exile Cunning
Solo exhibition by Alan Johnston.

"While Alan Johnston's reputation continues to grow in Europe, Japan and America he is rarely given the opportunity to exhibit at home. This is an unfortunate irony given that his work is founded on a desire to contextualise the integration of art, architecture and philosophy into a kind of holistic cultural gestaltism based firmly in the profoundly egalitarian setting of Scottish commonsense philosophy." Ross Sinclair (February 1991)

01/04/91–20/04/91 Volatile Components
An installation of new work by Neil Chapman consisting of several hundred vacuum-formed objects.

05/04/91 New Music From London
Orchestre Murphy, The Honkies, No Rules O.K! at the Vic Bar, Glasgow School of Art.

01/05/91–31/05/91 Workers City
Events and debate.

20/5/91–30/05/91 National Virus
Euan Sutherland and Ross Sinclair.

10/06/91 Speed

With work by Paul Maguire, Ewan Morrison, Theresa Quinn, David Allen, Stephen Harty, Julie Roberts, Iain Kettles, Bryndis Snaebjornsdottir, Colin MacFarlane, Suse Wiegand, Stuart McGlinn, Melissa A Newgass, Stuart Gow, Helen-Marie Nugent, Colin Pettigrew, Claire Barclay, Douglas Gordon, Lesley Punton, Craig Richardson, Anne Quinn, Derek Scanlan, Anne Elliot, Roderick Buchanan, Tracy McKenna, Nathan Coley, Elsie Mitchell, Tim Cullen, Calum Stirling, Jonnie Wilkes, Kevin Hobbs, Heather Allen, Martin Boyce, Christine Borland and Jim Buckley.

08/07/91–03/08/91 Temporary Duration

Collaboration between French, Italian and German artists Elise Parre, Gianni Piacentini, Charlotte Moerker, all of whom had lived in Glasgow for six months as part of the 'Pepiniere' European residency programme.

13/08/91–30/08/91 Angus Hood, Simon Patterson, Thomas Walsh

"Although the artists are working within the broad tradition of painting, the differences in method, presentation, and purpose indicate a healthy diversity in current attitudes towards the debate on painting/not painting…from Thomas Walsh's 'traditional' interiors, to Angus Hood's combination canvases, to Simon Patterson's wall drawing." (from press release)

(05/8/91–25/8/91 'Windfall': At the Seamen's Mission, Glasgow with Sylvie Reynaud, Niels Staal, Elsie Mitchell, Martin Boyce, Edwin Janssen, Julie Roberts, Claire Barclay, Norman Regler, Boris Achour, Jens Heise, Emma McMullan, David McMillan, Michael Lapuks, Roderick Buchanan, Iain Kettles, Anita Drachman, Gerard Byrne, Josep Darana, Blan Ryan, David Allen, Nathan Coley, Douglas Gordon, Jim Hamlyn, Achim Bertenburg and Craig Richardson.)

10/09/91–28/09/91 Missing Persons

Recent collaborative photographic works by Jo Spence.

"The images are in effect, a 'theatre of the self', in which Spence explores the ways in which identity is constructed historically and politically…Spence pictures herself as the sexual object of a male gaze and the medical object of modern medicine; her images concerning her own breast cancer are also a means of reclaiming power over definitions imposed by a male-dominated society as much as they are a form of therapy" Ewan Morrison (*The List*, 31 January–13 Feburary 1992, p. 40)

08/10/91–26/10/91 Like Moth

Installation, film and video by Cathy Wilkes.

02/11/91–23/11/91 Specific Rooms

Sculpture by Yuji Takeoka using bronze, terracotta and highly lacquered surfaces.

27/11/91–12/91 Lawrence Weiner

Large gallery specific text work and public sticker campaign.

14/01/92–08/02/92 In Here

David Shrigley, Rachel Mimiec, Rory Donaldson, Leila Galloway, Brigid Teehan.

"In Here, explores the private, the confessional and the perverse. Five artists present brand new works, five very different approaches…" (Beatrice Colin, *The List*)

07/02/92–15/03/92 Really Saying Something
David Allen, Jacqueline Donachie, Jonathan Monk, Michael S McGlinn, Colin Pettigrew and Derek Scanlan visit Flanders.

18/02/92–21/03/92 Outta Here
Jonnie Wilkes, Annette Heyer, Martin Creed, Gianni Piacentini, Willy Doherty, David Wilkinson.

"'Outta Here' was conceived in tandem with 'In Here' which ran through January. Whilst the earlier exhibition brought together works which reflected the experience of the individual, 'Outta Here' will focus on artists whose practice utilises elements related to a shared environment." (press release)

01/04/92–09/04/92 New Visions Videoteque
Transmission presents film and video work in conjunction with the New Visions International Festival.

With New Visions Videoteque Archive—a library of submitted video works, available for viewing in the gallery.

01/04/92 *LSD*: Screening by Hungarian filmmaker Gabor Csaszari; 09/04/92 Independence Day: Featuring the video programmes 'International Zeitgeist' and 'Communities of Resistance'. "Thursday 9th April, the final day of the Festival and the day of the General Election, has been designated 'Independence Day'. From 12 noon there will be continuous screenings of the films constituting the main 'International Zeitgeist' programme, interspersed with live election broadcasts." (press release)

01/05/92–23/05/92 Three New Works
Paul Maguire and Simon Starling collaborate on geometric structures made from white fluorescent strip lights, Michael McDonough and Donald Urquhart each produce a new series of photographs.

08/06/92–27/06/92 Contact: 552-4813
Work by Colin MacFarlane, Paul Marsden, Toby Webster, Adrian Wiszniewski, Craig Richardson, Oladele Bamgboye, Kirsty Ogg, Andrew Lockhart, Thomas Walsh, Iain Kettles, Marchant & Guest, John Shankie, Andrew Miller, Richard Wright, Jim Hamlyn, Jonathan Cassells, David Allen, Michael Ellis, Colin Pettigrew, Jim Suttie, Claire Barclay, Kenneth Mackay, Stephen Hurrell, Jonathan Monk, Louise Crawford, Eva Arrighi, Melissa A. Newgass, Jill Henderson, Karen Vaughan, Emma Kay, Neil Chapman, Christine Borland, Meredith Crone, Raymond Lee, Martin Boyce, Mike Ellen, Simon Patterson, David Shrigley, Douglas Gordon, Jacqueline Donachie, Roderick Buchanan and Kevin Henderson.

+ a reading by David Shrigley from his new book *Merry Eczema*.

14/07/92–08/08/92 Skins
Installation by Edwina Fitzpatrick.

05/08/92 Talks
Ross Sinclair and Nathan Coley speak about time spent in Los Angeles and Saint Andrews respectively.

01/09/92–04/10/92 City Racing at Transmission
Work from London's best known artist-run space by John Burgess, Keith Coventry, Matthew Hale, Paul Noble and Peter Owen.

07/09/92–04/10/92 Transmission at City Racing
Work from Scotland's best known artist-run space by Annette Heyer, Andrew Lockhart, Julie Roberts and Ross Sinclair.

24/09/92 Sell and Be Damned—Book Launch

13/10/92–31/10/92 Zoo
Gallery residency by Iain Kettles resulting in the production of several large scale cardboard sculptures.

"Artist Iain Kettles will be squids-in if he manages to sell his unusual range of sculptures. The 26 year old's exhibition at the Transmission Gallery is a bizarre range of animals crafted from corrugated cardboard. Iain will be making the pieces throughout the duration of the show and has already modelled a giraffe, a 21-foot high giant squid and a star-gazing mongrel. He still hopes to have time to make a massive hippo." (the *Glaswegian*, 22 October 1992)

10/11/92–05/12/92 Démesures
Exhibition of work by Marcel Duchamp, Marcel Broodthaers, Georges Touzenis, Phillippe Favier, Petra Werle, Gilbert Lascault, Gerard Collin-Thiébaut, Gilles Ghez, Michel Sauer and Patrick Neu, concerned with miniaturisation. Curated by The French Institute, Edinburgh.

15/12/92–23/01/93 Bodies of Water
New works for Transmission by David Shanabrook involving film, sculpture and troughs of water beneath the gallery floor.

02/02/93–27/02/93 Landscape Painting
An exhibition of appropriated landscape imagery by Graham Gussin, Andrew Forrester, Nigel Stewart and Jonathan Monk.

"Landscape Paintings at Transmission Gallery, Glasgow, are not your traditional fields and hills but a radical look at the politics of place by four young artists. Jonathan Monk takes the jokey conceptual approach, using billboard ads for bucketshop flights to foreign parts. Nigel Stewart translates photos of Dachau then and now, Graham Gussin lifts science fiction book-jacket imagery full of clouds and sky. I like Andrew Forrester's shaped canvases if only because their 1960s colours are unpretentious and with no holds barred." Clare Henry (the Glasgow *Herald*, 12 February 1993, p. 12)

09/03/93–27/03/93 Transmission Gallery
A site-specific architectural intervention by Zeyad Dajani and Robin Lee.

06/04/93–24/04/93 The Daily Planet
Melissa A Newgass, Jonathan Barnbrook & Tamoko Yoneda, Alan Dunn & Alex Dempster, Thomas Gidley, Andrew Lockhart, Stephen Murphy, Kirsty Ogg and Jane & Louise Wilson. Curated by Andrew Lockhart on the theme of the daily newspaper.

04/05/93–29/05/93 Works on Paper
Exhibition of graphic works and prints by Wolf Vostell, one of the main exponents of Fluxus, organised by the Goethe Institute, London.

08/06/93–03/07/93 Hors-champs
Video installation by Vancouver based artist Stan Douglas.

13/07/93–31/07/93 Trasna
The first part of an exchange project with Belfast including works by Derval Fitzgerald, Sandra Johnston, Terry McAllister, Aine Nic Giolla Coda and Karen Vaughan.

07/09/93–25/09/93 3 Projects, 3 Talks
"In September Transmission will present 3 projects. These projects will be installed in the gallery in quick succession. Each will run for 5 days only. Each project will include an artist's talk related to the work presented in the gallery. These talks will be held each Thursday at 7.30pm. Refreshments will be served." (press release)

07–11/09: Ross Sinclair—'We Don't Love You Anymore'; 14–18/09: Craig Richardson—'Euphoria of Destruction'; 21–25/09 Edwin David—'The Defense of Utopia'.

24/09/93–15/10/93 Transmission in Belfast
Second part of the exchange with work by Gerard Byrne, Jacqueline Donachie, Anna Milsom, Emma Neilson and Richard Wright—installed in a Belfast shop unit.

05/10/93–31/10/93 Itself
Max Fenton, David Griffith, Nigel Prince and Hermione Wiltshire. Curated by Max Fenton.

05/11/93–27/11/93 Transmission—Artemisia
Oona Ball, Nathan Coley, Michael Ellis, Craig Richardson and Heather Allen travel to Chicago to take part in the first part of a gallery exchange project.

16/11/93–04/12/93 Querweltein
Cologne based artist Heike Weber produces new sculpture during a Glasgow residency while Transmission member Colin MacFarlane works and exhibits in Cologne.

11/12/93–22/01/94 Nu Smell
Works by Matthew Crawley, Keith Farquhar, Matthew Leahy, Diane Main, Eva Rothschild, John Russell and Toby Webster.

02/02/94–26/02/94 Vernet's Studio
Lubaina Himid re-created 'The Studio', an etching by nineteenth century artist Horace Vernet, using cut-out figures of various female artists and their representations of women in place of characters (all male) portrayed in the original etching.

04/03/94–05/03/94 30 Secs. plus title
An exhibition of 35mm slide works by artists from Glasgow and Los Angeles organised by David Allen.

Featuring the work of Sam Ainsley, David Allen, Dewey Ambrosino, Christine Borland, Martin Boyce, Roderick Buchanan, Michael Buckland, Anthony Burdin, James Chinlund, Jackie Donachie, Julie Fowells, Amy Harlan-Blount, Paul Maguire, Jonathan Monk, Victoria Morton, Jeff Nelson, Kirsty Ogg, Rolf Pilarski, Marina Rosenfeld, Steven Schultz, John Shankie, David Shrigley, Ross Sinclair, Simon Starling, Eugenio Dittborn, Jill St Jacques, Michael Jarmon, Lisa Ward, Susan Ward, Dave Hughes and Richard Wright.

08/03/94–26/03/94 Richard Wright
New gallery specific wall paintings by Richard Wright.

05/04/94–30/04/94 Silencium

Installation by Lothar Baumgarten.

+ 'The Reading Room' with texts and installations by Janice Galloway, Jackie Kay and Michael Bracewell.

+ 30/04 'Reading Room' Symposium.

'The Reading Room' was a project initiated by BookWorks which set out to examine historical, cultural, social, racial and political perspectives that effect artists and art practices, with reference to books, reading and knowledge through reading.

10/05/94–28/05/94 Artemisia at Transmission

Second leg of the exchange with Artemisia Gallery, Chicago including works by Linda James, Eileen Ryan, Nancy Hild, Silvia Malagrino, Elaine Scheer and Jo Hockenhull.

07/06/94–02/07/94 Modern Art

Jonnie Wilkes, Stephanie Smith, Cath Whippey, Fiona Wright, Simon Starling, Kirsty Stansfield, Jeremy Stevenson, James Thornhill, Brigid Teehan, Toby Webster, Stella Tobia, Mike Ellis, Karen Vaughan, Graham Fagen, Aoise Faren, Mark Orange, Anne-Marie Copestake, Stuart Gow, Derval Fitzgerald, Douglas Gordon, Victoria Morton, Angus Hood, Emma Neilson, Rachel Evans, Loretta Hayes, Kenny Mackay, Mark Haddon, Linda Neilson, Stephen Hurrell, Iain Kettles, Michael Kirkham, Kirsty Ogg, Dez Lawrence, Sally Barker, Graham Ramsay, Christine Frew, Christine Borland, Louise Brown, Michael McGraw, Susan Hunter, Colin MacFarlane, Judy Spark, Jonathan Monk, Heike Weber, Andy Miller, Gerry Mitchell, Craig Richardson, Simon Shaw, Ross Sinclair, David Shrigley, Hinrich Sachs, Paul Maguire, Matthew Leahy, Martin Boyce, Will Bradley, Jakki Cunningham, Roderick Buchanan, Graham Gussin, Eva Rothschild, Julie Roberts, John Clark, Deirdrie McCloskey, Martin Creed, Douglas Gibb, Caroline Woodley, Russell McEwan, Sandra Johnston, Robert Montgomery, Kevin Henderson, Jeremy Millar, Oona Ball, Emily Bates, Karen Bauld, Donna Jamieson, Anna Milsom, Nathan Coley, Jackie Donachie, Tim Cullen, Melissa A Newgass.

12/07/94–06/08/94 Detached Bell Tower

Stefan Gec installs eight bells cast from the steel of eight Soviet submarines.

06/09/94–01/10/94 Claire Barclay

Solo exhibition of new sculpture made for Transmission.

12/10/94–22/11/94 Good House Keeping—4 event-based projects

12–22/10: 'Couch Potatoes'—new video work. David Allen, Colin Andrews, Simon Aeppli, Jason E. Bowman, David Cooke, Anne-Marie Copestake, Alan Currall, Edward Dorrian, Russell McEwan, Alan Frame, Simon Fildes, Nicky Gogan, Douglas Gordon, Geraldine Kirk, Shiona McCubbin, Jonathan Monk, Kirsty Ogg, Bob and Roberta Smith with Jessica Voorsanger, Stephanie Smith, Gillian Wearing, Alex Wood and Martin Young. Flower arrangement by Hilary Stirling; 27–29/10: Rachel Evans—'Rhapsody on a Theme d'Amour'; 09–16/11: Mike Nelson—'Charity Shop'; 19–26/11: 'That We Know'—Invited guests: Lisa Goodfriend, Hugh O'Donnell and Karen Lury contribute to a discussion organised by Hinrich Sachs.

26/11/94–22/12/94 Don't Look Back

Works by Paul Logue, Peter Lynch, Darren Marshall, Hayley Tompkins and Sue Tompkins at Oldknows Gallery, Nottingham—the first half of an exchange project.

06/12/94–21/01/95 Airmail Painting No. 96, *Liquid Ashes*, and Airmail Painting No. 103, *To Return (RTM)*

Two large 'Airmail Paintings' sent to Transmission by Eugenio Dittborn from Santiago, Chile.

31/01/95–18/02/95 Making Out

This exhibition presents the work of nine young artists from four European cities: Berlin, Glasgow, London and Paris.

Michel Blazy, Brigid Teehan, Tim Marr, Joanne Tatham & Tom O'Sullivan, Rolf Pilarsky & Lisa Ward, Lawrence Harvey and Mark Jones.

25/02/95–11/03/95 Kevin Henderson—**Weighing from Land**
21/03/95–08/03/95 Hanne Darboven—**Friedrich II, Harburg 1986**
Two projects linked to musical performance.

25/04/95–20/05/95 New Rose Hotel

Art and design fusion with works by Rudolph Fila, Victoria Morton, Julian Opie, Paul Maguire, Su Grierson, Andrew Miller, Allford Hall Monaghan Morris Architects, Stephen Harty, Chris Downs, Ron Arad, Susan Hunter, Philippe Starck, Nigel Prince, Hiroshi Sugimoto, Jonathan Ambrose, Dene Happell, Martin Boyce, Andrew Megaw, Eva Grubinger, Dr Jives, Jonnie Wilkes, Hamish McChlery, Martin Young and Toby Webster.

30/05/95–24/06/95 Chase Me

'Chase Me' brings together three artists—Mark Haddon (Borders of Scotland), Katrin von Maltzahn (Berlin) and Erlend Williamson (London)—whose work deals in different ways with the search for an identity in changing geographical, social, political and cultural conditions.

11/07/95–28/07/95 In Stereo

New works made for the gallery by four local artists: Jim Lambie, Robert Montgomery, Mary Redmond and James Thornhill.

+ in the basement: screening of a new work by Heather Allen.

+ 22/07/95 Taste (Sense and Sensibility): an exhibition of small sculptures by Alan Kane made for the Val d'Oro Restaurant, 12 London Road, Glasgow.

+ 28/07/95 Guitar Amp Action: Transmission kicks off the summer with a crazy punk rock party featuring local bands Hello Skinny, Lungleg, Superstar and Par Cark.

05/09/96–30/09/96 Map of the Sewer
New work by David Shrigley.

07/10/95–04/11/95 Art Club 2000
Work by this collaborative group of New York based artists concerned with New York based Scottish artist Jackie McAllister. Part of the Fotofeis Festival of Photography.

20/10/95–19/11/95 Transmission at La Capella
Iain Kettles, Diane Main, Andrew Miller, Eva Rothschild, Hilary Stirling and Judith Weik exhibit work at La Capella in Barcelona as the first leg of this Transmission exchange.

14/11/95–2/12/95 Forget Brown Spot, Save The World
First half of an exchange project with the Toronto based artists' group Brown Spot with work by Michael Buckland, Jill Henderson, Slim Pickings, Marc Streifling and Shannon Wadsworth.

12/12/95–20/01/96 Call of the Wild
Justin Carter, Caroline Kirsop, Liza May Post, Sarah Tripp, David Zerah and Torbjørn Rodland investigate contemporary attitudes to nature.

27/01/96–24/02/96 21 Days of Darkness
Vito Acconci, Lee Miller, Art Club 2000, Glenn Brown, Simon Periton, Fanni Niemi-Junkola, Gregory Green, Jason Fox, Pierre Molinier, Susan Harper, Andrew McWhinney, Adam Chodzko, The Royal Observatory prints, Neil Miller, Mabel Palacin, Weegee, Christine Borland, Søren Martinsen, Douglas Gordon.

05/03/96–13/03/96 With Love, Filthy Swan
Transmission hosts the artists' group Filthy Swan: Iain Dickinson, Robert Johnston, Gary Rough, Scott Waugh, Douglas Payne and Toby Paterson—recent graduates from Glasgow School of Art.

+ in the basement: 'The Tower'—construction by Joanne Tatham.

19/03/96–06/04/96 A Grapefruit in the World of Park
Works by Judith Dean, Tracey Emin, Yoko Ono and Mary Heilmann. Curated for Transmission by Cathy Wilkes.

+ in the basement: 'Untitled 1995'—an installation using high-frequency ultra-violet neon and low temperature refrigeration units by Steve Hollingsworth.

16/04/96–04/05/96 Espais De Desig—La Capella at Transmission
Anna Estany, Carles Congost, Ester Partegas, Javier Penafiel from La Capella in Barcelona exhibit as the second leg of a gallery exchange. Curated by Manel Clot.

+ in the basement: Graham Fagen sound installation in collaboration with Dennis Hopper and Sydney Devine.

14/05/96–25/05/96 Art for People*
The first open submission show of gallery members.

+ in the basement: films by Michel Auder: *My Last Bag of Heroin (for real), The Valerie Solanas Incident, Chelsea Girls with Andy Warhol (1971–1976).*

+ 'Frack'—project by Austrian artist Peter Friedl involving garment exchanges in various gallery spaces around Europe.

04/06/96–29/06/96 Karen Kilimnik—Me and the Boys
New Yorker Kilimnik made her own little disco in this installation dedicated to the Beatles.

09/07/96–27/07/96 Mere Jelly

Second half of an exchange project between Nottingham and Glasgow which included Clair Chinnery, Stephen Craighill, Anthony Hall, Jez Noond, Irene Rogan and Denise Weston.

06/07/96–21/07/96 Jackie Derrida—24 hr TV

Performance and video event held in the basement space with Jackie Derrida (aka Graham Bell).

21/07/96 Rocket Event

Rocket launch event in Pollok Park with Michael Mulvihill.

07/96 Sick Building

Transmission participated in this show in Copenhagen, part of a project called 'Compartments'. Darren Marshall, Graham Ramsay, Heather Allen, Iain Kettles, Simon Starling, Jim Lambie and the Transmission Committee exhibited (amongst others).

10/09/96–05/10/96 Victoria Morton

Solo show of paintings.

24/09/96–05/09/96 Viper—incorporating Bank TV

London artists Bank present 'an ever changing programme of video produced in London and Manchester and brought direct to you every day in the Transmission basement'.

05/10/96–05/01/97 Life/Live

Transmission participate in an exhibition concerning artist-run spaces in Britain at the Musée d' Art Moderne de la Ville de Paris. The artists showing were Richard Wright, Martin Boyce, Susan Tompkins, Heather Allen and Roderick Buchanan. The show toured to Lisbon in January 1997.

13/10/96–09/11/96 **Stay on your own for slightly longer**

One of four exhibitions of Swedish artists curated by Maria Lind as part of a project called 'I am Curious'. Artists who exhibited at Transmission were Lotta Antonssonn, Henrik Håkansson, Annika von Hausswolff and Anders Widoff.

+ Turner Prize Discussion: Transmission took part in the events surrounding the Turner Prize by showing documentary videos and hosting a panel discussion.

19/11/96–14/12/96 SEETHROUGHBRAIN

Maura Biava (Italy), Yasue Ichige (Japan), David Noonan (Australia), Alastair MacKinven (Canada), Dierdre McCloskey (Ireland), Katie McKee (Scotland) and Mark Waller (England).

"Most of our knowledge is predominantly verbal whether it is literary or scientific. For example, education can be seen to fail as it can produce students who are completely unaware of the world as a primary fact of experience." (press release)

+ in the basement: 'Klick', an exhibition of giant photo posters, enlarged from the archives of thirteen artists. Curated by Kate Daw and including work by Karen Bauld, John Beagles, Martin Boyce, Paul Carter, Kate Daw, Kate Gray, Deborah Holland, Billy McCall, Janice McNab, David Noonan, Graham Ramsay, Abigail Simmonds and Clara Ursitti.

11/01/97–08/02/97 Hong Kong Island
A group show based around propositions of unrealisable projects by Alan Currall, Chris Evans, Claire Barclay, Kevin Kelly, Billy Clark, Aoise Farren, Kate Gray, David Wilkinson, Andrew Miller and Simon Polli.

+ Preview night: 'Blueprints and pipe dreams'—David Michael Clarke gives a rapid-fire slide presentation with help from the Duchess of York, Damon Hill, Douglas Gordon and the Spice Girls; 18/01: 'Unrealisable Hope'—Stefano Pasquini holds a slide talk and discussion on his work, utopian projects and 'Hong Kong Island'; 01/02: 'Finding Things Out'—Billy Clark expands on his investigative work presented in the exhibition; 08/02 *Metropolis*: Screening of the film by Fritz Lang.

17/02/97–15/03/97 JOYJOY
Gitte Villesen, David Burrows, Gary Perkins, Stuart Purdy, Karen Reynolds, Peter Kapos and Paul McCarthy exhibited work in this show which presented innocence as the harbinger of deception.

+ Videos in the basement—*Ren and Stimpy*, Manga, Throbbing Gristle live at Oundle School for boys; 27/02: Screening of Kenneth Anger's *Scorpio Rising* and John Waters' *Female Trouble*; 08/03: Martin McGowan discusses Paul McCarthy's work in the context of 'JOYJOY'; 13/03: Screening of *Scorpio Rising* and Charles Laughton's *Night of the Hunter*.

22/03/97–31/03/97 Young Parents
Transmission participated in an exhibition in Manchester of artists and artist-run spaces with City Racing (London), Three Month Gallery (Liverpool) and hosted by The Annual Programme and Castlefield Gallery. Transmission's contribution was curated by Tom O'Sullivan and Joanne Tatham from proposals by Transmission members and included Amanda Bindley, Jamie Burroughs, Alex Frost, Steve Hollingsworth, Eva Rothschild, Tom O'Sullivan, Joanne Tatham, Beáta Veszely, Toby Webster, David Wilkinson and Caroline Woodley.

25/03/97–12/04/97 New York Public Access Experience
Hundreds of hours of clips, shows and interviews from New York's public access cable TV stations organised by Alex Bag, Patterson Beckwith and Sam Soghor.

+ in the basement: 'Non Stop Body Rock'—Dave Beech, Dave Burrows, Sue Webster & Tim Noble. Curated by Graham Ramsay.

19/04/97–31/05/97 Four Projects, Four Talks
19–26/04: Nicolas Floc'h—sculptures and video documentation of Floc'h's 'Écriture Productive'—land/sea art concerned with language; 01–08/05: Beáta Veszely—"You are cordially invited for a cup of tea in a stable on Sunday 4th May between 3–5pm". Event to accompany three video projections in the gallery, recorded in three Scottish racehorse stables; 13–20/05: Liam Gillick—'Another Shop in Tottenham Court Road'—set construction for the production of a short documentary. Volunteers were filmed reading from the artist's books *Erasmus is Late* and *Ibuka!*, as the third part of a series of documentaries produced in different cities; 24–31/05: Clara Ursitti—'The Smell of Fear Part 1 and 2: Judy Garland'—a scent portrait of the late Judy Garland, created with the help of Dr George Dodd.

+ in the basement: 01–20/05/97: 'Diva(s)'—project by Robin Bagnall and George Toth, preview performance with String Quartet.

+ Transmission also took part in the Glasgow Art Fair, exhibiting and selling work by various members.

07/06/97–05/07/97 Russell Crotty and Jonnie Wilkes

Local artist Jonnie Wilkes exhibited new sculptural installation work alongside the giant star-atlas book works of California's Russell Crotty.

13/07/97–02/08/97 European Couples and Others*

The annual members' open show, with over 200 exhibiting including guests invited by members. The theme was dedication—each work being dedicated to a person, event, idea or object.

06/09/97–04/10/97 Simon Starling—Blue Boat Black

First solo show in Scotland by Glasgow-based artist Simon Starling.

+ Transmission took part in 'Connected', an artist-run-space survey at the Northern Gallery for Contemporary Art in Sunderland. Paul Carter and Anne-Marie Copestake made new work for the exhibition space. Video footage of the installation and opening of 'Blue Boat Black' was also shown.

11/10/97–01/11/97 The Unconditioned State of Search

Corey McCorkle (New York City) exhibits along with Peter Zimmermann (Cologne) and Brits Dean Hughes and Peter Walsh. Zen Ikebana flower arrangements by Vera Ferguson tie lifestyle-ism to transcendence.

15/11/97–13/12/97 Olympic Village

Padraig Timoney, Alan Michael, Joanne McGonigal and Roddie Mathieson show in the second leg of an exchange between Transmission and Three Month Gallery in Liverpool.

Transmission members Sophie Macpherson and Roger Hiorns exhibited in Liverpool along with Yiannis Grigoriadis from 3–26 October.

13/01/98–31/01/98 Henry VIII's Wives

Rachel Dagnall, Jonas Eggen, Bob Grieve, Simon Polli, Lucy Skaer and Per Sander, all recent graduates from the Environmental Art Department at Glasgow School of Art, create a collaborative multi media show over the festive period.

10/02/98–07/03/98 I love this life

Paul Johnson, Hayley Tompkins, Michael Fullerton, Joe Brainard, Jonny Redding, Lindsey Orr and Simon Mcauley.

+ 26/2/97 Slide talks by Michael Fullerton, Kirsty Ogg (talking about her flat-based curatorial activities in Norwich), Lucy Byatt and Julia Radcliffe (co-directors of Visual Arts Project, Glasgow).

14/03/98–05/04/98 Something Ahhh… Nothing

Three weeks of live chaos at Transmission in conjunction with the newly opened 13th Note Bar. This varied and hectic programme of performances, music, readings and talks included Rob Mitchell, Rose Thomas & Sophie Macpherson, The James Orr Complex, Fukuyama, Richard Maddalena, Dario Kavara, Kevin Henderson, Robert McShane, Cut Joey, Cylinder, MCDJ AB-Normal Tupperware, Badgewearer, Gael McDougall, David Hopkins, Ricky Campbell Allen and the DeepFried DJs.

+ Transmission at the Stockholm Art Fair.

07/04/98–18/04/98 Alex Frost — Theme Show
Over the course of this project Alex Frost constructed a full size geodesic dome within the gallery, plotting this utopian form of architecture's assimilation into both the establishment and 'drop-out' subcultures.

04/98 Philosophical Inquiry at Transmission
The first of ten weekly meetings facilitated by Catherine McCall and Howard Robinson.

25/04/98–16/04/98 Helen Beckman and Graham Little
New Yorker Helen Beckman's blue gouache drawings of monkeys explore the line between human and animal whilst Graham Little's colourful sculptures do the same with regard to fine art and design in this two person show.

+ in the basement: Dan Shipsides and Peter Richards — 'Still to Real'.

23/05/98–13/06/98 Never Been in a Riot
Superflex, AdBusters, Ralph Rumney, Undercurrents, Negativland plus video and audio library.

+ in the basement: video work and posters by Billy McCall and Paul Carter.

17/06/98–27/06/98 In Order of Appearance
For a week Transmission was converted into a cinema and local artists and film buffs were asked to introduce their favourite movies. Including Bob Grieve, Lucy Mackenzie, John McKeown, Douglas Gordon, Clare Barclay, Sarah Tripp and the Fleapit Film Club.

+ in the basement: 'Mise-en-scene', an exhibition by Kevin Hutcheson.

04/07/98–31/07/98 Tronway Arts Centre *
The annual Transmission members' open exhibition. This year the gallery was converted into an Arts Centre, complete with sculpture garden and cafe bar.

05/09/98–03/10/98 Fritz Welch and Anne-Marie Copestake
Massive improvisational wall drawings by Brooklyn-based Fritz Welch dominated the upstairs gallery while Anne-Marie Copestake showed a new video work in the re-jigged basement space.

10/10/98–07/11/98 Eurocentral
Manfred Pernice, Boris Ondreicka, Matthew Harrison, Yvonne Fontijne, Orla Ryan, Chad McCail and Andy Shaw.

21/11/98–28/11/98 and **05/12/98–12/12/98** The Janus Programme
Two short group shows each featuring the same selection of artists. Featuring Robb Mitchell, Anne-Louise Kieran, Hanneline Visnes, Kevin Hutcheson, Mark Vernon, Fred Pedersen, Lindsey Orr and Michael Wilkinson.

09/01/99–30/01/99 Voidoid
Jim Lambie caused psychedelic eye-mayhem by covering the floor area of Transmission with concentric lines of multi-coloured vinyl tape. His first solo show also included video piece 'Ultralow' in the basement.

06/02/99–27/02/99 Tobias Rehberger—Standard Rad
Tobias Rehberger created an environmental portrait of his friends, Standard Rad (a design company based in London and Frankfurt).

+ in the cellar: Videos by Annika Ström who played a live set of her songs on the opening night.

06/03/99–27/03/99 Where the Wild Roses Grow
David Noonan and Daniel von Sturmer with collaborators Elizabeth go (Cathy Wilkes, Hayley Tompkins, Sue Tompkins, Victoria Morton, Sarah Tripp).

03/04/99–24/04/99 Euroride: The Pineapple Goes Transmission
The first leg of an exchange project with The Pineapple, a mobile project room from Malmo, Sweden. Artists: Lena Mattsson (who presented a performance in the Mitre bar on the preview night), Magnus Wallin, Elisabet Apelmo, David Krantz, Torbjørn Limé, Bjørn Wangen, Axel Lieber.

+ screening of the new Fugazi film, presented by Glasgow Music Collective in the gallery basement.

+ 14/04/99: Slide talks by Clare Barclay and Lucy McKenzie in the 13th Note bar.

29/04/99–02/05/99 Transmission at the Glasgow Art Fair
Mary Redmond represents the gallery.

08/05/99–29/05/99 Sounds of Grass
Glasgow-based Hayley Tompkins and Sue Tompkins.

"The white cube of the Transmission space has been reworked with a diagonal chipboard partition and squares of hessian sackcloth are hung over the walls. Elsewhere, there are a number of colourful and exact wall paintings, a display of painted eggs and a hanging group of magazine pages that have been crumpled in the palm of the hand until they assume a soft and shiny form, like leaves." Sarah Lowndes (*The List*, 13–27 May 1999, p. 73)

+ in the basement: Neal Beggs—'Dead Flat Vertical'.

+ 19/05/99: Slide talks by Scott Myles and Stephen Hurrell at the 13th Note bar.

12/06/99–03/07/99 Hundred Years Egg
Group show of artists who make junctions between uncanny technology and popular culture; Mats Adelman, Michael Fullerton, Simon McAuley and Magnus Wassborg.

+ 23/06/99: Slide talks by Alex Frost and Richard Wright.

+ 08/07/99 *Wavelength*: screening of Michael Snow's 1967 film.

17/07/99–08/08/99 Transmission Open*
Members' show.

+ 28/07/99: Talks by The Modern Institute (Toby Webster and Will Bradley) and Michael Wilkinson at the Mitre Bar.

04/09/99–02/10/99 Atelier van Lieshout—AVL Equipment
Rotterdam based Joep Van Lieshout presented a selection of equipment, furniture and weaponry produced by his artists' workshop collective.

+ related talk by Lars Bang Larson.

+ in the basement: 'Personal Worlds' installation by Thomas Seest, followed by 'New Works', a sound installation by Sally Osborn.

16/10/99–06/11/99 Fields and Rays and Green Numbers
Part 2 of the exchange with Pineapple Project Room, Malmo. The exhibition took place in a cinema space and featured the work of Duncan Campbell, Hayley Tompkins, Sue Tompkins, Scott Myles, Anne-Marie Copestake and Sarah Tripp.

16/10/99–13/11/99 Day of The Donkey Day
A group show loosely based around ideas about humour and failure featuring works by Rebecca Warren, Chris Evans, Matti Suuronen, Mika Tannila, Glenn Brown and Caro Bensca. With a short accompanying essay by Matthew Goulish.

+ Talks by Cathy Wilkes and Duncan Campbell at the Mitre Bar.

17/11/99–20/11/99 Participation in Vienna Austrotel Art Fair
A new art fair in a hotel in Vienna, Transmission's room featured the work of Keith Farquhar, Neil Bickerton & Lorna Macintyre, Eva Rothschild, Stuart Purdy, Roger Hiorns, Duncan Campbell, Alex Frost, David Shrigley, Michael Wilkinson and Lucy McKenzie.

20/11/99–18/12/99 Enrico David, Clare Stephenson, Roger Hiorns
Three person show featuring woven and embroidered pictures by Enrico David, spray paintings/sculptures by Clare Stephenson and ceramic bubble vessels by Roger Hiorns.

+ in the basement: a raised concrete floor and related video by Zeyad Dejani.

29/01/00–05/02/00 Neil Bickerton and Lorna MacIntyre—Complecity 11
12/02/00–19/02/00 Luke Fowler—The Social Engineer
Two one-week projects by young artists.

+ in the basement (throughout): Knut Åsdam—sound installation and video.

26/02/00–18/03/00 Crack is Wack
Group show featuring the work of Jonas Eggen (Oslo), Stuart Purdy (Glasgow), Maria Finn (Paris), Brian Dawn Chawkley (London), Dimitra Barba (Athens), Ulrik Hansen (Copenhagen).

25/03/00–08/04/00 e.g. Sometime Instant
A wide-ranging project and broadcast by Glasgow-based sometime pirate radio initiators radiotuesday (Alex Frost, Mark Vernon and Duncan Campbell).

In the gallery: Film screening and *Touch* installation presented by Anne-Marie Copestake; *Doodle-Scanner-Chanter* by Paul Mulvihill; *The Wilsons*, an ongoing project by Crystal Collins; Ian Balch presents *Gift*, a new choral artwork in collaboration with composer Stephen Davismoon, chorus master Frikki Walker and the choir of Saint Mary's Cathedral; Life without buildings perform live.

Closing Night: 'Doktor Barnes Advocaat' with Diskono.

In the studio: Calum Stirling, Tony Swain, Cylinder, Robin Bagnall, James McLardy & David Young, Clare Stephenson, Mutti Geld, Caroline Woodley—interview with Liam Gillick.

Talk: Sarah Lowndes hosts a discussion on the ins and outs of independent music production with Emma Pollock (The Delgados & Chemical Underground), Hubby (El Hombre Trajeado & Doityerself.co.uk) and Douglas McIntyre (Creeping Bent Records).

Around the city: 26/03: 'Stilletto' with Sally Chapman at the 13th Note; 01/04: 'Give the DJ a break' with Scott Myles, Sarah Lowndes, Anna J and Hannah's Barber at the Buff Club; 06/04: Gilded Lil live at 13th Note; 09/04: Capt K vs Pukey (Ewan Imrie and Rob Kennedy), Ideal Home (Torsten Lauschman and Michael Wilkinson) at the Cross Bar.

Broadcast contributions also came from Marc Baines, Fergus Kelly, Carol McGuigan, Sikkerhet, John Beagles and Graham Ramsay, Deaf and Dummy, David Fulford, Orla Ryan, Barry Burns, AMMM, Wendy Wilmurt Brown, Zoe Irvine & Gerald Lopez Straub, David Bellingham, Neil Bickerton, Scott Simpson, Johny Hi'way, Ektor Virite, Aku Raskie, Thomas Seest and MC Sorensen, Voukkoset, Falkirk, Alekseij Konstantinoff, Cuzner, Rishaug & Arm, Senor Cockroach, O Samuli A, Heather Minchin, People Like Us vs The Jet Black Hair People, Vex, Vengloss Advocaat, Nick E Melville, John Nicol, Brian Lavelle & Richard Youngs, Chris White, Hayley Newman & Kaffe Matthews, Duncan MacQuarrie and Poison Sisters.

13/04/00–16/04/00 Transmission at the Glasgow Art Fair
Transmission's stall featured works by Hayley Tompkins, Keith Farquhar, Michael Wilkinson, Sue Tompkins, Roger Hiorns, Scott Myles, Mary Redmond, Chris Evans, Duncan Campbell, Clare Stephenson, Alex Frost and Kevin Hutcheson.

15/04/00–13/05/00 Ellen Cantor
Video and installation of works on paper.

+ in the basement 15/04–22/04: Claudine Hartzell—'Fragile Paradise'; 02/05–13/05: Rob Kennedy—'Movers and Shakers'.

27/05/00–24/06/00 The Glamour
Glasgow based collaborators Joanne Tatham & Tom O'Sullivan produced a large sculptural installation for the upper gallery and basement.

11/07/00–06/08/00 It may be a Year of Thirteen Moons but it's still the Year of Culture
Curated by Charisma (Lucy McKenzie and Keith Farquhar) and featuring the work of Markus Selg (Hamburg), Lucy McKenzie (Glasgow), Steven Campbell (near Stirling), Merlin Carpenter (London), Keith Farquhar (Glasgow) and Albert Oehlen (Cologne).

10/08/00–13/08/00 Some Moved Pictures of Lawrence Weiner
Transmission presented *Hearts and Helicopters*, a new video work by Lawrence Weiner. On the closing day of the project four earlier films by Weiner were shown at a special event in the gallery attended by the artist. The project was a collaboration between Transmission and independent curator Barbara Clausen.

12/09/00–07/10/00 Good Luck For You
Julia Schmidt (Liepzig), Peter Wüthrich (Zurich), Alex Frost (Glasgow), Liz Craft (Los Angeles) and Elizabeth Kent (London).

+ in the basement: 'amoebase'—new work by New Zealand-born, London-based artist Lyndal Jefferies.

14/10/00–04/11/00 Members' Show*
The annual showcase of works by Transmission's membership.

10/11/00–15/12/00 Me, We—Transmission at Project Space, Athens
Duncan Campbell, Chris Evans, Luke Fowler, Michael Fullerton, Andrew Kerr, Michelle Naismith, Clare Stephenson and Cathy Wilkes.

19/11/00–16/12/00 Ideas About A Place
In association with 'Vivre Sa Vie', a Glasgow/Edinburgh based survey of contemporary art from France. Transmission's contribution featured graphic designer Laurent Fétis, sculptures by Mathieu Mercier, design products by BLESS and a video by film maker Frederick Wiseman.

06/01/01–13/01/01 Lucy Skaer
'Like a circle in a spiral
or
The cotton was high and the corn was growing fine,
but that was another place and another time.
or
A modern pig of Iron age type'

A one week project by Lucy Skaer featuring a series of drawings and hand painted objects.

+ 17/01/01: slide talks by Mark Titchner and Chris Evans in the Mitre Bar.

20/01/01–17/02/01 Best Eagle
A three person show featuring two Glasgow-based artists Michelle Naismith and Duncan MacQuarrie and Mark Titchner from London.

+ 13/02/01–19/02/01 Transmission participate in ARCO, an art fair in Madrid. We show work by gallery members Claire Barclay, Anne-Marie Copestake, Alex Frost, Michael Fullerton, Kevin Hutcheson, Duncan MacQuarrie, Scott Myles, Lucy Skaer and Clare Stephenson.

03/03/01–31/03/01 Dub'L-intROOdER
Glasgow-based duo John Beagles and Graham Ramsay curated and participated in a project focusing on collaborative art practice. Other artists included Muntean & Rosemblum (Austria), Bob & Bob (USA), Paul McCarthy & Mike Kelley (USA), Bob and Roberta Smith & Dave Burrows (London) and BANK (London).

05/04/01–08/04/01 Glasgow Art Fair

Transmission show work by Alan Michael, Michelle Naismith, Michael Fullerton, Duncan MacQuarrie, Katy Dove and Duncan Campbell.

14/04/01–05/05/01 The Tattooed Room

'The Tattooed Room' is an ongoing artwork by Gerd Aurell and Anneli Furmark. This project consisted of a series of wall paintings in the gallery space along with narrative slide shows. The exhibition also included two short performances on the opening night.

02/05/01-13/05/01 Rencontres Video

An international programme of video screenings in Annecy, France organised by imagespassages. This included work by gallery members Katy Dove, Luke Fowler, Duncan Campbell, Torsten Lauschmann.

12/05/01 Noir

Torsten Lauschmann and Michael Wilkinson presented a gothic mix of music and video in the basement.

26/05/01–16/06/01 Hair on One Side is Swept Back

Miriam Cahn, Mary Chong, Laurence Figgis and Michael Mallett.

+ in the basement: *Open Day*—A film by Rosalind Nashashibi.

01/07/01–31/07/01 Cathy Wilkes

Solo exhibition by the Glasgow-based artist.

+ 26/07/01: slide talks by Laurence Figgis and Victoria Morton in the Mitre Bar.

*Over a hundred artists take part in the annual members' shows—comprehensive records of all exhibitors don't exist.

Note: Brackets denote exhibitions organised with assistance from Transmission.

Transmission Committee Members

1983

Alastair Magee, Lesley Raeside, John Rogan, Michelle Baucke, Alastair Strachan (first committee), Gordon Muir, Malcolm Dickson, Carol Rhodes, Graham Johnstone, Peter Thompson, Simon Brown, Douglas Aubrey (second committee), Richard Walker, Jayne Taylor, Tommy Lydon, John Main, Billy Clark, Karen Strang, Gillian Steel, Scott Paterson, Anne Elliot, David Allen, Christine Borland, Mike Ellen, Pete Gilmour, Euan Sutherland, Anne Vance, Douglas Gordon, Craig Richardson, Claire Barclay, Elsie Mitchell, Roderick Buchanan, Katrina Brown, Jacqueline Donachie, Martin Boyce, Simon Starling, Kirsty Ogg, Eva Rothschild, Will Bradley, Toby Webster, Tanya Leighton, Judith Weik, Caroline Kirsop, Toby Paterson, Sarah Tripp, Robert Johnston, Ewan Imrie, Julian Kildear, Lucy Skaer, Sophie Macpherson, Rose Thomas, Alan Michael, Fred Pedersen, Anna McLauchlan, Danny Saunders, Alex Pollard, Clare Stephenson, Lorna Macintyre, Laurence Figgis...

2001

This is a list of everyone who has served as a Transmission committee member from 1983 to the present. The second committee entirely replaced the first but after that the groupings are less defined. Some people stayed for the standard two years (occasionally more), others left after a few months. At times there were only two people on the committee; the standard is now six.

This book has been produced by the current Transmission committee

Design and layout by Robert Johnston

Cover image from a painting by Alan Michael

Photo credits: Alan Dimmick; Fred Pedersen; Robert Johnston; Will Bradley; Simon Starling; David Allen; Oladele Bamgboye; Billy Clark; Transmission members

Black Dog Publishing Limited
5 Ravenscroft Street
London E2 7SH, UK
t: +44 (0)20 7613 1922
f: +44 (0)20 7613 1944
e: info@bdp.demon.co.uk

Architecture Art Design Fashion History Photography Theory and Things

Printed in the European Union

ISBN 1 901033 13 9

A catalogue record of this book is available from The British Library

Transmission
28 King Street
Trongate
Glasgow
G1 5QP
United Kingdom
t: +44 (0) 141 552 4813
f: +44 (0) 141 552 1577
e: info@transmissiongallery.org
www.transmissiongallery.org

Transmission is a registered charity in Scotland. Charity No. SCO 16442

Transmission is supported by the Scottish Arts Council and Glasgow City Council
This publication was funded by the Scottish Arts Council and Glasgow City Council

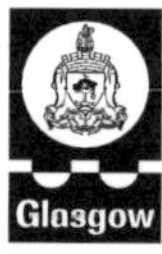
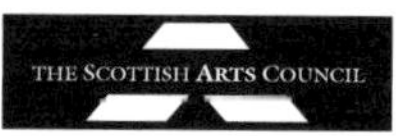